CHILDREN'S NEEDS – PARENTING CAPACITY

Child abuse: Parental mental illness, learning disability, substance misuse and domestic violence

2nd edition

HEDY CLEAVER, IRA UNELL AND JANE ALDGATE

D1579447

WITHDRAWN FROM
THE LIBRARY

UNIVERSITY OF
WINCHESTER

LONDON: TSO

KA 0352802 2

information & publishing solutions

Published by TSO (The Stationery Office) and available from:

Online
www.tsoshop.co.uk

Mail, Telephone, Fax & E-mail
TSO
PO Box 29, Norwich, NR3 1GN
Telephone orders/General enquiries: 0870 600 5522
Fax orders: 0870 600 5533
E-mail: customer.services@tso.co.uk
Textphone: 0870 240 3701

TSO@Blackwell and other Accredited Agents

UNIVERSITY OF WINCHESTER

0353022 | 3627
| CLL

Published for the Department for Education under licence from the Controller of Her Majesty's Stationery Office.

All rights reserved.

© Crown Copyright 2011

You may re-use this information (excluding logos) free of charge in any format or medium, under the terms of the Open Government Licence. To view this licence, visit http://www.nationalarchives.gov.uk/doc/open-government-licence/ or e-mail: psi@nationalarchives.gsi.gov.uk.

Where we have identified any third party copyright information you will need to obtain permission from the copyright holders concerned.

This publication is also available for download at www.official-documents.gov.uk

ISBN: 9780117063655

Printed in the UK by The Stationery Office Limited
J2441707   C2.5   09/11   11130

Contents

UNIVERSITY OF WINCHESTER
LIBRARY

List of figures and tables

Figures

Tables

Preface

It is probably true to say that, for most people, childhood is a mixed experience where periods of sadness and loss are balanced with moments of happiness and achievement. Such complexity, however, is rarely represented in the literature of childhood. Indeed, much of the written word in the nineteenth and twentieth centuries depicts childhood in one of two contrasting ways. For example, A.A. Milne's poem 'In the Dark', first published in 1927, (Milne 1971) shows childhood as a golden era where children are loved and nurtured by caring parents. It is a time characterised by innocence, unqualified parental love, irresponsibility, peer friendships and a thirst for adventure and knowledge.

I've had my supper,

And had my supper,

And HAD my supper and all;

I've heard the story

Of Cinderella,

And how she went to the ball;

I've cleaned my teeth,

And I've said my prayers,

And I've cleaned and said them right;

And they've all of them been

And kissed me lots,

They've all of them said 'Good-night.'

But never far away is the alternative experience, typified by parental desertion, illness, isolation and poverty. James Whitcomb Riley (1920), who penned uplifting poems of perhaps questionable quality for children during the 1890s, paints a much bleaker picture in his poem 'The Happy Little Cripple'.

I'm thist a little cripple boy, an' never goin' to grow

An' get a great big man at all! – 'cause Aunty told me so.

When I was thist a baby onc't, I falled out of the bed

An' got "The Curv'ture of the Spine" – 'at's what the Doctor said.

I never had no Mother nen – fer my Pa runned away

An' dassn't come back here no more – 'cause he was drunk one day

An' stobbed a man in thish-ere town, an' couldn't pay his fine!

An' nen my Ma she died – an' I got "Curv'ture of the Spine!"

Acknowledgements

We acknowledge with sincere thanks the many people who gave generously of their time to help us with this work. We particularly appreciate the expertise and advice offered by Arnon Bentovim, Richard Velleman, Lorna Templeton, Carolyn Davies and Sheena Prentice. The work has been funded by the Department for Education and we thank staff in the department, particularly Jenny Gray who supported us throughout the work with her interest and valuable comments.

The work was assisted by an advisory group whose membership was:

Isabella Craig and Jenny Gray (Department for Education); Christine Humphrey (Department of Health) and Sian Rees (NICE); Arnon Bentovim (consultant child and adolescent psychiatrist at the Great Ormond Street Hospital for Children and the Tavistock Clinic); Marian Brandon (reader in social work, University of East Anglia); Carolyn Davies (research advisor, Institute of Education, University of London); Jo Fox (social work consultant, Child-Centred Practice); David Jones (consultant child and family psychiatrist, Department of Psychiatry; University of Oxford); Sue McGaw (specialist in learning disabilities, Cornwall Partnership Trust); Sheena Prentice (specialist midwife in substance misuse, Nottingham City PCT); Wendy Rose (The Open University); Lorna Templeton (manager of the Alcohol, Drugs and the Family Research Programme, University of Bath); and Richard Velleman (University of Bath and director of development and research, Avon and Wiltshire Mental Health Partnership NHS Trust).

Introduction

This second edition of *Children's Needs – Parenting Capacity* provides an update on the impact of parental problems, such as substance misuse, domestic violence, learning disability and mental illness, on children's welfare. Research, and in particular the biennial overview reports of serious case reviews (Brandon et al 2008; 2009; 2010), have continued to emphasise the importance of understanding and acting on concerns about children's safety and welfare when living in households where these types of parental problems are present.

> *Almost three quarters of the children in both this and the 2003-05 study had been living with past or current domestic violence and or parental mental ill health and or substance misuse – often in combination.*

(Brandon et al 2010, p.112)

These concerns were very similar to those that prompted the first edition of this book, which was commissioned following the emergence of these themes from the Department of Health's programme of child protection research studies (Department of Health 1995a). These studies had demonstrated that a high level of parental mental illness, problem alcohol and drug abuse and domestic violence were present in families of children who become involved in the child protection system.

Research context

The 2010 Government statistics for England demonstrate that, as in the 1990s, only a very small proportion of children referred to children's social care become the subject of a child protection plan (Department for Education 2010b). However, the types of parental problems outlined above are not confined to families where a child is the subject of a child protection plan (Brandon et al. 2008, 2009, 2010; Rose and Barnes 2008). In many families children's health and development are being affected by the difficulties their parents are experiencing. The findings from research, however, suggest that services are not always forthcoming. Practically a quarter of referrals to children's social care resulted in no action being taken (Cleaver and Walker with Meadows 2004). Lord Laming's progress report (2009) also expressed concerns that referrals to children's services from other professionals did not always lead to an initial assessment and that *'much more needs to be done to ensure that the services are as effective as possible at working together to achieve positive outcomes for children'* (Lord Laming 2009, p.9, paragraph 1.1). Practitioners' fear of failing to identify a child in need of protection is also a factor driving up the numbers of referrals to children's social care services which result in no provision of help. *'This is creating a skewed system that is paying so much attention to identifying cases of abuse and neglect that it is draining time and resource away from families'* (Munro 2010, p.6). Munro's Interim Report (2011) draws attention once again to the highly traumatic experience for children and families who are drawn into the Child Protection system where maltreatment is not found, which leaves them with a fear of asking for help in the future. A finding which was identified by earlier research on child protection (Cleaver and Freeman 1995).

Evidence from the 1995 child protection research (Department of Health 1995a) indicated that when parents have problems of their own, these may adversely affect their capacity to respond to the needs of their children. For example, Cleaver and Freeman (1995) found in their study of suspected child abuse that in more than half of the cases, families were experiencing a number of problems including mental illness or learning disability, problem drinking and drug use, or domestic violence. A similar picture of the difficulties facing families who have been referred to children's social care services emerges from more recent research (Cleaver and Walker with Meadows 2004). It is estimated that there are 120,000 families experiencing multiple problems, including poor mental health, alcohol and drug misuse, and domestic violence. *'Over a third of these families have children subject to child protection procedures'* (Munro 2011, p.30, paragraph 2.30).

Children's services have the task of identifying children who may need additional services in order to improve their well-being as relating to their:

(a)   physical and mental health and emotional well-being;

(b)   protection from harm and neglect;

(c)   education, training and recreation;

(d)   the contribution made by them to society; and

(e)   social and economic well-being.

(Section 10(2) of the Children Act 2004)

The Common Assessment Framework (Children's Workforce Development Council 2010) and the Assessment Framework (Department of Health et al. 2000) enable frontline professionals working with children to gain an holistic picture of the child's world and identify more easily the difficulties children and families may be experiencing. Although research suggests that social workers (Cleaver et al. 2007) and health professionals are equipped to recognise and respond to indications that a child is being, or is likely to be, abused or neglected, there is less evidence in relation to teachers and the police (Daniel et al. 2009).

The identification of children's needs may have improved, but understanding how parental mental illness, learning disabilities, substance misuse and domestic violence affect children and families still requires more attention. For example, a small in-depth study found less than half (46%) of the managers in children's social care, health and the police rated as 'good' their understanding of the impact on children of parental substance misuse, although this rose to 61% in relation to the impact of domestic violence (Cleaver et al. 2007). The need for more training on assessing the likelihood of harm to children of parental drug and alcohol misuse was also highlighted by a survey of 248 newly qualified social workers (Galvani and Forrester 2009). A call for more high-quality training on child protection across social care, health and police was also made by Lord Laming (2009). Munro's review of child protection in exploring *'why previous well-intentioned reforms have not resulted in the expected level of improvements'* (p.3) highlighted the *'unintended consequences of restrictive rules and guidance'*, which have left social workers feeling that *'their professional judgement is not seen as a significant aspect of the social work task; it is no longer an activity which is valued, developed or rewarded'* (Munro 2010, p.30, paragraph 2.16).

The experience of professionals providing specialist services for adults can support assessments of children in need living with parental mental illness, learning disability, substance misuse or domestic violence. Research, however, shows that in such cases collaboration between adults' and children's services at the assessment stage rarely happens (Cleaver et al. 2007; Cleaver and Nicholson 2007) and a lack of relevant information may negatively affect the quality of decision making (Bell 2001). An agreed consensus of one another's roles and responsibilities is essential for agencies to work collaboratively. The evidence provided to the Munro review (2011) found *'mixed experiences and absence of consensus about how well professionals are understanding one another's roles and working together'* and argues for *'thoughtfully designed local agreements between professionals about how best to communicate with each other about their work with a family...'* (Munro 2011, p.28, paragraph 2.23). Although research shows that the development of joint protocols and information-sharing procedures support collaborative working between children's and adults' services (Cleaver et al. 2007), a survey of 50 English local authorities found only 12% had clear family-focused policies or joint protocols (Community Care 2009).

The multi-agency approach

In many of the cases that are referred to children's social care, no single agency will be able to provide all the help required to safeguard and promote the welfare of the child and meet the needs of their parents. Social workers, in partnership with families and other agencies, must judge what services, from which agencies, are called for. A research-based typology of families has been developed to help social workers identify the range, type and duration of services required to meet the needs of the child and support the family (Cleaver and Freeman 1995). Three categories in the typology are particularly relevant:

- **Families experiencing multiple problems:** these families are well known to children's services and welfare agencies linked to the Criminal Justice System. They experience a range of problems, many of which are chronic. Difficulties may include parental learning disability, poor mental and physical health, domestic violence, severe alcohol problems, drug abuse, poor housing, long-term unemployment and financial and social incompetence.

- **Families experiencing a specific problem:** these families are rarely known to statutory agencies and come to their attention because of a specific issue, for example acute parental mental illness or a parental drug overdose. Families are not confined to any social class and, on the surface their lives may appear quite ordered.

- **Acutely distressed families:** these families normally cope, but an accumulation of difficulties has overwhelmed them. Families tend to be composed of single or poorly supported and immature parents, or parents who are physically ill or disabled.

The above typology makes a clear distinction between families who normally cope well but have been recently overwhelmed by problems and those who have many chronic problems which require long-term multi-service input. To ensure children's safety and welfare, many of these families will require support from both children's and adults' services. A collaborative approach would ensure that not only are parents recognised as having needs in their own right, but the impact of those needs on their children becomes part of a multi-agency response. Research suggests that the value of such inter-agency collaboration is widely accepted by professionals (Cleaver et al. 2007). A review of the literature on neglect by Daniel and colleagues (2009) highlighted the importance of developing more effective integrated approaches to children where all professions regard themselves as part of the child well-being system. However, ensuring that practice reflects these principles is not always easy, despite the support of national policy and guidance.

> *Despite considerable progress in interagency working, often driven by Local Safeguarding Children Boards and multi-agency teams who strive to help children and young people, there remain significant problems in the day-to-day reality of working across organisational boundaries and cultures, sharing information to protect children and a lack of feedback when professionals raise concerns about a child.*

(Lord Laming 2009, p.10, paragraph 1.6)

The importance of an integrated professional group being accountable for local child protection rather than confining the responsibility to children's social care was stressed in Munro's first two reports on the child protection system (2010, 2011).

Reluctance to admit problems

In addition to identifying and responding to the issues that can affect parenting capacity, the original child protection research also revealed that parental problems themselves could influence the process of enquiries under section 47 of the Children Act 1989, which are undertaken when there are concerns that a child may be suffering significant harm (Department of Health 1995a). A number of key factors were identified, many of which remain pertinent. The first of these was parents' anxiety about losing their children. Cleaver and Freeman (1995) noted that in the early stages of a child protection enquiry, families were reluctant to admit to a history of problem drinking or drug use or mental illness because they assumed it would result in social workers taking punitive action. Subsequent research reinforces this finding (see, for example, Booth and Booth 1996; Cleaver et al. 2007; Gorin 2004).

For similar reasons, families were eager to conceal domestic violence. Farmer and Owen's (1995) research suggests, firstly, that hidden domestic violence may account for many mothers' seemingly uncooperative behaviour and, secondly, that confronting families with allegations of abuse could compound the mother's vulnerable position. Indeed, child protection conferences were often ignorant of whether or not children lived in violent families because in the *'face of allegations of mistreatment couples often formed a defensive alliance against the outside agencies'* (Farmer and Owen 1995, p.79). In fact, the authors found that the level of domestic violence (52%) discovered during the research interviews was twice that disclosed at the initial child protection conference. *'Problems which parents thought would be discrediting were not aired in the early stages – especially those which included domestic violence and alcohol and drug abuse'* (Farmer and Owen 1995, p.190).

The fear that children will be taken into care and families broken up if parental problems come to light may be felt more acutely when the mother is from a minority ethnic group. Difficulties in communication and worries over cultural norms being misinterpreted increase women's fears, and official agencies may be seen as particularly threatening if the mother is of refugee status (Stevenson 2007). Parents value professionals who are non-judgemental in their approach, who communicate sensitively and who involve the parents and keep them informed during all stages of the child protection process (Cleaver and Walker with Meadows 2004; Komulainen and Haines 2009). Evidence suggests that parents are able to discuss their own concerns about their parenting when professionals approach them openly and directly (Daniel et al. 2009). Unfortunately, many parents feel they are treated less courteously by medical staff once concerns of non-accidental injury are raised (Komulainen and Haines 2009).

Working in partnership with children and key family members

Statutory guidance, produced for professionals involved in assessments of children in need under the Children Act 1989, acknowledges the importance of involving children and families and seeks to ensure that all phases of the assessment process are carried out in partnership with key family members.

> *The quality of the early or initial contact will affect later working relationships and the ability of professionals to secure an agreed understanding of what is happening and to provide help.*

(Department of Health et al. 2000, p.13, paragraph 1.47)

The implementation of the Assessment Framework has affected practice. Parents' and children's understanding of the assessment process has improved as has their involvement in assessments, plans and reviews. Research shows that many social workers go to considerable lengths to explain things to parents (particularly those with learning disabilities) and children, and to involve them as much as possible in all stages of the child protection process (Cleaver and Walker with Meadows 2004). A second finding is that professionals tend to evade frightening confrontations; a feature which continues to be identified in serious case reviews (Brandon et al. 2009, 2010; Department for Education 2010c; Lord Laming 2009). Research suggests that when professionals feel unsupported or must visit alone, visiting and child protection enquiries might not always be as thorough as they could be (James 1994; Denny 2005; Farmer 2006).

Gender

Few of the 1995 child protection studies explored parental problems in terms of gender and whether the gender of the parent with the problem influenced social work intervention. Irrespective of which parental figure was presenting the problem, professionals focused their attention on working with mothers. In some cases, despite prolonged domestic violence directed from a father figure to the mother and suspicions that the man was also physically abusive to the children, fathers were rarely involved in the child protection work. *'The shift of focus from men to women allowed men's violence to their wives or partners to disappear from sight'* (Farmer 2006, p.126). However, for some families the possibility of social workers engaging with the father figure was difficult because he refused to discuss the child with the worker, was always out during social work visits or no longer lived in the household (Farmer 2006).

Interpreting behaviour

A final factor identified by the original child protection studies, and still pertinent today, is that social workers may misinterpret parents' behaviour (Department for Education 2010c; HM Government 2010a; C4EO 2010). For example, research has shown that social workers were likely to assume that guilty or evasive behaviour of parents was related to child abuse. But such behaviour was, on occasions, found to be the result of parents wanting to keep secret a history of mental illness, learning disability, illicit drug use or other family problems (Cleaver and Freeman 1995).

In contrast, the apparent co-operation of some parents may result in practitioners applying the 'rule of optimism' (Dingwell et al. 1983). This stems from a number of assumptions – the strongest being that parents love their children and want the best for them, and that children's lives are better if they stay at home, even if that home is very dysfunctional. The application of the rule of optimism may result in overly positive interpretations of what parents say and of the behaviour and circumstances observed. Research suggests that *'over-confidence in "knowing" the parent or carer, might lead to misjudgement, over-identification with parents or GPs not seeing concerns about children'* (Tompsett et al. 2009, p.3). In these circumstances practitioners may too readily accept parents' explanations of events and be reluctant to challenge them (Cleaver and Nicholson 2007; Brandon et al 2010; Department for Education 2010c). Professionals' sympathy for parents can lead to expectations for children being set too low. Lord Laming stresses, *'It is not acceptable to do nothing when a child may be in need of help. It is important that the social work relationship, in particular, is not misunderstood as being a relationship for the benefit of the parents, or for the relationship itself, rather than a focused intervention to protect the child and promote their welfare'* (Lord Laming 2009, p.24, paragraph 3.2). Practitioner support which benefits the parents but does not promote the welfare of the children was also a concern highlighted in Munro's first report of the child protection system. She identified *'a reluctance among many practitioners to make negative professional judgments about a parent....In cases where adult-focused workers perceived their primary role as working within their own sector, failure to take account of children in the household could follow'* (Munro 2010, p.17, paragraph 1.27). A key finding from a review of evidence on what works in protecting children living with highly resistant families was the need for authoritative child protection practice.

> *Families' lack of engagement or hostility hampered practitioners' decision-making capabilities and follow-through with assessments and plans ... practitioners became overly optimistic, focusing too much on small improvements made by families rather than keeping families' full histories in mind.*

(C4EO 2010, p.2)

A lack of knowledge about different cultures within minority communities can also be a barrier to understanding what is happening to the children. Inquiry reports and research have highlighted that stereotyping of families from different backgrounds, linked with difficulties in attributing the correct meaning to what parents say, may have a negative impact on social work assessments and judgements (Dutt and Phillips 2000). For example, in the case of Victoria Climbié, a child who came to England from the Ivory Coast of Africa, professionals assumed the unusual, exceptionally respectful and frequently frozen response to her 'mother' was normal in the family's culture, when in fact it was a sign that Victoria was afraid of her abusive carer (Cm 5730 2003; Armitage and Walker 2009). Communication and understanding can be eased when parents have the opportunity to use the language of their choice (Gardner and Cleaver 2009). The following conclusion, drawn from analysing child deaths and serious injury, is relevant to all those professionals who have concerns about the welfare and safety of a child.

> *In order to have a better chance of understanding how difficulties interact, practitioners must be encouraged to be curious, and to think critically and systematically.*

(Brandon et al. 2008, p.98)

Legal and policy context

Safeguarding and promoting children's welfare

The Children Act 1989 places a duty on local authorities to provide a range of appropriate services for children to ensure that those 'in need' are safeguarded and their welfare is promoted. Children are defined as 'in need' when they are unlikely to reach or maintain a satisfactory level of health or development, or their health and development will be significantly impaired without the provision of services (s17(10) of the Children Act 1989).

Although many families cope adequately with the difficulties they face, others need the assistance of services and support from outside the family to 'safeguard and promote the welfare of the children', which is defined as:

- *protecting children from maltreatment;*

- *preventing impairment of children's health or development;*

- *ensuring that children are growing up in circumstances consistent with the provision of safe and effective care;*

  and undertaking that role so as to enable those children to have optimum life chances and to enter adulthood successfully.

(HM Government 2010a, p.34, paragraph 1.20)

The Department of Health *'regards safeguarding vulnerable children as a high priority and is supporting the NHS to improve safeguarding arrangements'* (Department of Health 2010a, p.6). Providing support to parents in order to improve outcomes for children is part of the Government's strategy to improve public health. In the White Paper *Healthy Lives, Healthy People* (Cm 7985 2010) the Government seeks to give *'every child in every community the best start in life'* through reducing child poverty, increasing the numbers of families reached through the Family Nurse Partnership programme and the number of Sure Start health visitors (p.7, paragraph 11(c)). The strategy acknowledges that improving the health and wellbeing of women before, during and after pregnancy is a *'critical factor in giving children a healthy start in life and laying the groundwork for good health and wellbeing in later life'* (p.17, paragraph 1.17). There is also a commitment to invest in early years support in order to improve children's development; a key factor in their future health and wellbeing. The value of supporting good parent-child relationships in order to build the child's self esteem and confidence and reduce the risk of children adopting unhealthy lifestyles is also recognised. For families with complex needs the strategy sets out a commitment to locally co-ordinated support to prevent problems from escalating.

The Government-commissioned report on early intervention provides much evidence *'to suggest that the first three years of life create the foundation in learning how to express emotion and to understand and respond to the emotions of others'* (Allen 2011, p.5, paragraph 15). There is an emphasis on early intervention packages which have a proven track record, and a recommendation that a new, Early Intervention Foundation is created.

Past governments have also sought to respond to the needs of vulnerable families with the aim of improving the wellbeing of children. The Children Act 1989 recognised that to promote children's welfare, services may need to address the difficulties that parents experience.

> *Parents are individuals with needs of their own. Even though services may be offered primarily on behalf of their children, parents are entitled to help and consideration in their own right... Their parenting capacity may be limited temporarily or permanently by poverty, racism, poor housing or unemployment or by personal or marital problems, sensory or physical disability, mental illness or past life experiences...*

(Department of Health 1991, p.8)

Under the Children Act 2004 *'a children's services authority in England must have regard to the importance of parents and other persons caring for children in improving the well-being of children'* (Section 10(3) of the Children Act 2004).

The National Framework for Children, Young People and Maternity Services stressed the importance of providing support to parents and the need for collaboration between adults' and children's services.

> *In addition to meeting the general needs of parents from disadvantaged backgrounds, it is important to consider the more specialised forms of support required by families in specific circumstances, such as support for parents with mental health difficulties or disabilities, or with substance misuse problems. Good collaborative arrangements are required between services for adults, where the adult is a parent, and children's services, in particular, where children may be especially vulnerable.*

(Department of Health and Department for Education and Skills 2004, p.69, paragraph 3.4).

The needs of vulnerable children were addressed in the Department of Health's revised code of practice which provides guidance to doctors, relevant hospital staff and mental health professionals on how they should proceed when undertaking their duties under the Mental Health Act 1983. The code of practice notes that practitioners should ensure that:

- children and young people are provided with information about their parents' illness;

- appropriate arrangements are in place for the immediate care of dependent children;

- the best interests and safety of children are always considered in arrangements for children to visit patients in hospital; and

- the safety and welfare of dependent children are taken into account when clinicians consider granting leave of absence for parents with a mental disorder.

(Department of Health 2008)

Improving child protection and reforming frontline social work practice is a priority for the Government. Although past governments were committed to protecting children, statistical returns on the numbers of children subject to a child protection plan continue to increase suggesting more needs to be done (Department for Education 2009 and 2010a). At March 2010 39,100 children were subject to a child protection plan, an increase of 5,000 (15%) from the 2008-09 figures (Munro 2011, p.25). Three principles underpinned the recent review of child protection which the Government asked Professor Munro to undertake: '*early intervention; trusting professionals and removing bureaucracy so they can spend more of their time on the frontline; and greater transparency and accountability*' (Munro 2010, p.44).

The Children Act 2004 placed statutory duties on local agencies to make arrangements to safeguard and promote the welfare of children in the course of discharging their normal functions. Ensuring effective inter-agency working is a key responsibility of Local Safeguarding Children Boards (LSCBs). LSCBs should ensure that agencies demonstrate good collaboration and co-ordination in cases which require input from both children's and adults' services. Services for adults include GPs and hospitals, learning disability and mental health teams, drug action teams and domestic violence forums.

A survey of the organisations responsible for safeguarding and promoting the welfare of children under section 11 of the Children Act 2004 suggested that although significant progress has been made, two-thirds of organisations did not yet have *all* the key arrangements in place (MORI 2009). The Government's statutory guidance *Working Together to Safeguard Children* makes clear that safeguarding and promoting the welfare of children '*depends on effective joint working between agencies and professionals that have different roles and expertise*' (HM Government 2010a, p.31, paragraph 1.12).

> *Adult mental health services – including those providing general adult and community, forensic, psychotherapy, alcohol and substance misuse and learning disability services – have a responsibility in safeguarding children when they become aware of, or identify, a child at risk of harm.*

(HM Government 2010a, p.65, paragraph 2.102)

Parental mental illness

The Government is committed to

> '*protecting the population from serious health threats; helping people live longer, healthier and more fulfilling lives; and improving the health of the poorest, fastest; and lifting families out of poverty.*'

(Cm 7985 2010, p.4(1))

Poor mental health is a key component of the overall burden of longstanding illness within the general population and is responsible for the greatest proportion of working days lost (Health and Safety Executive 2010). In its strategy for improving public health in England, the Government has identified the need to target a range of issues including mental illness, heavy drinking and drug misuse (Cm 7985 2010). It recognises that no single agency can do this alone. '*Responsibility needs to be shared right across society – between individual, families, communities, local government, business, the NHS, voluntary and community organisations, the wider public sector and central government*' (Cm 7985 2010, p.24, paragraph 2.5). The Cross-Government mental health outcomes strategy sets out plans to ensure mental health awareness and treatment (for children as well as adults) are given the same prominence as physical health. Six objectives are highlighted:

(i)   *More people will have good mental health*

(ii)   *More people with mental health problems will recover*

(iii)   *More people with mental health problems will have good physical heath*

(iv)   *More people will have a positive experience of care and support*

(v)   *Fewer people will suffer avoidable harm*

(vi)   *Fewer people will experience stigma and discrimination*

(HM Government 2011, p.6, paragraph 1.5)

Children are at the heart of this strategy. It acknowledges that some parents '*will require additional support to manage anxiety and depression during pregnancy and the child's early years...*' (HM Government 2011, p.39, paragraph 5.5). The aim is to intervene early with '*vulnerable children and young people in order to improve lifetime health and wellbeing, prevent mental illness and reduce costs incurred by ill health, unemployment and crime*' (p.9, paragraph 1.15). It is anticipated early intervention will bring benefits not only to the individual during childhood and into adulthood, but also improve his or her capacity to parent.

Adults may experience a single or a combination of issues, such as poor mental health and learning disability, substance misuse and domestic violence, and require a range of services in order to remain independent. *A Vision for Adult Social Care* acknowledges that some people will need social care support because of the effects of long term conditions.

'Good partnership working between health and social care is vital for helping them to manage their condition and live independently' (Department of Health 2010b, p.13, paragraph 3.13).

Parents with a learning disability

The Equality Act 2010 prohibits service providers discriminating on a number of criteria including disability. Disability is defined in the following way.

(1) A person (P) has a disability if—

> *(a) P has a physical or mental impairment, and*
> *(b) the impairment has a substantial and long-term adverse effect on P's ability to carry out normal day-to-day activities.*

(Section 6(1) of the Equality Act 2010)

Section 47(1) of the National Health Services and Community Care Act 1990 places a duty on local authorities to consider the needs of disabled persons, including those with learning disabilities. This is supported by practice guidance.

> *In general, councils may provide community care services to individual adults with needs arising from physical, sensory, learning or cognitive disabilities, or from mental health needs.*

(Department of Health 2010b, p.18, paragraph 43)

Supporting disabled adults in their role as parents is highlighted in this practice guidance. For example, in determining eligibility, all four levels include the situation in which *'family and other social roles and responsibilities cannot or will not be undertaken'* (Department of Health 2010b, p.20, paragraph 54). Local authorities are enjoined to consider the additional help those adults with, for example, mental health difficulties or learning disabilities may need if they have parenting responsibilities. This includes identifying whether a child or young person is acting in a caring role and the effect this is having on them and exploring whether there is a need to safeguard and promote the welfare of the child.

Parental substance misuse

In the Government's drug strategy, the impact of drugs and alcohol misuse on society is recognised.

> *From the crime in local neighbourhoods, through families forced apart by dependency, to the corrupting effect of international organised crime, drugs have a profound and negative effect on communities, families and individuals.*

(HM Government 2010b, p.3)

Prevention and supporting recovery is at the heart of this strategy. A 'whole-life' approach is proposed in order to break the *'inter-generational paths to dependency by supporting vulnerable families'*, providing good quality education and advice, intervening early and supporting people to recover. Relevant agencies are expected to work together to address the needs of the whole person. To prevent substance misuse amongst children and young people (some of whom will have parents who misuse drugs and alcohol) the strategy advocates the use of family-focused interventions (HM Government 2010b, p.11).

It has been estimated that there are between 250,000 and 350,000 children of problem drug users in the UK (Advisory Council on the Misuse of Drugs 2003) and a third of adults in treatment have child care responsibilities (HM Government 2010b). The Government's drug strategy places a particular focus on the children of parents with drug and alcohol problems. The need to be aware of the harm, abuse and neglect, as well as the inappropriate caring roles, some children may experience is stressed. The strategy is clear that *'where there are concerns about the safety and welfare of children, professionals from both adult and children's services, alongside the voluntary sector, should work together to protect children, in accordance with the statutory guidance Working Together to Safeguard Children (2010)'* (HM Government 2010b, p.21).

A range of relevant practice guidance is available to local authorities. For example, the Department of Health has produced guidance which focuses on people with severe mental health problems and problematic substance misuse.

> *Substance misuse is usual rather than exceptional amongst people with severe mental health problems and the relationship between the two is complex.*

(Department of Health 2002, p.4)

The guidance supported joint working and improved co-ordinated care between mental health services and specialist substance misuse services (Department of Health 2002).

Models of Care for Alcohol Misusers (Department of Health and National Treatment Agency for Substance Misuse 2006) provided practice guidance for local health organisations and their partners in the commissioning and provision of assessments, interventions and treatment of adults who misuse alcohol. The guidance acknowledged the impact of parental alcohol misuse on children. This is clearly stated in the foreword by the then chief medical officer, Sir Liam Donaldson:

> *There is no doubt that alcohol misuse is associated with a wide range of problems, including physical health problems such as cancer and heart disease; offending behaviours, not least domestic violence; suicide and deliberate self-harm; child abuse and child neglect; mental health problems which co-exist with alcohol misuse; and social problems such as homelessness.*

(Department of Health and National Treatment Agency for Substance Misuse 2006, p.5)

However, the recommendations relating to screening and early assessments did not include the children of parents who misuse alcohol, although the guidance did recommend that comprehensive risk assessments should be targeted at, among others, users with complex needs including women who are pregnant or have children 'at risk'. The Department of Health has recently trialled a range of alcohol screening and brief intervention approaches to evaluate their delivery, effectiveness and cost-effectiveness (Screening and Intervention Programme for Sensible Drinking (SIPS) see www.hubcap.org.uk/F25W.)

Domestic violence

The Government is also concerned about violence against women and children and is committed to improving the standards of care and support.

> *As well as the government's commitment to support existing rape crisis centre provision on a stable basis and to establish new centres, the Home Office has allocated a flat cash settlement of over £28m over the next four years for work to tackle violence against women and girls.*

(HM Government 2010c, p.15, paragraph 2.1)

The Department of Health's action plan *Improving services for women and child victims of violence* (HM Government 2010c, p.15, paragraph 2.1) is part of the cross-Government approach to tackling such violence. The plan acknowledges that *'violence and abuse can also be a risk factor in families with multiple problems .... the Spending Review makes a commitment for a national campaign to support and help turn around the lives of families with multiple problems, improving outcomes and reducing costs to welfare and public services'* (p.10).

With the aim of improving the response to the victims of violence, the Government's action plan proposes to:

- raise awareness: amongst health professional of their role in addressing the issues, and through providing patients with information that helps them access relevant services quickly and safely;

- improve the competency and skills of NHS staff through developing a training matrix;

- improve the quality of services to victims of violence; and

- improve the data collection on violence and support health professionals to appropriately share information.

(Department of Health 2010a)

The Domestic Violence, Crime and Victims Act 2004 amended part 4 of the Family Law Act 1996 and the Protection from Harassment Act 1997. The 2004 Act extended the powers of the court in protecting the partners in a relationship. Furthermore, it created a new criminal offence of *'causing or allowing the death of a child or vulnerable adult'* (Section 4 of the Domestic Violence, Crime and Victims Act 2004).

Section 24 of the Crime and Security Act 2010 also seeks to protect women and children who are the victims of domestic violence. Senior police officers have been given the power to issue domestic violence protection notices (DVPN). Such a notice can be used to ban violent men from the family home, initially for 24 hours, to prevent women from future violence or the threat of violence. The safety of the child must also be taken into consideration. Before issuing a DVPN the officer must consider *'the welfare of any person under the age of 18 whose interests the officer considers relevant to the issuing of the DVPN (whether or not that person is an associated person)'* (Section 24(3) of the Crime and Security Act 2010).The issuing of a DVPN triggers the application to the magistrates court for a domestic violence protection order. This is an order, lasting between 14 and 18 days, which prohibits the perpetrator from molesting his victim.

There is also statutory and practice guidance available to support professionals in safeguarding women and children from domestic violence. For example, *Working Together to Safeguard Children* reinforced the role of the police in identifying and safeguarding children living with domestic violence; *'patrol officers attending domestic violence incidents, for example, should be aware of the effect of such violence on any children normally resident within the household'* (HM Government 2010a, p.71, paragraph 2.126). To ensure police officers working in child protection at all levels have access to specialist training on domestic violence, an updated training module has been made available to police forces since December 2009 (Cm 7589).

The 2009 Home Office guidance and practice advice and *Working Together to Safeguard Children* (HM Government 2010a) both advocate the use of multi-agency risk assessment conferences (MARAC) as a process for *'helping to address an issue of domestic violence; for managing PPOs, including those who are problematic drug users; or for identifying children at risk'* (Home Office 2009a, p.14-15, paragraph 2.3.3). (PPOs refer to Prolific and other Priority Offenders). MARAC meetings are expected to involve representatives of key statutory and voluntary agencies, who might be involved in supporting a victim of domestic abuse.

Another example of multi-agency working in cases of domestic violence is the Specialist Domestic Violence Court (SDVC) programme. These special courts, within the Criminal Justice System, bring together a similar range of bodies to MARAC.

> *Agencies work together to identify, track and risk assess domestic violence cases, support victims of domestic violence and share information better so that more offenders are brought to justice.*

(Her Majesty's Court Service et al. 2008, p.3, paragraph E1.1)

Limitations of the research drawn on in this publication

Different laws and cultures

Much of the research on mental illness, learning disability, domestic violence and substance misuse comes from the US, which has different laws, traditions, and social institutions from the United Kingdom. For example, a major difference which exists in relation to substance misuse is the commitment to harm minimisation in the United Kingdom. This approach is not universally shared in the US, which has followed an abstinence-only policy for the last 30 years. As a result there are unique services in the United Kingdom, such as consistently available methadone treatment and needle and syringe exchange schemes for problem drug users, and controlled-drinking programmes for problem alcohol users. In the US, abstinence-based programmes, especially in alcohol services, are more available than controlled drinking, and methadone maintenance programmes are more restrictive in the US compared to the United Kingdom. This has implications for services for women in the US, where many treatment programmes for pregnant drug and alcohol users require women to be abstinent in order to take part in the programme. In many American states, pregnant mothers who use drugs or alcohol risk prison sentences while pregnant on the grounds of physical child abuse.

Focusing on a specific issue

Most research is centred on a specific issue such as domestic violence, depression, learning disability or heroin use. However, in practice, many problem drug users will use a variety of drugs and alcohol (polydrug use). Similarly, many of those experiencing domestic violence also suffer depression and may use alcohol or drugs as a way of coping; or those who are perpetrating the violence may be under the influence of alcohol or drugs. Moreover, a learning disability does not inure an individual to drug misuse, domestic violence or mental illness. In this publication, although each issue is taken individually when describing the psychological and physical symptoms, when discussing the findings from research in relation to the impact on parenting capacity a more pragmatic and inclusive approach has been taken.

Time-limited research

Research on these issues usually looks at the influence on parenting capacity over a relatively short period. This approach does not take into account the differing needs of the child at various times in their life or the fluctuating nature of drug and alcohol use, learning disability, mental illness or domestic violence on the parents themselves. Longitudinal studies would help minimise this limitation, but they are few and far between.

Sampling bias

The samples used in many research studies are taken from specific groups such as parental cocaine or alcohol users in treatment, mentally ill parents in hospital, parents in receipt of services for learning disability, or mothers in refuges. Far less is known about parents in the general population who experience these problems but do not seek help; it would be dangerous to assume that the populations studied are representative.

Research on the impact of parental problems on children tends to be biased towards women as carers. There are more studies on maternal parenting capacity than paternal capacity, and often the influence of other family factors, such as the role of grandparents or siblings, or the impact of divorce or separation, is not considered.

Many of the studies focus on specific problems, such as children's drug and alcohol use, violence, mental health, education, offending and behavioural problems, rather than a more holistic approach or the identification of signs of resilience or coping strategies.

It is often not possible to accurately measure the quantities of drugs and alcohol being used by parents, the degree of violence experienced, or the extent of mental illness or learning disability. For example, some parents may feel threatened by services which can take action on the care of their children and underestimate their difficulties. In other situations parents may overestimate their problems. For example, drug use may be exaggerated and presented as mitigating circumstances in criminal court cases or in an attempt to maximise a methadone prescription.

A further limitation of the research is the dependence on client recall. Drugs and alcohol, domestic violence, mental illness and learning disabilities all adversely affect the capacity to remember, and many studies rely not only on recent memory but memory over many months or years. It is questionable how accurate these measurements are. Finally, it is essential to remember that the majority of parents who experience these issues, especially those who present for services, are usually also suffering from multiple forms of deprivation and social exclusion. These factors should not be underestimated in their net effect on parenting capacity.

With all of the above limitations in mind, there is a great deal of consistency in the results of research on some aspects of parenting capacity and the influence of these parental problems on children, while other aspects are less consistent. One of our objectives is to help place the research in context, taking account of the limitations.

Structure of the book

In considering how parental mental illness, learning disability, problem drinking, drug misuse or domestic violence may affect the child, a holistic and developmental model is applied. Research findings are disaggregated through applying the conceptual framework designed to assess and measure outcomes for children in need (Department of Health et al 2000). The three domains of the child's developmental needs, parenting capacity and family and environmental factors constitute the framework. The three inter-related domains incorporate a number of important dimensions (see Figure 1.1).

Figure 1.1 The Assessment Framework

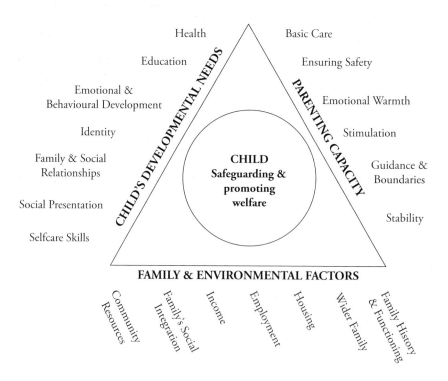

(Department of Health et al. 2000)

The evidence is explored in relation to these domains and dimensions, with particular emphasis on how parental mental illness, learning disabilities, substance misuse and domestic violence have an impact on children's health and development, and whether there is evidence that children are suffering, or likely to suffer, significant harm. Because the impact on the child will depend on a variety of factors including age and developmental stage, the age bands first used in the Integrated Children's System (Department for Children, Schools and Families 2010) have been applied. For example, with regard to the educational development of children aged 3–4 years, it is important to identify when parents' problems substantially restrict the child's access to stimulating toys and books, or prevent parents spending sufficient time talking, reading or playing with their children. Alternatively, assessing the impact of these same parental issues on the education of adolescents aged 11–15 years needs to focus on different themes – for example, school attendance and involvement in other learning activities such as sport, music or hobbies.

Within each dimension and for each age group, evidence is used to highlight both the adverse impact on children and the factors which act as protectors, such as the strategies children use to cope with stressful family situations and the support and influence of the wider family and community.

The book is divided into three parts, Parts I, II and III.

Part I includes Chapters 1–3 and explores the following general issues:

Chapter 1: questions whether concern is justified, and explores the problems of definition and prevalence.

Chapter 2: explores the ways in which mental illness, learning disability, problem drug use (including alcohol) and domestic violence affect parenting capacity.

Chapter 3: identifies which children are most vulnerable.

Part II includes Chapters 4–6, with a specific focus on children of different ages and stages of development:

Chapter 4: discusses the impact of parental problems for children under 5 years.

Chapter 5: focuses on the issues for children aged 5 to 10 years.

Chapter 6: focuses on young people aged 11 years and over.

Part III includes Chapters 7 and 8 which draw together the findings and implication for policy and practice:

Chapter 7: discusses the conclusions from the study.

Chapter 8: outlines the implications for policy and practice.

PART I: GENERAL ISSUES AFFECTING PARENTING CAPACITY

1 Is concern justified? Problems of definition and prevalence

To understand whether the present concerns over parental mental illness, learning disability, problem alcohol and drug use or domestic violence are justified, this chapter examines the problems with terminology and the prevalence of these issues. General population studies provide evidence of their prevalence and the relevance of gender, culture and class. Findings from child protection research are used to identify associations between these parental problems and children's health and development, including the extent to which they may pose a risk of significant harm to the child.

Problems with terminology

Understanding the degree of these parental problems is difficult because different research studies use different terms and there are few definitions provided. For example, in the Department of Health's 1995 studies on child protection (Department of Health 1995a) it is unclear whether Sharland et al.'s (1996) parents who have 'relationship problems' are a similar group to Thoburn et al.'s (1995) parents who are in 'marital conflict', or Farmer and Owen's (1995) families who are experiencing 'domestic violence'. Difficulties also arise because, for example, different countries use different ways of measuring drug and alcohol use. For instance, the 'unit of alcohol' in the United Kingdom has little meaning in the US where different measures of alcohol are used in peer-reviewed journals and research. In addition, the purity of drugs used in different countries may differ. For example, a gram of heroin in New York may be more or less pure than a gram of heroin in London.

In discussing the impact of these issues on families, the term 'parent' is generally used in a generic way to refer to any adult responsible for parenting the child. Thus the mentally ill 'mother' could be the birth mother, stepmother, foster mother, father's female cohabitee or female relative who is bringing up the child. The precise relationship of the carer to the child has been noted when the findings from research suggest this is relevant. Identifying the relationship between the child and parent figure can be important because it can affect children's perspectives on events. For example, in examining why some children who had witnessed domestic violence were more resilient than others, Sullivan et al. (2000) found children's adjustment was affected by their relationship to the abuser; stepfathers and father figures were more emotionally abusive and instilled more fear in the children than birth fathers or non-father figures.

When scrutinising the literature on mental illness, learning disability, problem alcohol and drug use, and domestic violence the authors have been guided in the use of terms by the following policy and practice documents.

Mental illness

Clinical studies of adults generally define mental illness either by using the European system: *The ICD-10 Classification of Mental Illness and Behavioural Disorders* (World Health Organisation 1992) or the US classification: *Diagnostic and Statistical Manual of Mental Disorders* (American Psychiatric Association 2000). Unfortunately, the quality of information from community-based records may preclude such a precise diagnosis. In addition, there continues to be considerable dispute over whether 'personality disorder' is a psychiatric illness as such or merely a description of extremes of normal variation (see Kendell 2002 for a discussion of this issue). Moreover, because *'personality dysfunction has been repeatedly described in anecdotal case reports, clinical studies and surveys of the parents of maltreated children'* (Falkov 1997, p.42) it was thought that to omit it in a study of the impact on children of parental problems would be remiss. In some ways, the recent amendments to the Mental Health Act 2007 simplify the issue in clinical terms with the use of a new expression – 'mental disorder' – which is defined as *'any disorder or disability of the mind'* but excludes both alcohol and drug dependence and *'learning disabilities unless with abnormally aggressive or seriously irresponsible behaviour'*.

Learning disability

The Department of Health's definition of learning disability encompasses people with a broad range of disabilities. *Learning disability includes the presence of:*

- *a significantly reduced ability to understand new or complex information, to learn new skills (impaired intelligence); with*

- *a reduced ability to cope independently (impaired social functioning);*

- *which started before adulthood, with a lasting effect on development.*

(HM Government 2010a, p.279, paragraph 9.56)

Mencap also provides a clear description of learning disability.

> *A learning disability is caused by the way the brain develops. There are many different types and most develop before a baby is born, during birth or because of a serious illness in early childhood. A learning disability can be mild, moderate, severe or profound, but all are lifelong. Many people with a learning disability, however, live independent lives.*

(Mencap www.mencap.org.uk)

The cause of learning disabilities includes genetic factors, infection before birth, brain injury at birth, brain infections or brain damage after birth. Examples include Down's syndrome, Fragile X syndrome and cerebral palsy (Royal College of Psychiatrists 2004a).

Problem drinking

The National Institute for Health and Clinical Excellence (2010) in their public health guidance on alcohol-use disorders provides the following definitions:

Hazardous drinking - A pattern of alcohol consumption that increases someone's risk of harm.

Harmful drinking - A pattern of alcohol consumption that is causing mental or physical damage.

Higher-risk drinking - Regularly consuming over 50 alcohol units per week (adult men) or over 35 units per week (adult women).

In the United Kingdom one unit is equivalent to half a pint of ordinary-strength lager or beer or one shot (25 ml) of spirits, while a small (125 ml) glass of wine is equal to 1.5 units. The unit measure has lost some of its value and simplicity because few pubs or restaurants serve 125 ml glasses of wine (they are now either 175 ml or 250 ml). Also, when the unit was devised wine was calculated as having on average 9% alcohol, while most wines these days are 12–15%. Similarly, the alcohol content of many beers and lagers is now more than it was when the unit system was established. Previously, the alcohol content of beer and lager was estimated at 3.5–4.0%. Now most beers are stronger, 3.5–9.0%, with many popular beers at 5%. The pub 'measure' of spirits has, in some pubs, been replaced by a 35 ml measure. Recently, the number of units of alcohol in a bottle of wine has been printed on the label.

The Government strategy for public health (Cm 7985 2010) acknowledges the deleterious impact of heavy drinking on health and the negative effect on others. *'Drunkenness is associated with almost half of assault and more than a quarter of domestic violence incidents'* (p.20, paragraph 1.31).

Problem drug use

Research into problem drug use employs a bewildering range of terms in its descriptions including drug use, drug misuse, drug dependence, addiction, drug abuse and problem drug use. These terms are not always defined, which makes it difficult to compare the findings from one study with another. For instance, someone can be a problem drug user (having problems as a result of drug use) but not suffer from addiction (suggesting physical and psychological dependence).

With regard to problem drug use, this publication follows the lead taken by the Advisory Council on the Misuse of Drugs (2003).

UNIVERSITY OF WINCHESTER
LIBRARY

By problem drug use we mean drug use with serious negative consequences of a physical, psychological, social and interpersonal, financial or legal nature for users and those around them. Such drug use will usually be heavy, with features of dependence.

(Advisory Council on the Misuse of Drugs 2003, p.7)

Domestic violence

When considering domestic violence, the 2009 definition used by the Home Office was found to be helpful.

Domestic violence is 'Any incident of threatening behaviour, violence or abuse (psychological, physical, sexual, financial or emotional) between adults who are or have been intimate partners or family members, regardless of gender or sexuality.' This includes issues of concern to black and minority ethnic (BME) communities such as so called 'honour based violence', female genital mutilation (FGM) and forced marriage.

(Home Office 2009b)

This definition of domestic violence does not confine itself to physical or sexual assaults but includes a range of abusive behaviours which are not in themselves inherently violent. As a consequence, some authors prefer to use the term 'domestic abuse'. It should also be noted that domestic violence recognises few social boundaries. For example, research on female victims of domestic violence reports that *'violence against women is the most democratic of all crimes, it crosses all religious, class and race barriers'* (Women's Aid 1995).

Child abuse and neglect

Child abuse and neglect are forms of child maltreatment and result from anyone (but more commonly a parent or carer) inflicting harm or failing to act to prevent harm. Statutory guidance provides the following descriptions of abuse and neglect.

Physical abuse *may involve hitting, shaking, throwing, poisoning, burning or scalding, drowning, suffocating, or otherwise causing physical harm to a child. Physical harm may also be caused when a parent or carer fabricates the symptoms of, or deliberately induces, illness in a child.*

Emotional abuse *is the persistent emotional maltreatment of a child such as to cause severe and persistent adverse effects on the child's emotional development. It may involve conveying to children that they are worthless or unloved, inadequate, or valued only insofar as they meet the needs of another person. It may include not giving the child opportunities to express their views, deliberately silencing them or 'making fun' of what they say or how they communicate. It may feature age or developmentally inappropriate expectations being imposed on children. These may*

Is concern justified? Problems of definition and prevalence

27

include interactions that are beyond the child's developmental capability, as well as overprotection and limitation of exploration and learning, or preventing the child participating in normal social interaction. It may involve seeing or hearing the ill treatment of another. It may involve serious bullying (including cyber bullying), causing children frequently to feel frightened or in danger, or the exploitation or corruption of children. Some level of emotional abuse is involved in all types of maltreatment of a child, though it may occur alone.

Sexual abuse *involves forcing or enticing a child or young person to take part in sexual activities, not necessarily involving a high level of violence, whether or not the child is aware of what is happening. The activities may involve physical contact, including assault by penetration (for example, rape or oral sex) or non-penetrative acts such as masturbation, kissing, rubbing and touching outside of clothing. They may also include non-contact activities, such as involving children in looking at, or in the production of, sexual images, watching sexual activities, encouraging children to behave in sexually inappropriate ways, or grooming a child in preparation for abuse (including via the internet). Sexual abuse is not solely perpetrated by adult males. Women can also commit acts of sexual abuse, as can other children.*

Neglect *is the persistent failure to meet a child's basic physical and/or psychological needs, likely to result in the serious impairment of the child's health or development. Neglect may occur during pregnancy as a result of maternal substance abuse. Once a child is born, neglect may involve a parent or carer failing to:*

- *Provide adequate food, clothing and shelter (including exclusion from home or abandonment);*

- *Protect a child from physical and emotional harm or danger;*

- *Ensure adequate supervision (including the use of inadequate care-givers); or*

- *Ensure access to appropriate medical care or treatment.*

- *It may also include neglect of, or unresponsiveness to, a child's basic emotional needs.*

(HM Government 2010a, p.38-39, paragraphs 1.33-1.36)

Prevalence

One of the first questions to address is how prevalent is parental mental illness, learning disability, drug or alcohol misuse and domestic violence in families with dependent children. Many adults have times when they suffer from anxiety or depression, develop unstable relationships with partners or drink alcohol, and increasing numbers have used drugs, both licit and illicit, but this does not mean they are poor parents. Moreover, research has consistently failed to show any clear relationship between intelligence – until it falls below a certain level, usually taken to be an IQ of 60 or less – and parenting (Booth and Booth 2004; Tymchuck 1992). It is the extremity or combination of these situations, particularly the association with violence, which may impair parents' capacity to meet their children's needs and, in some situations, result in child abuse and neglect.

Unfortunately, the ability to accurately gauge the extent of parental mental illness, learning disability, problem alcohol or drug use, and domestic violence is hampered not only by problems of terminology but also because prevalence depends upon the population group being studied. For example, community-based samples such as the household survey carried out by the Office for National Statistics will be more representative than research which focuses on specific groups, such as hospital patients, women and children in refuges, or those who attend clinics or courts. Moreover, the severity of the condition under study is likely to be much greater in specific sample groups as is the coexistence of a variety of additional problems. But regardless of the type of sample group under consideration, any generalisations to samples beyond that being studied should be made with considerable caution.

The following sections explore, in turn, the existing evidence on the prevalence of:

- parental mental illness

- learning disability

- problem drinking and drug use

- domestic violence.

Two sources are examined for each category:
- general population studies

- child protection research.

Prevalence of parental mental illness: general population studies

There is wide variation in the morbidity of different types of mental illness. For example, the General Household Survey (Office for National Statistics 2003) shows that one in six adults in Great Britain had a neurotic disorder during the week surveyed in 2000. In contrast, the prevalence of a psychotic disorder was much lower – during the same time frame only 1 in 200 had a disorder such as psychosis and schizophrenia (Singleton et al. 2001). Table 1.1 compares the rate of different types of mental illness within the general population derived from community-based studies.

Table 1.1: **Prevalence of mental illness among adults in the general population**

Type of mental illness	Rate	Source of data
Mixed anxiety and depressive disorder	8.8%	Singleton et al. 2001 (based on data from the General Household Survey)
Generalised anxiety disorder	4.4%	Singleton et al. 2001
Depression	2.5–6.6%	Singleton et al. 2001; Kandal et al. 2000; Kessler et al. 2003
Phobia	3.5%	Singleton et al. 2001
Obsessive compulsive disorder	3.3%	Singleton et al. 2001; Hollander 1997
Panic disorder	0.7%	Singleton et al. 2001
Schizophrenia	0.5–1.0%	Office for National Statistics 2006a; Singleton et al. 2001
Personality disorder	4.4–13.4%	Singleton et al. 2001; Torgersen et al. 2001; Coid and Yang 2006
Postnatal depression	9–27%	O'Hara 1999; Royal College of Psychiatrists 2010; Netmums 2005

It is encouraging to note that the proportion of people receiving treatment for mental health difficulties has increased from 14% in 1993 to 24% in 2000. In the main this was the result of a doubling in the proportion of those receiving medication, whereas access to psychological treatment has remained constant (Office for National Statistics 2005).

The picture is complicated because mental illness frequently exists alongside other disorders. For example, US research indicates that half of those with a diagnosis of schizophrenia (Swofford et al. 2000) and nearly a third of those with a mood disorder also misused or were dependent upon alcohol or drugs (Regier et al. 1990). The work of Rosenthal and Westreich (1999) in the US also suggests that half of individuals who experience alcohol or drug problems or mental health disorders will have two or more of these disorders over their lifetime. Work in the United Kingdom which focused on those attending mental health services found 44% of patients self-reported problem use of drugs and/or were assessed to have used alcohol at hazardous or harmful levels in the previous year (Weaver et al. 2002).

Research would suggest that 30% of adults with a mental disorder have dependent children and 7% live in lone-parent households (Falkov 1998; Melzer 2003). There are an estimated 50,000 to 200,000 children and young people in the UK caring for a parent with a severe mental illness (Mental Health Foundation 2010). The OPCS survey (Office of Population and Censuses and Surveys 1996), which broke down the data by the type of family unit, showed psychiatric morbidity to be associated with family characteristics. Couples living with children have a greater morbidity for both neurotic disorder (155 per thousand) and functional psychoses (4 per thousand) than couples without children (134 per thousand for neurotic disorder and two per thousand for functional psychoses). The data also show a higher rate of mental illness for lone parents than for adults living as a couple with children (see Table 1.2). These findings suggest that children may be more vulnerable to harm and neglect when living with a lone parent who suffers from mental illness, because when the parent is experiencing the disorder there is likely to be no other caring adult living in the home to take on the parenting role.

Table 1.2: **Prevalence of mental illness among parents in the general population**

Type of mental illness	Couple and child(ren)	Lone parent and child(ren)
Neurotic disorders	15.5%	28%
Functional psychoses	0.4%	1.1%

Parental mental illness: issues of gender, culture and class

Research on fathers or male carers with mental health problems is sparse. What is clear is that men who live either as a couple with children or in a lone-parent situation have a lower rate of neurotic disorder and functional psychoses than do women in similar situations (Singleton et al. 2001; Coid and Yang 2006).

In contrast, there is a considerable body of work which records the rate of mental illness in mothers. Somewhat surprising is that the prevalence of maternal mental illness appears to vary from country to country. For example, an American study suggests as many as 25–39% of women suffer depression following childbirth (Centre for Disease Control and Prevention 2004), whereas British studies have traditionally placed the figure at around 10% (O'Hara and Swain 1996). However, a more recent online survey suggests depression following childbirth has increased significantly over the past 50 years in Britain, up from 8% in the 1950s to 27% today (Netmums 2005). One might question whether the variance in reported rates of mental illness is due to real differences in prevalence, in how mental illness manifests itself, or in the methods of assessment and recording. For example, the US study (Centre for Disease Control and Prevention 2004) of 453,186 women recorded depression in terms of its severity and found 7.1% of mothers reported experiencing severe depression, and just more than half reported experiencing low to moderate depression following childbirth.

Research into the impact of race, class and culture suggests a further complicating factor in gauging prevalence. Mental illness is linked to social class and poverty. Data from the General Household Survey (Singleton et al. 2001) showed that those with a mental illness were more likely than those without to have no formal educational qualifications and to come from social class V (unskilled, manual occupations) and be economically inactive. Adults with mental health problems have the highest unemployment rates for any of the main groups of disabled people; only 21% are employed (Office for National Statistics 2006b). The impact of class and poverty are exacerbated when adults are parents caring for children. '... *among those with children at home, working-class women were four times more likely to suffer from a definite psychiatric disorder*' than comparable middle-class women (Brown and Harris 1978, p.278).

Vulnerability to mental disorders may be the result of adverse life events such as poverty, poor environment, sexism or racism and other forms of social disadvantage (Centre for Disease Control and Prevention 2004; Ghate and Hazel 2002; Propper et al. 2004). For example, research based in 15 electoral wards in London found the incidence of schizophrenia in non-white minorities was related to the proportion of the ethnic minority living in the area; the smaller the minority group the greater the incidence of schizophrenia (Boydell et al. 2001). Of significance are individual experiences, particularly those involving long-term threat (Brown and Harris 1978; Sheppard 1993).

The picture is further clouded because mental illness is perceived differently by different cultural groups (NSPCC 1997a; Anglin et al 2006). For example, the literature seems to suggest that in some south Asian cultures mental illness is expressed in terms of physiological ailments. As a result, symptoms may be reported as problems requiring medical rather than psychiatric services. Likewise, in some cultures outside the Western world schizophrenia is interpreted as a possession of the sufferer by malevolent spirits, and the services of priests rather than doctors are sought (Littlewood and Lipsedge 1997).

This cumulative body of evidence, although illustrating some of the difficulties in assessing prevalence, suggests that a considerable number of children are living in families where at least one parent is suffering from a mental illness.

Prevalence of parental mental illness: child protection studies

The majority of parents who experience mental illness do not neglect or harm their children simply as a consequence of the disorder (Tunnard 2004). Children become more vulnerable to abuse and neglect when parental mental illness coexists with other problems such as substance misuse, domestic violence or childhood abuse (Cleaver et al. 2007).

Studies in the field of child protection suggest that the prevalence of identified mental illness, which in many cases exists alongside other parental difficulties, increases with the level of enquiry. At the referral stage prevalence is low. Cleaver and

Walker with Meadows' (2004) study of 2,248 referrals to children's social care found, on re-analysing their data, that parental mental illness was recorded in 10.4% of referrals, a finding similar to the 13% identified by Gibbons et al. (1995). However, prevalence increases with greater knowledge of the family circumstances. Following an initial assessment, social workers recorded parental mental illness in 16.9% of cases (Cleaver and Walker with Meadows 2004). When cases come under greater scrutiny and a child protection conference is held, prevalence increases once again. Parental mental illness was identified in a quarter of cases coming to conference (Farmer and Owen 1995). There is a further rise in prevalence for children involved in care proceedings. Parental mental illness had been noted in some 43% of cases where children are the subject of care proceedings (42% in Hunt et al. 1999; and 43% in Brophy et al. 2003).

Early research on child murder recorded particularly high rates of maternal mental illness. Resnich's (1969) review of 131 cases of parental child murder identified 71% of mothers as being depressed and Gibson's (1975) study of maternal filicide noted 90% of the mothers had a psychiatric disorder. More recent research into extreme cases of child abuse tempers these findings, although there remains considerable variation. Falkov's (1996) study of fatal child abuse found 32% of parents had a psychiatric disorder, a finding similar to the rate (28%) identified in families subject to serious case reviews during 2007–8 (Ofsted et al. 2008). However, this is likely to be an underestimate. The analysis of an intensive sample of 40 serious case reviews found almost two-thirds (63%) of children lived in a household with a parent or carer with current or past mental illness (Brandon et al. 2009 and 2010), a figure rather higher than the 43% found in Reder and Duncan's 1999 study of fatal child abuse.

The focus on mothers, common in much of the child protection research, might suggest that they are more prone to killing their children. However, filicide is not the prerogative of mothers. Except for neonates, fathers and father figures are more likely to murder a child in their care than are mothers (Marks and Kumar 1996; Stroud 1997; Cavanagh et al. 2007).

> *Father admitted shaking the baby ... Both parents have a history of mental illness. Little known about family, but they have had frequent house moves and changes of name.*

(Brandon et al. 2008, p.46)

Parental mental illness and type of child abuse

There is a further important issue to be considered; the possible association between parental mental illness and type of child abuse. A search of the literature failed to identify any work which specifically explores this link. However, studies focusing on specific types of child abuse suggest parental mental illness is associated with emotional abuse. For example, when children are registered as emotionally abused, parental mental illness was recorded in 31% of cases (Glaser and Prior 1997).

Research on child sexual abuse also suggests a greater association with parental mental illness. Sharland and colleagues' (1996) study of child sexual abuse found 71% of families, where there were suspicions of abuse, were in a 'poor psychological state' using the General Health Questionnaire (Goldberg and Williams 1988) and there was a further increase when suspicions were confirmed. These findings are in line with Monck et al.'s (1995) study of families attending a specialised treatment and assessment day clinic for child sexual abuse. They found 86% of mothers (assessed using the General Health Questionnaire) showed symptoms of depression or anxiety and, for a considerable proportion, the symptoms had been of long duration.

Caution, however, must be exercised in relation to these findings because studies of physical abuse and neglect have tended not to use standardised measures of mental health and it is not possible to compare like with like.

Prevalence of parental learning disability: general population studies

The prevalence of learning disability among the general population is difficult to establish because no information is kept nationally. Emerson and Hatton (2008), using data from 24 local authorities estimated that there were 985,000 people in England with a learning disability, equivalent to an overall prevalence rate of 2% of the adult population.

However, McGaw and Newman (2005) raise a note of caution, pointing out how differences in classification result in confusion and inconsistency. Traditionally, scores on standardised intelligence tests have been used to define learning disability; approximately two-thirds of people (69%) fall within the normal range of 85 to 115 (average IQ being 100). Individuals whose results are two standard deviations below the mean, i.e. an IQ of 70 or below, are classified as 'learning disabled' (Dowdney and Skuse 1993). One difficulty in establishing the prevalence of learning disability relates to how those with borderline IQs (70 to 85) are classified. In addition, individuals may exhibit different ability levels across the components of IQ and other tests used. *'...in reality there is no clear demarcation between parents who have learning disabilities and those who do not'* (McGaw and Newman 2005, p.8).

Similar problems are encountered when trying to establish the number of adults with learning disabilities who are parents. Estimates in the United Kingdom vary widely from 23,000 to 250,000 (Booth and Booth 2004; Department of Health and Department for Education and Skills 2007). Further information comes from a survey in England during 2003–2004 of 2,898 adults with learning disabilities, which found that 1 in 15 (7%) was a parent (Emerson et al. 2005). The inconsistency in the estimates of parents with a learning disability probably reflects the difficulties in classification. *'What is clear, however, is that there are increasing numbers of parents with learning disabilities in contact with services'* (Department of Health and Department for Education and Skills 2007, p.36).

People with a learning disability have greater physical and mental health needs and are more likely to have experienced childhood abuse or neglect than the rest of the population (McGaw et al. 2007). For example, in the United Kingdom research indicates 25–40% of adults with a learning disability will experience a mental health problem at some point in their lives (MIND 2007). In particular, rates of schizophrenia are three times higher than in the general population, although there are few data on the prevalence of other types of mental illness (Hassiotis et al. 2000).

Parental learning disability: issues of gender, culture and class

Most reports and studies involving people with learning disabilities do not differentiate between men and women. As McCarthy (1999) explains *'It is as if having a learning disability overrides all other identities and it is, somewhat bizarrely, as if it is politically incorrect to draw attention to gender differences.'* Literature that does differentiate between men and women with learning disabilities tends to focus on sexuality and sexual abuse. Studies focusing on men with a learning disability are almost exclusively about their sexual behaviour, and those which focus on women highlight their sexual vulnerability (McCarthy 1999).

In contrast, much research has drawn attention to the vulnerability of families where one or more parent has a learning disability. Parents with learning disabilities have been found to be amongst the most socially and economically disadvantaged groups. The financial difficulties faced by these families are illustrated in the figures drawn together by Mencap. The data show that less than one in five people with learning disabilities are in work (compared with one in two disabled people generally) and that those who are working are mostly only working part time and are low paid. Just one in three people with learning disabilities take part in some form of education or training (Mencap 2008).

Prevalence of parental learning disability: child protection studies

Because parents with a learning disability account for a very small proportion of all parents, this group is rarely highlighted in large-scale studies of children referred to children's social care services. However, some data are available. Re-analysis of the 2,248 referrals to children's social care (Cleaver and Walker with Meadows 2004) found parental learning disability had been recorded in less than 1% (0.8%) of referred cases. Of those referrals that progressed to an initial assessment, social workers identified parental learning disability in 2.6% of cases. Hunt and colleagues' (1999) study found 22% of parents who were subject to care proceedings had a learning disability. Parental learning disability is frequently identified as one of the many co-current problems that impact on parents' capacity to safeguard and promote the welfare of their children (Cleaver and Freeman 1995; Cleaver and Nicholson 2007). Finally, in an intensive study of 40 serious case reviews 15% of children were living with a parent with a learning disability (Brandon et al. 2009).

A review of research suggests that between 40% and 60% of parents with learning disabilities have their children taken into care as a result of court proceedings (McConnell and Llewellyn 2002). A more recent survey of 2,893 people with learning disabilities in England found of those who were parents, just under half (48%) were not looking after their children (Emerson et al. 2005). However, this figure included children who had left home because they had grown up and, therefore, it must not be assumed that 48% of parents with a learning disability had had their children taken into care. These figures contrast greatly with the findings from an in-depth follow-up study of 64 cases referred to children's social care where one or both parents had a learning disability (Cleaver and Nicholson 2007). In this study most children continued to live with their parents following a referral to children's social care. Three years after the initial referral only 12 children (18.8%) had been removed from their parents' care, including two children who had been placed for adoption.

Parental learning disability and type of child abuse

Learning disability is not correlated with deliberate abuse of children '... *IQ by itself, is not a predictor either of the occurrence or of the non-occurrence of purposeful child abuse...*' (Tymchuck 1992, p.169). In fact, there is considerable evidence to show that an accumulation of the stressors relevant to all parents are more predictive of poor parenting than IQ scores. These include, for example, poverty, inadequate housing, marital disharmony and violence, poor mental health, childhood abuse, substance misuse and a lack of social supports (Craft 1993; Booth and Booth 1996; Cleaver and Nicholson 2007). In addition, parents may have the challenge of caring for a disabled child. Children born to parents with a learning disability are at increased risk of inherited learning disabilities and psychological and physical disorders (McGaw and Newman 2005).

While there is no association between parental learning disability and child abuse or wilful neglect, there is evidence that children may suffer neglect from omission as a result of a lack of parental education combined with the unavailability of supportive, acceptable resources (McGaw and Newman 2005). Research has identified that most concerns relate to inadequate levels of child care, and when children became the subject of a child protection plan it was usually under the category of neglect or emotional abuse (Tymchuck and Andron 1990; Cleaver and Nicholson 2007).

Fathers or father figures can play a key role in ensuring children's developmental needs are met in families where the mother has a learning disability (Cleaver and Nicholson 2007; Booth and Booth 2002). Unfortunately, in most cases where physical or sexual abuse occurs it is often the mother's male partner or husband who is responsible (Tymchuck and Andron 1990; Booth and Booth 2002). The finding that few of the abusive male partners had learning disabilities provides support to the premise that some mothers with learning disabilities are particularly vulnerable to the financial, practical and emotional support offered by men who are paedophiles and whose primary concern is gaining access to the children (Cleaver and Freeman 1995).

Prevalence of parents with problem drinking or drug misuse: general population studies

The majority of parents using alcohol or drugs will present no increased risk of harm to their children. Most (but by no means all) of the harm which is caused to children will be the result of problematic drug or alcohol use. Problems will not only be caused by the quantity of drugs and alcohol consumed but also by the types of drugs and the pattern of use.

Problem drinking

Alcohol is a common feature of many people's lives in the United Kingdom and the majority of people drink sensibly or only exceed Department of Health guidelines occasionally (Department of Health et al. 2007). Problematic alcohol use is much less common. The NHS Information Centre (2010), using data from the General Lifestyle Survey, reported that 7% of men and 5% of women were higher risk drinkers (defined as 50 units of alcohol a week for men and 35 units of alcohol a week for women). Data from the Office for National Statistics showed that between 2005 and 2007 there was little change in the proportion of men and women who drank heavily (Robinson and Lader 2007).

In addition to the problems caused by regular or habitual excessive drinking, problems can result from binge drinking, occasional intoxication or unsafe drinking such as drinking before driving (Velleman 1993). Just over a fifth of men (22%) and 15% of women were 'binge drinkers', defined as drinking more than twice the daily limit – over 6 units a day for women and over 8 units a day for men (NHS Information Centre 2010). The problem with this definition of binge drinking is that many people 'binge' drink from time to time, especially when they are in their 20s and 30s, with little resulting harm.

'The evidence suggests that a dependent drinker costs the NHS twice as much as other alcohol misusers..' (HM Government 2010b, p.7). NHS hospital admissions, where the primary diagnosis of disease specifically relates to alcohol, have risen

markedly over 10 years, from 39,996 in 1996/7 to 57,142 in 2006/7. Within these admissions, the number related to alcoholic liver disease almost doubled, from 7,810 to 14,668 (NHS Information Centre 2009). The consequences of hazardous patterns of drinking are also reflected in the steady rise in alcohol-related deaths from 6.9 per 100,000 in 1991 to 13.6 per 100,000 in 2006 (Office for National Statistics 2009).

With this evident increase in problem drinking, it is of concern to find that access to alcohol treatment has not kept pace. Many areas of England and Wales have inadequate treatment facilities, accompanied by long waiting periods. The findings from the Alcohol Needs Assessment Research Project (Department of Health 2005) found just 1 in 18 alcohol-dependent people were receiving treatment from a specialist alcohol treatment agency. Recent initiatives, however, may start to increase provision, especially at the level of primary care.

Adults with alcohol problems are more likely than those without to experience poor mental health. For example, Weaver and colleagues (2002) found 85.5% of users of alcohol services experienced mental health problems. Moreover, half of those in treatment for alcohol problems experienced 'multiple' morbidity that is the co-occurrence of a number of different psychiatric illnesses or substance misuse.

The OPCS (Office of Population and Censuses and Surveys 1996) household survey gives data on the rate of alcohol dependence by type of family unit. Unlike mental illness the rate of alcohol dependence for couples living together is similar (27 per thousand) irrespective of whether or not they have dependent children. Lone parents show a higher rate (38 per thousand) than that found for couples with children. These findings reflect those for mental illness and suggest that children living with a lone parent are more vulnerable to the impact of parental drinking than children in households where adults live as a couple.

Information on the numbers of children living with parents with alcohol problems comes from Brisby and colleagues (1997). Their admitted approximate calculation indicates some 7% of parents are drinking at harmful levels. Through extrapolating from census data they suggest that this indicates *'some 800,000 children in England and Wales, 85,000 children in Scotland and something under 35,000 children in Northern Ireland are living in a family where a parent has an alcohol problem'* (Brisby et al. 1997, p.7). More recent studies suggest the number of children living with parents who misuse alcohol exceeds these earlier estimates, *'more than 2.6 million children in the UK live with hazardous drinkers, 705,000 live with a dependent drinker'* (Munro 2011, p.26, paragraph 2.20; Manning et al 2009; Strategy Unit 2004). Extrapolating from census data has inherent problems and is likely to be an underestimation of the true picture, as the figures rely on parents acknowledging the extent of their alcohol consumption (Forrester 2000).

Although not all children living with a parent with alcohol problems will suffer significant harm, a retrospective study of adults who were the children of problem drinkers found that, as children, they experienced significantly more negative experiences, were less happy and had a less cohesive childhood than was reported by adults who made up the comparison group (Velleman and Orford 2001). The authors note *'that all the association between parental problem drinking and childhood problems might be mediated via parental family disharmony'* (p.156). The findings suggest that it is the link with family disharmony and violence that increases the risk of harm to children of problem-drinking parents.

Drug misuse

Drug use is not as common as alcohol consumption. Findings from the British Crime Survey 2009/10 indicate that one in three (36.4%) adults in the population have used illicit drugs at least once, suggesting that a large proportion of the adult population have had some experience of illegal drug use even if it was in the past (Hoare and Moon 2010). This is a rather smaller proportion than that noted by Leitner and colleagues (1993) who reported that at least half the adult population aged 19–59 had tried illicit drugs at some time in their lives. Cannabis remains the most likely drug to be used (the British Crime Survey estimates 6.6% of adults used cannabis in the last year); the next most commonly used drug was cocaine, taken by 2.4% of adults (Hoare and Moon 2010).

Overall, the use of illicit drugs has been falling in England and Wales for several years. According to the British Crime Survey 2009/10, 8.6% of the adult population (aged 16–59) of England and Wales had tried an illegal drug during the last year, a fall from the figure of 11.1% found for 1996. The use of the most dangerous drugs, Class A (under the Misuse of Drugs Act 1971) such as heroin and cocaine (during the last year), has also fallen from 3.9% in 2008/9 to 3.1% in 2009/10. Frequent illicit drug use is less prevalent, and the survey data suggested it applied to only 3.3% of the population (Hoare and Moon 2010).

Over the last 10 years, access to treatment for drug problems, especially heroin and to a lesser extent cocaine, has increased considerably. The development of the National Treatment Agency (a Special Health Authority within the National Health Service) has not only ensured increased funding for existing agencies but has made sure that there is now better access to services in all parts of the country. At the time of writing (2011), there are over 200,000 people being treated for drug problems in England and Wales, an increase of 4% on the previous year, and waiting times for treatment have fallen; nearly all clients wait less than three weeks to start treatment (National Treatment Agency 2010). In England, over half (55%) of problem drug users are currently in treatment (National Audit Office 2008, p.30).

Research has also identified the co-morbidity of substance misuse and mental illness. Three-quarters (74.5%) of users of drug services reported experiencing mental health problems (not formal mental illness); 30% experienced 'multiple' morbidity, the co-occurrence of a number of psychiatric disorders or substance misuse problems (Weaver et al. 2002).

The Office of Population and Censuses and Surveys (1996) survey breaks down the data on the prevalence of drug dependence in the general population into family units. This analysis reveals that couples living with a child have a lower rate of drug dependency than lone parents (9 per thousand for couples with a child compared with 24 per thousand for lone parents). Once again, the vulnerability of children to the impact of parental drug use when living with a lone parent, compared to those who live with two caring adults, is apparent.

It is hard to know with any degree of certainty how many children are living with parents who are using illicit drugs, as such behaviour is against the law and characterised by denial and secrecy. *Hidden Harm* (Advisory Council on the Misuse of Drugs 2003) estimated that there are up to 60,000 children in Scotland who have a parent with a drug problem (approximately 5% of the total population group for this age). In England and Wales there are estimated to be between 200,000 and 300,000 children (2–3% of children under the age of 16 years) who have parents who misuse drugs. Not all children will be living with their parents, only about a third of fathers and two-thirds of mothers with problem drug use are still living with their children; most of the children are living with other relatives (Advisory Council on the Misuse of Drugs 2003). Meier and colleagues (2004) surveyed the data collection statistics used by all drug treatment agencies in England and Wales and found that 42% of drug users had dependent children but only 47% of the children lived with their parents; about 9% were in care.

Epidemiological research also provides information on the number of babies born to drug-misusing mothers. The Advisory Council on the Misuse of Drugs (2003) estimated 1% of babies are born each year to women with drug problems, that is 6,000 babies born from 600,000 pregnant women who are misusing drugs. The numbers seem to be rising; most maternity units have reported an increase in the number of pregnant women with drug problems (Advisory Council on the Misuse of Drugs 2003). This concern was also highlighted in a Channel 4 *Dispatches* programme (3 November 2008), which reported a doubling in the number of babies born to drug-addicted mothers in four years. The programme noted that there were 1,970 such babies born in 2007 – compared to 1,057 in 2003 – and in more than half the cases the children were born with foetal withdrawal symptoms or neonatal abstinence syndrome; 3,500 babies were born to parents who problematically use heroin each year. While the reported number of babies born to problem drug users is clearly increasing, this could in part be due to the greater awareness among professional health care staff of problem drug-using mothers.

Problem drinking or drug misuse: issues of gender, culture and class

Population studies show that drug and alcohol misuse is more common among men than among women. Men are three times more likely to be drug dependent than are women (Department of Health et al. 2007). Similarly, in relation to alcohol dependency men are twice as likely to meet the criteria as are women (SAMHSA 2007). Men from social class V are the heaviest drinkers among men. However, women from social class V are significantly under the average for women's drinking as a whole (Royal College of Physicians 1991).

The issue of gender in parental drinking was highlighted by the work of ChildLine (1997). An analysis of all calls received in the year 1 April 1995 to 31 March 1996 shows 3,255 children talked about their parents' problematic drinking. The majority (57%) identified a male figure (fathers, stepfathers, or mother's boyfriend) as the problem drinker. Mothers also featured: a third (33%) of children mentioned their mother or mother figure had an alcohol problem. Just 7% indicated both parents had a drink problem.

Some studies (Seljamo et al. 2006) indicate that a father's drinking is more influential than a mother's when considering their children's drinking patterns at age 15. However, other studies (Macleod et al. 2008) suggest that heavy maternal drinking may be more influential in relation to children's drinking (at age 10) than a father's problem alcohol use. Research also suggests a link between mothers using cannabis and their children's use of the drug. Day and colleagues (2006) looked at prenatal maternal use of cannabis and children's cannabis smoking at age 14 and found that, compared to non-cannabis smoking mothers, their children experimented with cannabis at an earlier age and used cannabis more frequently. However, maternal tobacco smoking also showed a statistically significant association with cannabis use of the children at age 14.

Culture often determines attitudes towards alcohol and drugs and, therefore, the frequency and quantities used. For example, cultures in which religious beliefs eschew alcohol are likely to result in lower rates of problem drinking than those cultures where alcohol is freely available. An analysis of government statistics on alcohol consumption *'respondents from Pakistani or Bangladeshi origin were less likely to have drunk in the week prior to interview (5% and 4% respectively) compared to those recording their ethnicity as White British or White other (67% and 68% respectively)'* (NHS Information Centre 2009, p.18, paragraph 2.6.2). A comparative study of 91 people of Protestant background and 70 people of Jewish background showed that the Jewish culture and religion, where drunkenness itself or going to the pub and using alcohol as a social lubricant is not an inherent part of daily life, also make Jews less prone to drinking than Protestants (Loewenthal et al. 2003).

It is clear that drinking is seen to be more culturally appropriate in some ethnic groups compared to others. However, the cultural influence on drinking patterns has several layers which need to be examined. Most of the United Kingdom studies have traditionally focused on the alcohol use of immigrants, but immigrants constitute only a minority of ethnic groups. More recent work suggests that while the overall level of alcohol problems remains substantially lower in South Asian communities than in the general population, there is evidence that alcohol problems are on the increase among first-, second- and third-generation immigrant families (Gharial 2007). Similar trends were identified by Orford and colleagues (2004) in their small qualitative study of alcohol use by second-generation ethnic minorities. The results suggest that some second-generation immigrants develop similar drink patterns to the population at large, but Muslims, with some exceptions, are mainly abstinent.

Research has shown a significant positive correlation between the prevalence of problem drug use and deprivation (Marmot Review 2010). Social class, however, is a controversial issue when considering its impact on problem drug use. In 1987 a Nottinghamshire study compared the address of problem drug users with known indicators of social deprivation in the postal code and found a high correlation between the two. Also, there was a clear correlation between the growth in 'addicts notified to the Home Office' and indices of deprivation such as unemployment (Unell 1987). A correlation does not always mean a 'cause and effect' and by the 1990s the situation had altered. The 1990s demonstrated both a significant growth in problem drug use and a reduction in unemployment and growing prosperity. What has become clear is that those suffering the most deprivation, such as the homeless, are also at high risk of drug and alcohol misuse. In a survey of drug and alcohol problems among those provided with housing by a specialist housing association for the homeless in Nottingham, the rates of drug and alcohol problems were very high by any standard (Morris et al. 2004).

Although alcohol consumption may be increasing, access to services is more problematic. Orford and colleagues found that despite growing levels of alcohol use among second-generation migrant populations, awareness and perceived accessibility to sources of advice remain low (Orford et al. 2004).

Prevalence of parents with a drink or drug problem: child protection studies

Data from child protection studies show that, in general, the reported incidence of parental alcohol and drug misuse increases with the level of social work intervention. For example, 20% of families referred to children's social care services were found to have a history of drug or alcohol problems (see for example Gibbons et al. 1995; NSPCC 1997b). Other more recent research suggests a lower figure, but this may owe more to difficulties in identifying or recording the issue than in a real drop in incidence. Cleaver and Walker with Meadows' (2004) scrutiny of 2,248 consecutive referrals to children's social care found, on re-analysing their data, parental alcohol or drug misuse had been recorded in only 5.8% of referrals, and of those which went forward to an initial assessment, parental substance misuse was affecting families in 11.6% of cases. But earlier research by the author which focused on suspected child abuse found social workers identified parental substance misuse in a quarter of cases (Cleaver and Freeman 1995). This rate reflected that found in cases where children were the subject of a child protection conference (Thoburn et al. 1995; Farmer and Owen 1995). This figure may still be an underestimation as Brisby and colleagues (1997) found heavy drinking or intoxication was a factor in some 60% of cases at the child protection conference stage.

The figures also vary considerably at the point when children became the subject of a child protection plan. The Advisory Council on the Misuse of Drugs (2003) found that, on average, parental problem drug and/or alcohol use featured in a quarter of these cases. Once again, other studies suggest the incidence may be much greater. Forrester's sample of 50 families on the Child Protection Register in an inner London area identified parental substance misuse as a cause for concern in 52% of families (Forrester 2000). Turning Point (2006) suggests that half the child protection cases involved alcohol misuse by parents.

Hunt and colleagues' (1999) data suggest drugs and alcohol featured in 20% of cases where children were subject to care proceedings. Separating these issues indicates that 23% of cases subject to care proceedings included allegations of drug misuse and 20% alcohol misuse (Brophy et al. 2003). An intensive sample of serious case reviews identified that a third (33%) of children were living with a parent who had past or current drug or alcohol problems (Brandon et al. 2009). In some cases alcohol or drug misuse was closely linked to the child's death or serious injury. *'Drug or alcohol misuse was noted as a factor in most cases where "overlaying" was a positive cause of death'* (Brandon et al. 2009).

Problem drinking or drug misuse and the type of child abuse

Research which explores parents' problem drinking and drug misuse indicates an association with particular types of child abuse. For example, parental abuse of drugs or alcohol, or both, is found in more than half of parents who neglect their children (Dunn et al. 2002).

A focus on parental problem drinking also shows an association with violence within the family and the physical abuse of children (Famularo et al. 1992; Velleman 2001; Alcohol Concern 2010). A review by the Priory Group (2006) found 66% of children raised in alcoholic families reported physical abuse of which 26% had also experienced sexual abuse. But which parent is doing the drinking may also be relevant. Although alcohol was cited in 20% of cases when children reported physical abuse at the hands of their father, this was not the case when mothers drank excessively. Maternal problem drinking was more frequently linked to child neglect. *'One third of calls reporting neglect include a parent abusing drugs or alcohol. This was most often the mother. Alcohol was mentioned in two or three of these cases'* (NSPCC 1997b, p.35).

Research which explores the association between parental problem drug misuse and child abuse suggests parental drug use is generally associated with neglect and emotional abuse (Velleman 2001). Parents who experience difficulty in organising their own and their children's lives are unable to meet children's needs for safety and basic care, are emotionally unavailable to them and have difficulties in controlling and disciplining their children (Hogan and Higgins 2001; Cleaver et al. 2007). The chaotic lifestyle and tendency to allow other users into the home may also place children at risk of harm (Brophy 2006). Famularo and colleagues (1992) found cocaine addiction to be associated with the sexual maltreatment of children although not their physical maltreatment (see also Velleman 2004).

As with other parental problems, no systematic research into the association between problem drinking or drug misuse and child abuse exists. Further work is required to test whether there are links between parental problem drinking and drug misuse, and particular forms of child maltreatment.

Prevalence of domestic violence: general population studies

There are serious problems in accurately identifying the prevalence of domestic violence. The scale of the problem is likely to be greater than official statistics suggest because people are reluctant to reveal domestic violence and hesitant about seeking help. Dominy and Radford's (1996) study of 484 female victims of domestic violence found only one in three had previously told anyone of their experiences, a figure which reflects earlier findings by Dobash and Dobash (1980). The most recent crime survey found 7% of women and 4% of men reported having been the victims of domestic violence in the preceding year; more than one in four women in England and Wales had been affected by domestic violence since the age of 16 years (Flately et al 2010). Reported incidents of domestic violence are on the decline. Following a peak in reporting in 1996, reports of domestic violence have fallen by two thirds (Kershaw et al. 2008). The most common type of reported abuse is either non-physical (63%); that is emotional or financial abuse, or abuse through the use of physical force (61%). Women are more likely than men to experience all forms of intimate violence (Kershaw et al. 2008). Nonetheless, *'there are 120,000 victims in any year who are at high risk of being killed or seriously injured as a result of domestic abuse; 69% of high risk victims have children'* (Munro 2011, p.26, paragraph 2.20).

Research indicates there are strong links between intimate-partner violence and both 'drinking in the event' and 'problem drinking' (Finney 2004). Research using a self-completion questionnaire found 32% of victims of domestic violence said their attacker had been drinking. Drug taking is less likely to be an issue in domestic violence than alcohol but, where it is, drug misuse is more likely to be related to chronic victimisation. Where women had been subjected to chronic domestic violence, 8% said their assailant was under the influence of drugs (Mirrlees-Black and Byron 1999). There is considerable debate over whether there is a causal link between alcohol misuse and domestic violence. While it is recognised that alcohol consumption makes it more likely to predict violence or aggression, it should not be used to excuse such behaviour. People who are violent and aggressive will usually behave in these ways whether or not they consume alcohol (Galvani 2004).

The reluctance to report domestic violence makes it difficult to estimate the number of children living in violent households. Recent data suggest of the 11 million children in England, 200,000 live in households where there is a known risk of domestic violence or violence (Lord Laming 2009). Women's Aid offers women and children a safe refuge as well as non-residential support. During 2005/6 a total of 131,245 women and 95,960 children were supported by domestic violence services (Women's Aid 2008).

Domestic violence: issues of gender, culture and class

Povey's (2008) analysis of the self-reporting studies included in the British Crime Survey 2006/7 shows women are more likely than men to experience each type of partner abuse: non-physical abuse, threats or force, sexual assault and stalking. The difference between the sexes is starker when studying officially recorded incidents of domestic abuse, where the majority of victims are women, and men perpetrate the violence (Dobash and Dobash 1992). A US study involving 1,517 incidents of domestic violence where a child was present found 87% of victims were female and 86% of perpetrators were male (Fantuzzo and Fusco 2007).

Research suggests approximately a quarter of women experience domestic violence. A randomly selected sample of 1,000 men and women living in North London found that one in four women had been subject to domestic violence (Mooney 1994). A similar level (25%) of domestic violence was reported in a much larger Canadian telephone survey involving a random sample of 12,300 women (Statistics Canada 1993). Also in line with these trends is the Irish data which found 18% of women had been subjected to violence by an intimate partner at some stage of their lives (Office of the Tanaiste 1997).

Women are also more likely to be seriously injured as a result of domestic violence. A study by Povey (2008) found that 30% of women sought medical attention following an assault compared with 18% of men. Domestic abuse is also a significant aspect of the mortality figures for women; in practically a quarter of assaults (23%) by men, a weapon was used (Gilchrist et al. using Home Office data 2003). In 2008, 65% of female murder victims were killed by their partner, ex-partner or lover, compared with 11% of men (Povey 2008). On average two women per week are killed in England and Wales by partners or former partners (Home Office 2002). The men who perpetrate domestic violence are characterised by mental health problems (22% are depressed), alcohol misuse (49% have a history of problem alcohol use) and substance misuse (evident in 19% of cases) (Gilchrist et al. using Home Office data 2003).

Research has generally focused on violence perpetrated by men on female partners. Studies of violence by women against male partners or of relationships which are mutually violent are unusual. As a result, although there is a growing body of research which explores domestic violence from the women's perspective, the experiences of male victims remain largely unknown (Cook 1997). Moffitt and Caspi's (1998) research, which shows that partner violence is not role specific, highlights the ignorance which surrounds this aspect of domestic violence. They found the reason behind domestic violence is different for men and women. Generally, women's assaults were motivated by fear and a desire to get equal, whereas men were shown to use violence and fear in order to control their partners. However, the first ever American helpline for battered males suggests that women are capable of inflicting injuries on men, and there is little evidence to support the argument that this is generally to retaliate against or protect themselves from a violent male (Covell and Howe 2009).

Mutual combat may be the norm in many violent households, but attacks *by* women tend only to be reported when the attacks are very dangerous or result in serious injury (Cook 1997; Fergusson et al. 2005). Research in Canada, the US, Australia and New Zealand suggests that violence between couples is relatively common and may be an intimate part of the relationship. For example, from a Canadian sample of women, recruited on the basis of being victims of husband abuse, two-thirds admitted they also were perpetrators of violence to their husbands (Currie 2006). Similar findings were also reported in a US study of 258 children and their mothers, recruited from domestic-violence shelters; 61% of women who had been subject to severe intimate-partner violence reported committing one or more such acts themselves in the previous year (McDonald et al. 2009).

Intimate-partner violence exists also in same-sex relationships and US studies suggest prevalence rates are similar to those among heterosexual couples (Covell and Howe 2009). There is little research covering the impact on children of mutual violence or violence perpetrated by women. However, regardless of the gender of the perpetrator, witnessing adults hitting, pushing or shoving one another, even if no injuries occur, is frightening and gives children the message that violence is acceptable behaviour.

Prevalence of domestic violence: child protection studies

Child-focused research reveals strong links between child abuse and domestic violence. Gibbons et al.'s (1995) study of all child protection referrals noted that domestic violence occurred in approximately a quarter (27%) of cases. Cleaver and Walker with Meadows' study of 2,248 referrals to children's social care found, on re-analysing their data, that domestic violence was recorded in only 4.8% of all referrals; at the initial assessment stage social workers had recorded concerns about domestic violence in 16.7% of cases (Cleaver and Walker with Meadows 2004). Qualitative research suggests that this may be an underestimation, Cleaver and Freeman (1995) found domestic violence in 40% of cases where child protection concerns had warranted a visit to the family.

Thoburn et al. (1995) suggest a figure of 35% at the child protection conference stage, but acknowledge that much violence may be hidden, *'the amount of present and past marital conflict is almost certainly underestimated'* (Thoburn et al. 1995, p.38). This claim is substantiated by Farmer and Owen (1995) who found a similar rate of reporting by social workers at the child protection conference stage, although subsequent research interviews with families revealed the higher rate of 52%. This is in line with figures from the NSPCC (1997b), which estimated that domestic violence was present in over half (55%) of child protection cases they had dealt with.

The level remains fairly constant when children are the subject of care proceedings. Hunt et al. (1999) found that domestic violence was an issue in 51% of cases coming to court. Finally, an analysis of serious case reviews found evidence of past or present domestic violence in over half (53%) of the living circumstances of the children (Brandon et al. 2009).

Domestic violence and the type of child abuse

There is considerable evidence that *'adult partners who are violent toward each other are also at increased risk of abusing their children'* (Moffitt and Caspi 1998, p.137; Farmer and Pollock 1998; Hester et al 2007). Research suggests that men's severe interpersonal violence seldom occurs in isolation; women's violence to their partner, partner-child aggression, and mother-child aggression are also common (McDonald et al. 2009). Cavanagh and colleagues' (2007) study of 26 cases of fatal child abuse perpetrated by fathers found that in three-quarters of cases the man had also been violent towards his partner (the child's mother). The risk of child abuse is shown to be between three and nine times greater in homes where the adult partners hit each other (Moffitt and Caspi 1998). However, there is little agreement on the rates of overlap between domestic violence and child physical abuse: rates fluctuate between studies and range from 45% to 70% (Holt et al. 2008).

Additional evidence for a link between domestic violence and physical child abuse comes from feminist research. An American study of 'wife beating', using a voluntary sample of 1,000 women, found *'wife beaters abused children in 70% of families where children were present'* (Bowker et al. 1988, p.162). In contrast, the National Children's Home (NCH) Action for Children (1994) study of children living with domestic violence found only 27% of children were reported by their mother as *'hit or abused'*. The large disparity between these findings may be deceptive. The authors suggest the figure of 27% may under-represent the prevalence of physical child abuse because mothers are reluctant to disclose the abuse or are ignorant of it. In another study, less than half the mothers (44%) reported that their violent partners *'didn't touch the children'* (NCH Action for Children 1994, p.31). Evidence is also emerging that identifies a link between mothers who have experienced domestic violence and mother-child maltreatment. In a sample of 1,236 families entering the US child welfare system, almost half (44%) of the mothers who were reported for alleged child maltreatment had experienced physical violence by their partner (Casanueva et al. 2009).

There is also some evidence to suggest a raised incidence of co-occurrence of domestic violence and child sexual abuse, although rates vary due to sampling. For example, in a community sample of 54 mothers who had experienced domestic violence, 4% reported the sexual abuse of their child by their ex-partners (Smith et al. 1997). Humphreys and Stanley's (2006) analysis of case files where there was evidence of child sexual abuse, found the presence of domestic violence in over half the cases. Fathers and father figures were more likely to sexually abuse their child when they were violent and abusive to the mother. Similar findings come from Hester et al. (2007) who found over half the children who had been sexually abused and attending an NSPCC centre had been living with domestic violence.

It has been argued that witnessing and living with the abuse of one parent, usually the mother, can be considered a form of emotional abuse (Holt et al. 2008). Webster and colleagues' (2002) study on the emotional effects of domestic violence on children found 9 out of 10 children were present in the next or same room as the domestic violence incident. Other research found that 71% of children who had experienced domestic violence had witnessed the physical assault of their mother and 10% the rape of their mother (McGee 2000).

Summary of the evidence for a link between parental disorders and child abuse

This review of the research literature has revealed a similar pattern for the known prevalence of parental mental illness, learning disability, problem alcohol and drug use and domestic violence. When families come to the attention of social work services because of concerns about the children, the rate of parental problems shows a considerable increase from that found in the general population. Moreover, the findings from a number of different research studies cited above show the known prevalence generally continues to rise with the seriousness of the child protection enquiry (see Table 1.3).

Table 1.3: **Relationship between the rate of recorded parental problems and the level of social work intervention**

Parental problems	Referral stage	First enquiry or initial assessment	Child protection conference	Care proceedings	Serious injury or death
	%	%	%	%	%
Mental illness	10.4[1]	16.8[1]	25[2]	42[3]	63[4]
Learning disability	0.8[1]	2.6[1]	N/K	22[5]	15[4]
Alcohol/drugs	5.8[1]	11.4[1]	25[6]	23[5]	33[4]
Domestic violence	4.8[1]	16.7[1]	55[7]	51[5]	53[4]

1. Cleaver and Walker with Meadows 2004
2. Falmer and Owen 1995
3. Brophy et al. 2003
4. Brandon et al. 2009
5. Hunt et al. 1999
6. Advisory Council on Misuse of Drugs 2003
7. NSPCC 1997b

Caution is needed in interpreting these data, because we do not know whether the increase reflects a true picture of what is happening or simply that parental problems had not been recognised or recorded at an earlier stage in the assessment procedure.

To sum up

- Prevalence is difficult to assess. Community-based samples often preclude a precise diagnosis of the issue, whether it be mental illness, learning disability, substance misuse or domestic violence. Moreover, different studies use different terminology and it is not clear, for example, whether 'domestic violence' is synonymous with 'marital conflict'.
- The information concerning the prevalence of mental illness, learning disability, problem alcohol/drug use, or domestic violence in families with dependent children is incomplete, and figures vary depending on the population group being studied.
- Community-based samples suggest:
  - One in six adults in Great Britain have a neurotic disorder and 1 in 2,000 have a psychotic disorder.
  - Of the adult population in England, 2% have learning disabilities.
  - In the United Kingdom 3.7% of the adult population are drug dependent, and 9.2% of men and 6% of women are chronic drinkers. Overall, the findings suggest that drug use has fallen slightly over the past decade and those with problems are increasingly likely to be in treatment.
  - Practically a quarter of adults in England and Wales are victims of partner abuse. Women are more likely than men to be seriously injured as a result of domestic violence.
- Adults frequently experience a number of problems:
  - Nearly half of those attending mental health services (44%) report alcohol or drug problems.
  - Poor mental health affects 25% to 40% of adults with a learning disability, 86% of those using alcohol services, and 75% of those attending drug services.
  - Practically a quarter (22%) of men who perpetrate domestic violence are depressed, 49% have a history of problem alcohol use, and 19% a history of substance misuse.
  - Lone parents are more likely to experience mental health problems or drug problems than couples with children.
  - The data from child protection research suggest that the prevalence of reported parental mental illness, learning disability, problem drug use including alcohol, and domestic violence increases in relation to the degree of child protection concerns and the level of assessment and investigation.

2 How mental illness, learning disability, substance misuse and domestic violence affect parenting capacity

Chapter 2 explores how parental mental illness, learning disability, substance misuse and domestic violence affect parents' capacity to meet the needs of their children. The evidence is examined in relation to three aspects.

- The physical and psychological consequences of these issues for parents. This includes:
    - a brief description of the symptoms of different forms of mental illness
    - the impact of a learning disability on an individual's health and well-being
    - the effects on users of different types of substances, including alcohol
    - the impact of domestic violence.
- The ways that single and multiple disorders affect parenting capacity. This is examined in relation to:
    - parenting skills
    - parents' perceptions
    - control of emotions
    - neglect of physical needs
    - parent–child attachment relationships
    - separation.
- The final aspect to be examined is the social consequences of parental problems. The focus is on:
    - living standards
    - friends and family
    - family relationships.

Physical and psychological impact on parents' health and well-being

Before exploring the physical and psychological impact of the various disorders it is important to acknowledge all may have a common underlying cause. Chronic depression, psychiatric disorders or substance dependence are common long-term consequences of childhood abuse. Multi-generational research has demonstrated that the children of parents who themselves experienced childhood abuse are at increased risk of being abused or neglected (Noll et al. 2009).

Physical and psychological impact of mental illness

The following section attempts to give details of the sufferer's experience of the most common forms of mental illness, although it is inevitable that the symptoms described are those perceived by both patients and clinicians. Nonetheless, it is an attempt to show the impact of symptoms on the daily lives of parents and their children.

Schizophrenia

Schizophrenia is an episodic illness. With the onset of the illness sufferers often become socially withdrawn, lacking in energy or initiative and self-neglectful. Relationships with friends and colleagues are curtailed and the sufferer spends increasing amounts of time alone. They experience difficulties in functioning, frequently neglect their personal hygiene, behave in an odd manner and are plagued by strange ideas. Mood disturbance can include depression, anxiety and irritability commonly with a *'flattening of mood'* in which the person reacts as if their emotions are blunted (Falkov 1998). During a schizophrenic episode the sufferer loses contact with objective reality and becomes increasingly preoccupied with his or her inner, private life.

The symptoms experienced by people with schizophrenia are usually grouped as positive and negative.

Positive symptoms highlight a change in the usual thinking process and can include:

- Hallucinations – hearing, smelling, feeling or seeing something that isn't there. Voices which appear utterly real; although they can be pleasant, they are more often rude, critical, abusive or annoying.

- Delusions – totally believing things that others find strange, unrealistic and unbelievable.

- Difficulty in thinking clearly – concentration is hard and there is a tendency to drift from one idea to another.

- Feeling controlled – feeling psychologically and/or physically controlled by someone else.

Together these symptoms are called psychosis.

Negative symptoms show a reduction or absence of usual mental functions and can include:

- Loss of interest, energy and emotions.

- Social withdrawal, not bothering to get out of bed or go out of the house.

- Lack of motivation, not getting round to routine jobs like washing, cleaning or tidying.

(Royal College of Psychiatrists 2008)

There can be a great deal of variation in how schizophrenia affects the life of the sufferer and the children. Many schizophrenics find that their symptoms can be controlled well by anti-psychotic drugs and good treatment. Often there is a reduction in severity as people become older. In other cases, symptoms seem to be resistant to available drug regimes and treatment has a much less positive effect.

Unipolar affective disorder (depression)

Those who are depressed experience a pervasive and sustained change in mood, which leaves them feeling persistently sad, worthless and helpless. Depression is often cyclical and in most cases will resolve or improve with time. Often there is no clear single cause. Without treatment the symptoms can last for weeks or even years, rendering life meaningless and hopeless for the sufferer.

People who suffer from depression find it affects all aspects of their life: sleep is disturbed; appetite lost; thoughts are heavy, slow and gloomy; concentration becomes difficult and decisions impossible; actions slow down; and many sufferers are overwhelmed with feelings of exhaustion and worthlessness. Some are defeated by torpor and even the most mundane aspect of living, such as getting out of bed, appears momentous. A slowing down is not a characteristic symptom for all those with depression; some become agitated and restless.

Finally, depression can deprive the suffering parent of the capacity to care about themselves or about those whom they love. Life for the depressed appears hopeless, and sufferers present a picture of misery and helpless worry.

Bipolar affective disorder (manic-depression)

> *The disorder is characterised by mood fluctuations that include mania, hypomania, depression, and mixed episodes. It is chronic and highly recurrent, and associated with significant distress and disability.*

(Berk et al. 2005, p.662)

About a quarter of people with major depression will also experience a manic episode. Although the depression is similar to that in the unipolar affective disorder, manic episodes are experienced as overwhelming surges of physical and mental energy. It is as if the floodgates have burst allowing a multitude of different thoughts and ideas to vie for expression. As a result, sufferers become over talkative, frequently to the point of incoherence. Others can become argumentative, dictatorial and haughty as a result of inflated self-esteem or grandiosity. The feeling of extreme physical energy can result in restlessness and excitability, and the manic depressive feels driven to continual activity. When in this state sleep appears unnecessary, for some impossible, and eating an inconvenience that can be dispensed with.

Manic depression is often associated with substance abuse, and personality and anxiety disorders and as many as 25–50% of patients with bipolar disorder attempt suicide during their lifetime (Berk et al. 2005).

Anxiety disorders

There are various types of anxiety disorder including generalised anxiety disorder, panic disorder, agoraphobia, phobias, social-anxiety disorder, obsessive-compulsive disorder and post-traumatic stress disorder (Royal College of Psychiatrists 2008). Sufferers of anxiety disorders experience a range of fear symptoms in the absence of a dangerous situation, including increased arousal, restlessness, sweating, heart palpitations and shortness of breath, trembling and difficulties in concentration. They may experience chest pains and fear that they are dying or having a mental breakdown.

Generalised anxiety disorder is characterised by long-lasting unrealistic or excessive worries that are not focused on any particular object or situation. The constant fear and inability to control their worries may result in sufferers experiencing heart palpitations, dizziness, insomnia, and chest pain. When such physical symptoms are combined with intense and long-term anxiety, sufferers find it difficult to cope with everyday life. Generalised anxiety disorder affects more women than men. A review of 41 prevalence studies on anxiety disorders in the adult population found a lifetime prevalence of 18.5% for women compared with 10.4% for men (Somers et al. 2006).

A **panic attack** is usually a brief recurrent attack of terror and apprehension which has no identifiable cause. It is often accompanied by physical symptoms such as shortness of breath, trembling and shaking, confusion, dizziness, nausea, feelings of impending doom, fear of losing control, of going crazy, of having a heart attack or even of dying (Plewa 2008). Panic attacks commonly last 15–30 minutes although on rare occasions they may last for some hours. Those experiencing panic disorder have a four-fold risk of alcohol misuse and an eighteen-fold higher risk of suicide than the general population (Plewa 2008).

Phobias can be classified into three categories:

- social phobia

- specific phobias

- agoraphobia.

With social phobia (or social-anxiety disorder) sufferers fear or are acutely embarrassed about performing everyday actions such as eating in public. With a specific phobia the trigger for panic is precise, such as spiders, lifts or flying. Sufferers of agoraphobia experience anxiety about being in a place or situation where escape is difficult or embarrassing. As a result, public or unfamiliar places may be avoided, and in severe cases the sufferer may become confined to the home.

Obsessive-compulsive disorder is characterised by the compulsive need to repeatedly do certain things, such as hand washing or cleaning the house, in order to relieve anxiety. Obsessions are distressing, repetitive, intrusive thoughts or images that the individual often realises are senseless; however, affected people cannot control their thoughts or actions. As a result, they may take longer to complete certain tasks and have difficulty with personal relationships. Obsessive-compulsive disorder is a chronic illness with periods of remission and relapse. Like other disorders, there is a great deal of variation in the severity of symptoms and susceptibility to treatment.

Post-traumatic stress disorder results from a traumatic experience, such as being involved in warfare, rape, a hostage situation or a serious accident. It can also result from long-term exposure to a severe stressor. The sufferer may experience flashbacks, avoidant behaviour, depression, anxiety, irritability and other symptoms.

It is common for those who are undergoing drug or alcohol withdrawals to suffer from depression and/or anxiety, which usually resolves as their withdrawal symptoms diminish.

Personality disorder

Personality disorder implies abnormality in the sufferer's personal and interpersonal functioning. Research has shown that personality disorders tend to fall into three groups, according to their emotional 'flavour' (Royal College of Psychiatrists 2008).

- Suspicious – sufferers often experience feelings of deep suspicion and paranoia, are emotionally cold and have inappropriate emotional reactions.

- Emotional and impulsive – sufferers don't care about the feelings of others, tend to be aggressive and have a strong sense of their own self-importance.

- Anxious – sufferers tend to be perfectionists, rigid, judgemental, extremely sensitive to criticism, and feel insecure and inferior.

Both main mental health classifications, DSN-1V and ICD-10 (World Health Organization 1992) also identify borderline personality disorder. This is a *'severe and chronic disorder characterized by a pervasive instability of affect and interpersonal relationships, and impulsivity ... Co-occurring anxiety and mood disorders are common'* (Hill et al. 2005, p. 345).

The roots of adult personality and borderline personality disorders are thought to lie in attachment relationships and the impact of early negative childhood experiences, including emotional, physical and sexual abuse (Fonagy et al. 2003). Personality disordered parents frequently have coexisting physical and mental health problems. Sufferers can experience long-term after-effects and react in a variety of ways, including suicide attempts and self-harm (Hill et al. 2005). Alternatively, individuals may act out their stress through actual violence towards others (which can include partners or children), problem drinking or drug misuse, eating disorders and sexual disinhibition.

In 2009 the National Institute for Health and Clinical Excellence published guidelines to improve the treatment and management of people with antisocial and borderline personality disorder.

Physical and psychological impact of learning disability

Learning disability makes the acquisition of skills, at every stage in life, more difficult; children are slower to learn, understand and do things compared to other children of the same age. The degree of disability can vary greatly. Some children who have a severe learning disability will never learn to speak and will need help with looking after themselves in terms of feeding, washing, dressing and toileting throughout their lives.

Children with a moderate learning disability are likely to have a limited ability to understand and communicate, and find it hard to express themselves. Speech problems can make it even harder for other people to understand their wishes and feelings. This can be a frustrating and upsetting experience, and comparisons with their peers can leave children with a learning disability feeling very inadequate. Some children with a mild learning disability learn to read and write, and go on to hold down a job and live independently. In the main, adults with a learning disability who become parents will have a mild to moderate disability.

Many adults with learning disabilities will have experienced difficulties in their childhood, which will have left them with low self-esteem and a poor sense of their own worth. The very talents that are prized within childhood, such as good co-ordination and a talent for sports; communication skills and the ability to empathise with others; quick wittedness and high academic achievement, are beyond them. Consequently, many adults will have had a childhood characterised by bullying, scapegoating and isolation from their peers.

People with learning disabilities are more likely than other people to have other disabilities and certain health problems (Royal College of Psychiatrists 2008). For example, they are six times more likely than other people to have a mental health problem; up to a third of adults with learning disabilities may have epilepsy and half are likely to have problems with hearing and/or eyesight (Foundation for People with Learning Disabilities 2009). However, gaining access to services may be hampered by the difficulties many people with learning disabilities have in expressing their feelings in words, and by professional or service attitudes to working with people with learning disabilities within generic mental health services (Hassiotis et al. 2000).

Learning disability also affects opportunities to learn how to parent. For example, some adults with a learning disability will have spent their childhood and adolescence in institutions of one kind or another, although this is much less likely today than previously. Others will have experienced poor parenting themselves (McGaw et al. 2007) or been brought up in a very sheltered and protected environment, possibly having been assigned the role of the perennial child where there was no expectation that they might become parents themselves. Many young people with learning disabilities will have received inadequate sex education and are unaware of the significance of changes to their body. There is still a widely held belief that adults with learning disabilities should not have children.

> *People try to stop them having a relationship, having sex, having a baby, keeping the baby. Why are some professionals so shocked that people with learning difficulties want to start a family?*

(Andrew Holman, quoted in Community Care 2006)

Finally, the life experiences of parents with learning disabilities have left many feeling particularly powerless to deal effectively with the negative attitudes and prejudices from those with whom they come into contact. Small-scale studies (e.g. Cooke 2005) and messages from parents with learning disabilities themselves (e.g. CHANGE 2005) indicate that harassment and bullying, and sometimes violence and financial or sexual exploitation, can be a major problem for parents with learning disabilities and their children (Department of Health et al. 2007).

> *Shortage of money, debt, unemployment, chronic housing problems, fraught relationships, the hardships of single parenthood, personal harassment, victimization and skill deficits all contribute to their vulnerability.*

(Booth and Booth 1996)

Physical and psychological impact of drugs, including alcohol

Alcohol, and to a lesser extent drug use, is well integrated into the lives of many parents. For example, drinking alcohol is an intrinsic element of most religious ceremonies, festive celebrations, meals and everyday entertainment. Drinking or drug use may also be used to alter undesirable states such as depression, anxiety, withdrawal, symptoms of mental illness or the low self-esteem resulting from domestic violence. In examining the impact of different drugs it is important to bear in mind that most people do not consistently consume excessive amounts of alcohol or drugs, and the occasional use of alcohol or some of the less harmful drugs such as cannabis result in few, if any, lasting adverse effects.

There are many types of drugs and each has an individual profile in terms of its main effects. However, the same drug may affect different people in different ways. Excessive consumption of alcohol will cause some people to simply fall asleep while others become aggressive and violent. The situation is further complicated because the same drug may have very different behavioural consequences, even within the same individual, depending on their:

- current mental state

- experience and/or tolerance of the drug

- expectations

- personality

- means of administration (i.e. injecting, oral, smoking, nasal inhalation)

- dosage.

In some cases the way a drug is administered may be the main risk or cause of harm. For instance, intravenous drug use carries the additional risk of HIV/AIDS and hepatitis. Up to 50% of injecting drug users will have contracted hepatitis C (Foster 2008). There are long-term consequences of the hepatitis C virus, which include liver disease such as cirrhosis and cancer. Treatment for hepatitis C can be effective for most injecting drug users but the side effects can be difficult, including depression, low tolerance of frustration and low resistance to disease.

The severity of the withdrawal symptoms from any particular drug, whether physical or psychological, will depend on the type of drug and how much and for how long the drug has been used. With opiates (such as heroin) many physical symptoms can be reduced by substitute prescribing of methadone or bupremorphine. The psychological withdrawal symptoms often go on for longer than the physical symptoms and almost always include a degree of craving. Skilled professional interventions can help at this point through the use of psychological strategies and therapies. Anxiety, insomnia, difficulties in remaining attentive, frustration and depression (at least temporary) can be expected in almost all withdrawal states. They do not always require intervention, especially if the parent is well supported by family and friends. However, when symptoms are at their maximum they could interfere, at least for a while, with the capacity to carry out parenting responsibilities.

Analgesics

The results of using these substances (such as heroin, morphine and methadone) are highly dependent upon the individual's level of tolerance, means of administration, and nature of the particular analgesic. Those who inject heroin experience an almost overwhelming pleasure (a 'rush') which lasts for a few seconds followed by a dreamlike, unreal state. People have described feeling relaxed, elated, calm and clear. Low dosage may have little effect on parental functioning, although at higher levels it produces sedation, sleepiness and unconsciousness (Coleman and Cassell 1995).

Methadone

Usually prescribed in an oral linctus form, this induces a milder elation and no 'rush' because it is not ordinarily injected; prescribing methadone in tablet form is rarely justifiable and is best avoided (Department of Health et al. 1999). Those who use the same daily dose may have minimal impairment of consciousness and many hold down responsible jobs and successfully raise families. Withdrawals from heroin or other opiates like methadone can induce symptoms including nausea and vomiting, cramps, aches and pains, craving for the drug, sleeplessness, and lethargy. The experience has been likened to a severe case of the flu. If no new opiates are taken the symptoms will peak at some 72 hours after the last ingestion, although sleep problems, anxiety, and craving often continue.

Stimulants

Amphetamines, cocaine and 'crack' – a smokable form of cocaine – produce feelings of elation, confidence, and happiness. Users become talkative and feel competent and powerful when under the influence of the drug. However, this is frequently a misperception as concentration is often impaired and in the cold light of non-intoxication the users' efforts may not be as good as they had assumed. When used intravenously the impact is immediate, while oral or nasal intake results in a more delayed reaction. Smoking 'crack' cocaine also produces an almost instant reaction. As the drug leaves the system users often experience feelings of hopelessness and depression. The effect of amphetamines lasts for hours and, for the most part, cocaine and 'crack' is more intensive but shorter-acting. For some people the excessive use of these drugs results in paranoia, hallucinations and other symptoms reminiscent of psychotic illness. For those suffering from mental illness, stimulants may provoke a 'florid episode' leading to hospitalisation. Withdrawals can include depression, anxiety, craving and sleep problems (Coleman and Cassell 1995).

Depressants

Alcohol, tranquillisers, sedatives and solvents affect consciousness in different ways depending on the particular drug. Those who drink alcohol may, according to how much they drink, suffer from diminished capacity to concentrate, memory impairment and reduced psychomotor co-ordination. Speech is often slurred and inhibitions lost, which can result in diminished self-control and violence. The effects of alcohol are mediated by tolerance, expectation, personality and social setting.

Tranquilliser users can feel calm and relaxed on small doses but consciousness may be lost when using larger doses or when depressants are mixed with alcohol. Such a cocktail is particularly dangerous because it enhances the consequences of alcohol while increasing the risk of overdose. The same is true of sedatives such as sleeping pills. Withdrawals for alcohol range from the symptoms of a mild hangover to epileptic-type fits, hallucinations, heavy perspiration, vomiting and tremulousness in the most severe cases. Tranquilliser and sedative withdrawals can include anxiety, irritability, sleeplessness and depression (Coleman and Cassell 1995).

Hallucinogenic drugs

Cannabis is the mildest form of this group of drugs, which also includes LSD, Ecstasy and 'magic mushrooms'. Cannabis is most commonly ingested through smoking and the effects begin about 10 or 15 minutes after the first inhalation. The user usually feels calm, relaxed and has heightened awareness. Under the influence of cannabis memory is sometimes impaired, concentration becomes difficult and the user may lose all sense of time. LSD and magic mushrooms cause visual and other types of hallucinations, which can last for 12 hours or more (especially with LSD and shorter periods for magic mushrooms). Sensual experience will be enhanced or altered when under the influence of these drugs. Adverse reactions can be depersonalisation, hallucinations, paranoia and panic attacks but these are not common among those who use the drug moderately. Withdrawals tend to include sleep problems, anxiety and sometimes mild cravings. Flashbacks (a brief hallucinogenic experience – often less than a minute) can occur with LSD and less commonly with magic mushrooms, long after the initial experience.

For those with the most difficult and complex alcohol and drug problems, it is likely that problematic use will continue over time. Treatment may well prolong periods of abstinence or controlled use but relapse, in many cases, should be expected. The nature of most community services is such that many clients drop in and out of services according to their own needs, attitudes and behaviour. It should not be assumed that simply because a parent is receiving services they are abstinent or even in control of their alcohol or drug use. Nor can it be assumed that if they have dropped out of treatment they are problematically using alcohol or drugs.

Physical and psychological impact of domestic violence

Our earlier exploration of domestic violence and gender revealed that in the majority (87%) of reported incidents of domestic violence, women are the victims and men the perpetrators. However, epidemiological studies, which use the Conflict Tactics Scale (CTS) and involve self-report questionnaires such as the British Crime Survey (Walby and Allen 2004), question the role specificity of violence.

But one drawback to research findings based on the CTS is that the scale fails to take account of the social context, severity or consequences of the assault or the controlling effect on the women of threatened violence by their male partners (see for example Dobash and Dobash 1992; Ross 1996). Men's physical strength generally means that women are at much greater risk of sustaining injuries in domestic conflict. Domestic violence is the most frequent cause of women's injuries and is greater than the combined causes of all other injuries to women (Goldsmith and Vera 2000). The emphasis on men's violence against women is also reflected by findings from the Duluth Community Abuse Programme in Minnesota (Pence and McMahon 1998). Over an 18-year period, where female as well as male abusers were vigorously pursued within criminal justice strategies, women never comprised more than 7% of those attending the perpetrators' programmes.

Weighing the evidence from research (which suggests that on balance women are the main victims and survivors of domestic violence) and because little is known about the experiences of men in situations of domestic violence (either as victims or perpetrators), this section concentrates on women's experiences. A focus on violence against women is also relevant for the following reasons.

- In the majority of families which involve domestic violence it is the women's role to look after the children.

- Violent husbands or partners are less likely to be involved in parenting their children compared to their non-violent counterparts (Holt et al. 2008).

- When domestic violence results in family separation, children usually remain with the mother (Maidment 1976; Eekelaar and Clive 1977).

The mother's capacity to look after her children is affected by the severity of the violence she experiences. In the extreme it can result in her death, directly as a result of the assault or indirectly through suicide. Domestic violence can also lead to injury severe enough to warrant medical attention including hospitalisation. Nearly a third of cases reported to the British Crime Survey required medical attention: 59% resulted in an injury and 13% in broken bones (British Crime Survey 1996). Assault can take the form of slapping, punching, kicking, burns and stabbing, sexual abuse and rape, with the consequences being black eyes, bruising and broken bones (Mullender 2004; Cleaver et al. 2007).

> *I've seen him kick and punch, and pull her hair. Once he threw petrol over her. I remember him cutting my mum's lips.*

(Thirteen-year-old girl, quoted in Humphreys and Stanley 2006, p.55)

Domestic violence is rarely confined to physical assaults but involves a mixture of physical and psychological violence.

It was physical and mental. It was more mental violence ... (but) it was physical as well. He's knocked me unconscious a few times and strangled me. He stabbed me once with a knife, but it was more mental, you know. He was driving me mad. I thought I was going crazy...

(Mother, quoted in Malos and Hague 1997, p.402)

Female victims can be exposed to emotional abuse, constant criticism, undermining and humiliation (Hester and Radford 1995). Consequently, even when the impact is less obvious physically, domestic violence can have profoundly negative effects on women's mental health. There is considerable evidence that women exposed to domestic violence suffer a loss of confidence, depression, feelings of degradation, problems with sleep and increased isolation, and use medication and alcohol more frequently (Casanueva et al. 2009). Indeed, the experiences of women living in violent relationships have been likened to that of hostages and victims of torture (Graham et al. 1988). Holt and colleagues' (2008) review of the literature identified one- to two-thirds of abused women experience post-traumatic stress disorder, low self-esteem, depression and anxiety.

I was a nervous wreck. I was just like a gibbering idiot. I had no confidence, no self esteem. I thought I was the most useless thing ... because when you are being told all the time that you are crap, you sort of eventually begin to believe it.

(Mother, quoted in NCH Action for Children 1994, p.45)

Domestic violence emerges over time, often after the relationship has become well established. The initial incident is rarely unambiguous and frequently the man initially begs forgiveness, offering reassurances and promises to change. In response many women blame themselves for the situation, turning their anger and sense of failure upon themselves (Kirkwood 1993; Morely and Mullender 1994). Assaults, however, are rarely isolated incidents and, after the initial attack, domestic violence can become a recurring problem. A recognised pattern often develops, which may include a build-up of tension, an eruption of violence followed by pleas for forgiveness, a brief reunion and a return to former stability. Women's difficulties in leaving abusive men are reflected by the NCH report, which found the average duration of violent relationships to be 7.3 years (NCH Action for Children 1994).

Superficially, leaving a partner is an obvious solution for an abused woman. Although some women do take this route out, the decision is rarely easy. Most women feel committed to their relationship and responsible for the children; some feel emotionally and financially dependent and think they will be unable to survive on their own, and some believe that they or their children will be hurt or killed if they leave, or that their children will be taken into care (Office of the Tanaiste 1997). The decision to leave can place women and children in an increasingly vulnerable position. For many, the point of departure triggers a violent assault by their male partner as he tries to exert control and prevent her departure (Kirkwood 1993).

The fear that children will be taken into care is even more acutely felt when the abused woman is from an ethnic minority group. In these circumstances the woman may perceive official agencies as threatening (particularly if she is of refugee status), believe that her culture will be misinterpreted, or have little faith in her ability to explain her situation (Maitra 1995; Hyton 1997). Women's Aid provides specialist help and advice to women from different cultural groups and interpreters for those whose preferred language is not English (Women's Aid 2008). This fear of statutory agencies is understandable, particularly when considering the over-representation of black children in the public care system (Courtney et al. 1996; Bernard quoted in McGee 1996).

Greater hurdles must be overcome by disabled women seeking help. They may be dependent upon their abuser who may also be their carer and the main carer of the children, they may fear losing community care packages and find that much-needed adaptations to the home are not easily transferable.

In spite of the difficulties of leaving home, it would be misleading to assume that all women submissively accept living in a violent relationship. Research has shown that some women do try to discuss the abuse with their partner or talk to friends and relatives, while others call the police or seek refuge (Kelly 1988; Hoff 1990). The British Crime Survey showed that leaving was the best avenue of escape from domestic violence. However, separation does not always result in a cessation of violence; for 37% of women the violence increased, took a different form (for example stalking), remained the same or commenced following separation (Walby and Allen 2004). Men who were most violent when living with women continued to be the most violent following separation (Humphreys and Stanley 2006).

Impact on parenting

Parenting can be defined as those activities and behaviours of caregiving adults that are needed by children to enable them to function successfully as adults, within their culture.

(Jones 2009)

In order to achieve this, those who are responsible for parenting must provide the child with basic care, ensure their safety, provide emotional warmth, provide appropriate stimulation, offer guidance and boundaries and provide the child with stability (see the box on dimensions of parenting capacity for a detailed description).

UNIVERSITY OF WINCHESTER
LIBRARY

Dimensions of parenting capacity

Basic care

Providing for the child's physical needs, and appropriate medical and dental care.

> Includes provision of food, drink, warmth, shelter, clean and appropriate clothing and adequate personal hygiene.

Ensuring safety

Ensuring the child is adequately protected from harm or danger.

> Includes protection from significant harm or danger, and from contact with unsafe adults/other children and from self-harm. Recognition of hazards and danger both in the home and elsewhere.

Emotional warmth

Ensuring the child's emotional needs are met, and giving the child a sense of being specially valued and a positive sense of their own racial and cultural identity.

> Includes ensuring the child's requirements for secure, stable and affectionate relationships with significant adults, with appropriate sensitivity and responsiveness to the child's needs. Appropriate physical contact, comfort and cuddling sufficient to demonstrate warm regard, praise and encouragement.

Stimulation

Promoting the child's learning and intellectual development through encouragement and cognitive stimulation and promoting social opportunities.

> Includes facilitating the child's cognitive development and potential through interaction, communication, talking and responding to the child's language and questions, encouraging and joining the child's play, and promoting educational opportunities. Enabling the child to experience success and ensuring school attendance or equivalent opportunity. Facilitating the child to meet challenges of life

Guidance and boundaries

Enabling the child to regulate their own emotions and behaviour.

> The key parental tasks are demonstrating and modelling appropriate behaviour and control of emotions and interactions with others, and giving guidance which involves setting boundaries, so that the child is able to develop an internal model of moral values and conscience and social behaviour appropriate for the society within which they will grow up. The aim is to enable the child to grow into an autonomous adult, holding their own values, and able to demonstrate appropriate behaviour with others rather than having to be dependent on rules outside themselves. This includes not over-protecting children from exploratory and learning experiences.

Includes social problem solving, anger management, consideration for others and effective discipline and shaping behaviour.

Stability

Providing a sufficiently stable family environment to enable a child to develop and maintain a secure attachment to the primary caregiver(s) in order to ensure optimal development.

> Includes ensuring that secure attachments are not disrupted, providing consistency of emotional warmth over time and responding in a similar manner to the same behaviour. Parental responses change and develop according to the child's developmental progress. In addition, ensuring children keep in contact with important family members and significant others.

(Reproduced from Department of Health et al. 2000, p.21, paragraph 2.12)

Impact of a single disorder

To suggest that all parents who suffer from mental illness, learning disability, problem alcohol/drug use or are subjected to or perpetrate domestic violence present a danger to their children is misleading and dangerous. Indeed, much research indicates that, with adequate support, parents who are experiencing a single disorder are often able to be effective and loving parents and present little risk of significant harm to children.

Mental illness

Rutter and Quinton (1984) in their four-year follow-up study of children, found two-thirds of those in families where there was parental mental illness suffered no long-term behavioural or emotional difficulties. In fact, many parents with mental illness regard the bond between themselves and their children as especially strong and close (Ackerson 2003) and negative effects can be offset with adequate support.

> *A serious mental illness can adversely affect an individual's ability to parent, but it is possible, if provided with adequate resources, that many individuals with a serious mental illness are able to successfully care for their children.*

(Reupert and Maybery 2007, p.365)

Learning disabilities

Similarly, there is no foundation for presuming that parents with learning disabilities will inevitably neglect or abuse their children. Virtually all the available research suggests that most parents with a learning disability provide adequate care; much of the inadequate child care is the product of poverty, debt and poor housing (Booth and Booth 1996). With sufficient support parental learning disability does not affect child outcomes (Booth and Booth 1997).

> *...a key factor distinguishing children who remained living safely with their parents from those who did not show satisfactory progress and those who were removed was the presence of a non-abusive adult such as a partner or relative.*

(Cleaver and Nicholson 2007)

Problem substance use or domestic violence

Furthermore, there is considerable evidence that many, if not most, children of parents with problem alcohol and drug use eventually 'outgrow' their troubled childhood and develop into balanced, productive adults and parents (Tweed 1991; Velleman and Orford 2001; Daniel et al. 2009). Similarly, growing up in violent households does not automatically result in long-term problems for children. General population studies found that *'Although marital disharmony increases the risk to children of demonstrating psychiatric disturbance, most children in disharmonious homes do not show problems'* (Jenkins and Smith 1990, p.60).

Relationship between parents and children

Individual members of the family do not exist in isolation, and the child's own personality and needs will impact on their parents or carers, particularly when parenting takes place in an unsupportive environment (see Jones 2009 for a contemporary view of parenting). The relationship between parents and children is a two-way process that functions in a circular fashion; the emotions and behaviour of one player (i.e. the parent) affect the emotions and behaviour of the other (the child) and the consequent feedback results in each modifying their behaviour.

For example, adjusting to a new baby will test any parent, but parents face additional challenges when the infant is showing withdrawal symptoms (such as high-pitched crying and feeding difficulties) as a result of drugs taken by the mother during pregnancy. Furthermore, the mother's capacity to deal with her needy baby may be reduced by her own drug needs. The foundation of the developing relationship between parent and child will be stronger when parents have the capacity to respond to their baby's needs and find the reactions of their infant rewarding (Aldgate and Jones 2006).

Impact of multiple problems

While caution is needed in making assumptions about the impact on children of parental mental illness, learning disability, problem alcohol/drug use and domestic violence, it is important to acknowledge the ways in which these issues interact and the extent to which such problems may be associated with other parental experiences such as abuse, neglect or loss in childhood (Bifulco and Moran 1998).

Although a single issue such as mental illness may not detrimentally affect parenting capacity, there is considerable evidence that many parents also experience other difficulties (Cleaver and Walker with Meadows 2004; Velleman and Reuber 2007). For example, adults with mental health problems are more likely than those without to abuse drugs or alcohol; similarly, those who abuse drugs have a markedly increased lifetime occurrence of diagnosable psychopathology (Spotts and Shontz 1991; Beckwith et al. 1999).

> *Mum describes herself as having a series of difficult life experiences. She reports experiencing domestic violence in all her relationships and has a variety of physical health problems and has intermittent chronic depression, specific learning disabilities and agoraphobia. A family history of both learning difficulties and mental health problems exists.*

(Cleaver and Nicholson 2007, p.42)

It is the 'multiplicative' impact of combinations of factors that have been found to increase the risk of harm to children. For example, the risk of child abuse increased 14-fold when parents had themselves been abused in childhood, if the parent was under twenty-one, had been treated for mental health problems or had a partner with violent tendencies (Dixon et al. 2005a, 2005b). Research has shown that mothers who experience depression after childbirth, compared to those who do not, are 20% more dependent on alcohol (Woodcock and Sheppard 2002). Alcohol dependence linked to depression is generally associated with poorer, less consistent parenting. Research suggests that in such cases women's capacity to empathise with and respond to their children's needs is overwhelmed by their own needs where *'alcohol dependence is present alongside depression, there is greater concern about the 'dangerousness' of the situation'* (Woodcock and Sheppard 2002, p.243).

The prevalence of co-morbidity also places children of parents with learning disabilities at increased risk of abuse and neglect (McConnell and Llewellyn 2000). In most cases where there are concerns over the safety and welfare of the children, parents with learning disabilities also experience poor mental and physical health, domestic violence, problem alcohol or drug use, have a history of childhood abuse, growing up in care or a combination of these (Cleaver and Nicholson 2007).

Although there is substantial evidence showing that a combination of parental mental illness, learning disability and problem substance misuse increases the risk to children's safety and welfare, the best predictor of adverse long-term effects on children is the co-existence with family disharmony and violence. This is reinforced by the findings from serious case reviews '...*domestic violence, substance misuse, mental health problems and neglect were frequent factors in the families' backgrounds, and it is the combination of these factors which is particularly 'toxic'* (Brandon et al 2010, p.iii).

In contrast, when families remain cohesive and harmonious, research would suggest that many children, despite experiencing difficulties during childhood, are resilient and do not go on to have more problems in adulthood than other people (see Quinton and Rutter 1985 for mental illness; Velleman and Orford 2001 and Cleaver et al. 2007 for substance misuse; Cleaver and Nicholson 2007 for learning disability).

Aspects of parenting

To understand the ways in which parental mental illness, learning disability, excessive drinking, drug misuse, and domestic violence may affect children's health and development and indeed their safety, the following aspects of parenting are examined:

- parenting skills

- parents' perceptions

- control of emotions

- neglect of physical needs

- parent–child attachment relationships

- separation of children and parents.

Parenting skills

There is considerable research evidence which suggests that mental illness, learning disability, problem drinking or drug use and domestic violence affects parenting skills. For example, apathy and listlessness, classic symptoms of depression, which may be mirrored in those who use illicit drugs or are subject to domestic violence, mean parents have difficulty in organising day-to-day living. As a result they are often unpredictable, inconsistent and ineffective in their parenting (see Oyserman et al. 2000 for mental illness; Cleaver and Nicholson 2007 for learning disability; Barnard

2007 for problem substance misuse; Stanley et al 2009 for domestic violence). A sense of apathy, feelings of inadequacy or a poor skill-set can affect the quality of parents' interactions with their children. Devoting time to playing, talking, going out and taking an interest in their child's world may, at times, prove too difficult.

Research shows that when children are referred to children's social care services, initial assessments reveal that over half the children (57%) of parents with a learning disability were not being provided with adequate stimulation – the rate fell to 30% both for children living with substance-misusing parents and those living with domestic violence[1] (Cleaver et al. 2007; Cleaver and Nicholson 2007).

Parents with learning disabilities need much encouragement, support and training to acquire the necessary skills to bring up a child. Limited literacy means that information about how to parent cannot be gleaned from reading relevant leaflets and magazine articles; a restricted vocabulary and difficulty in understanding abstract concepts makes it harder to comprehend and retain the information given by professionals such as health visitors and midwives. When new skills are gained, parents with learning disabilities have more difficulty than other parents in generalising newly acquired skills to keep abreast of their child's developmental progress. Parenting is also hampered because a learning disability makes it hard to establish routines and to cope adequately with unexpected and unanticipated events; life can easily become disorganised.

A disorganised lifestyle will have a differential impact on children depending on their age, development and personality. A lack of supervision leaves babies, young children and disabled children particularly vulnerable, but older children are also at risk of neglect. For example, some parents who are opiate dependent allow others to inject heroin in their homes, despite believing that their drug dependence and associated lifestyle are potentially harmful to their children (Hogan 2003).

> *The children were being left to their own devices. Danielle (aged 8 years) was left in the bedroom alone and unsupervised with drug-using men in the house. She was at risk of anything. They could have abused her. They were high on drugs. Morgan (aged 4 years) was also unsupervised.*

> (Social worker's notes on a family referred to children's social care, quoted in Cleaver et al. 2007, p.87; mother depressed, her partner a drug misuser)

Initial assessments carried out by social workers in children's social care showed that parents were not adequately ensuring their child's safety in 93% of cases where children lived with substance-misusing parents, 73% of cases where children lived with domestic violence and 58% of cases where a parent had a learning disability[2] (Cleaver et al. 2007; Cleaver and Nicholson 2007).

---

[1] The statistics provided are the result of a re-analysis of data gathered for two research studies: Cleaver and Nicholson 2007 and Cleaver et al. 2007. The research did not cover children living with mentally ill parents and, consequently, such detailed information is not available.

[2] See footnote 1.

Difficulty in organising day-to-day living means that the rituals and routines which cement family relationships are difficult to sustain. For example, mental illness, learning disability, alcohol or drug misuse or domestic violence make it difficult for the family to plan anything in advance or to stick to familiar routines such as meal times, bedtimes and getting children off to school (Hogan and Higgins 2001).

> *Probably the only routine they had was my drug use and me getting my drugs, that was the only routine.*

(Drug-misusing parent, quoted in Barnard 2007, p.65)

Important events may be disrupted, for example birthdays forgotten, key events at school missed, Christmas and birthdays ruined and planned holidays abandoned.

> *A couple of Christmases ago, she was sober from the 18th to the 26th … And we went out shopping and we been skating. We done a lot within those days. But then she went back to the drink.*

(Rachel 17, mother alcohol misuser, quoted in Bancroft et al. 2004, p.21)

Parents' perceptions

Domestic violence, parental mental illness, learning disability and problem alcohol and drug use can all affect parents' perception of the world. Excessive drinking or drug use, epilepsy (a frequent concomitant with learning disability) or the consequences of a violent attack can cause a parent to lose consciousness. If there is someone else present to look after the children then this matters less to the physical care of the child, although the emotional impact is not necessarily diminished. However, when no provision has been made and there is no responsible adult present, parental unconsciousness means children must fend for themselves. If children incur injury or fall ill during this time it is unlikely that many will be able to adequately attend to their own needs or know how or where to get help.

> *Cos if I'm lying on the couch strung out, I'll not want to do nothing with him and if I'm lying full of it, I'll lie and sleep so … I've not done much with him cause he's always wanting to do stuff, play games with you or something.*

(Parent, quoted in Barnard 2007, p.77)

Further evidence that parents who misuse drugs are aware of the potential harm this may have on their children comes from a review of the literature on child neglect (Daniel et al. 2009).

Mental illness, learning disability, problem alcohol or drug use or domestic violence can result in parents having a warped view of the world. Distorted parental perceptions can impact on parenting in a number of ways:

- Depressed mothers may see themselves as inferior parents, less competent and adequate than non-depressed parents (see for example Reupert and Maybery 2007). Similar negative self-perceptions have been found for women who are subjected to domestic violence (Humphreys and Stanley 2006), those with an alcohol or drug problem (Hogan and Higgins 2001), and parents with a learning disability (Cleaver and Nicholson 2007).

  You just sit down and put needles in your arm, you don't care ... always trying to get money and wondering where you'll get your next hit. It's hard being with them crying in your face and you're sick, you're roaring and shouting at them... it's not fair on the kids. She used to go to me ma's a lot, she was happier with her.

  (Drug-using mother of 9-year-old girl, quoted in Hogan and Higgins 2001, p.11)

- Parental problems may lead parents to have a distorted view of their children. For example, in cases of maternal depression children may be perceived as having behaviour problems which are not substantiated by objective measures (Fergusson et al. 1995). In other circumstances, a particular child may be blamed for the parent's current distress, or alternatively, one child may be seen as a saviour and main source of solace (for mental illness see for example Rutter 1990; for domestic violence see Emery 1982).

A distorted view of the child can affect the parents' capacity to provide adequate guidance and boundaries. Initial assessments carried out by social workers showed that in 68% of cases parents with learning disabilities did not provide adequate guidance and boundaries for their children, this applied to over half of cases (54%) where the child lived with a substance-misusing parent and a similar proportion of cases (51%) where the child lived with domestic violence[3] (Cleaver et al. 2007; Cleaver and Nicholson 2007).

Control of emotions

Depression can make parents irritable and angry with children, and depressed mothers are less likely to be emotionally available and affectionate; parents with schizophrenia may have unusual or inappropriate affective responses to their children (Reupert and Maybery 2007). For example, a significant minority of mothers with post-partum psychosis expressed delusions that related directly to their infants, typically that the child was possessed, had special powers, or was medically unwell (Margison and Brockington 1982; Kumar et al. 1995).

---

[3] The statistics provided are the result of a re-analysis of data gathered for two research studies: Cleaver and Nicholson 2007 and Cleaver et al. 2007. The research did not cover children living with mentally ill parents and, consequently, such detailed information is not available.

A personality and borderline personality disorder also influences the ability to control emotions. Parents may experience inappropriate or intense anger or problems in controlling anger (Hill et al. 2005). Mothers with borderline personality disorder have been shown to have difficulty with sensitive and empathetic parenting (Newman et al. 2007). The impulsivity and rapid and extreme swings of mood can be very difficult for children to understand and may leave many in a state of perpetual vigilance. Extreme mood swings are particularly evident during periods of stress such as when parents have to deal with fractious infants or difficult adolescents (Norton and Dolan 1996). Research suggests that compared to other groups, children of mothers with borderline personality disorder showed a higher prevalence of emotional and behavioural problems and lower self-esteem (Barnow et al. 2006).

The intake of drugs such as cocaine and crack or excessive amounts of alcohol can also produce violent mood swings from, for example, caring, loving and entertaining to violent, argumentative and withdrawn. As a consequence, parents with a drink or drug problem may behave in an inconsistent and frightening manner towards their children (see for example ChildLine 1997).

When parents are preoccupied with their own feelings they may experience greater difficulty in responding to their child's needs, cues are missed and the parent appears withdrawn and disengaged (Martins and Gaffan 2000). Research suggests that the severity and chronicity of the issue affecting the parent is associated with its impact on parenting capacity (see for example Rogosch et al. 1992 for mental illness; Forrester 2000 for substance misuse; Booth and Booth 1996 for learning disability). In a quarter of cases initial assessments carried out by social workers found substance misuse affected parents' capacity to provide children with emotional warmth, a factor in 30% of cases where children lived with domestic violence, and in a fifth of cases involving a parent with a learning disability[4] (Cleaver et al. 2007; Cleaver and Nicholson 2007).

Neglect of physical needs

The effects of domestic violence, problem drinking or drug use, mental illness or learning disability may mean that parents neglect their own and their children's physical needs.

> *Greg (aged 11 years with a learning disability) was not always cleaned after soiling himself, all three children were losing weight and there was often no food in the house.*
>
> (Social worker's report about a single mother with a learning disability and her three children, quoted in Cleaver and Nicholson 2007, p.77)

---

[4] The statistics provided are the result of a re-analysis of data gathered for two research studies: Cleaver and Nicholson 2007 and Cleaver et al. 2007. The research did not cover children living with mentally ill parents and, consequently, such detailed information is not available.

Although most mothers, regardless of the problems they faced, reported that they had been able to continue to look after their children, for some there were periods of despair when they didn't care what happened to either themselves or their children.

Neglect is not restricted to young children. For example, when learning disability, mental illness, domestic violence or problem substance misuse means that money, ordinarily used for household essentials and clothes, is diverted to satisfying parental needs, children and young people may find it difficult to buy essential clothing, and friendships may be jeopardised.

A review of research by Stein and colleagues (2009) on the consequences of adolescent neglect suggests links between neglect and/or neglectful parenting during adolescence and negative outcomes for the young people in relation to all the *Every Child Matters* outcomes. For example, the authors (Stein et al. 2009) found evidence that neglect during adolescence was associated with:

- poorer mental health and well-being and risky health behaviours

- running away and bullying

- poorer educational engagement, conduct and achievement

- antisocial behaviours.

Neglect is a likely consequence of parents not providing children and young people with basic care. Research focusing on children referred to children's social care found that half of those living with a parent with a learning disability, subject to an initial assessment, were not provided with adequate basic care; this applied to 41% of children living with substance-misusing parents and 31% when children were living with domestic violence[5] (Cleaver et al. 2007; Cleaver and Nicholson 2007).

Parent–child attachment relationships

Attachment is concerned with the behaviour and emotions that occur in particular situations where a child is stressed or fearful of perceived danger and seeks the proximity of another who is seen as stronger and wiser ... When fear is activated in a young child, curiosity and exploration will be suppressed.

(Aldgate and Jones 2006, p.68)

In most cases parental problems influence how parents relate to their child. Weissman and Paykel (1974, p.121) observed that *'at the simplest level, the helplessness and hostility which are associated with acute depression interfere with the ability to be a warm and consistent mother'*. A psychopathic personality disorder may manifest itself

---

[5] The statistics provided are the result of a re-analysis of data gathered for two research studies: Cleaver and Nicholson 2007 and Cleaver et al. 2007. The research did not cover children living with mentally ill parents and, consequently, such detailed information is not available.

in a *'callous unconcern for others, a low threshold for frustration, a discharge of aggression and an inability to feel remorse'* (Stroud 1997, p.158). Similarly, excessive drinking or drug misuse can result in the parent being emotionally unavailable to the child. Mothers who have a problem with drugs are less responsive to their babies, less willing to engage in meaningful play and more likely to respond in a manner that curtails further engagement (see Kroll and Taylor 2003 for a review of the literature). Parents with learning disabilities may not readily recognise their baby's cues nor have sufficient understanding to know how to respond appropriately to reassure the baby and encourage further interaction (Cleaver and Nicholson 2007).

High levels of parental criticism are also associated with insecure attachments. Research suggests that children living with opiate-using parents are at increased risk of harm because these mothers were observed to rely on harsh verbal responses when communicating with their children (Hogan 1998).

> *I shouted at me son ... you know what I mean. I shouted at him when I was coming down and I felt dead guilty. I went into the other room and started crying ... it's not his fault I haven't got any speed.*

(Substance-misusing lone mother, quoted in Klee et al. 2002, p.154)

The experience of domestic violence can significantly undermine the mother's relationship with her children (Radford and Hester 2006; Humphreys et al. 2006). The capacity of mothers who have previously provided sensitive and competent parenting may decline rapidly with the arrival of a violent partner (Jones 2009). In an attempt to avoid further outbursts of violence, the mother may prioritise her husband's or partner's needs at the expense of her children's (Holt et al. 2008). A preoccupation with trying to control the domestic environment may result in the mother becoming emotionally distant, unavailable or even abusive to her children. Belittling and insulting a woman in front of her children undermines not only her respect for herself, but also the authority which she needs to parent confidently. Mothers in McGee's (2000) study describe being sexually assaulted and humiliated in front of their children, and 10% reported having been raped with their children present.

All these issues pose a considerable risk to the process of attachment and more general relationships between children and their parents. Insecure patterns of attachment may mean that children develop shaky internal working models, which can have adverse consequences for later relationships (Howe 1995). Moreover, when children experience a degree of rejection this may have implications for the child's sense of connectedness. This, in turn, can affect intellectual, emotional, social and psychological functioning (Owusu-Bempah 1995; Owusu-Bempah and Howitt 1997).

A further issue noted by Rutter (1989) is that depressed mothers have a tendency to seek comfort from a daughter. Although in some cases this can result in a warm and mutually satisfying relationship, in other instances the child may be used inappropriately for comfort, or be drawn into a behavioural style of distress and depression (Radke-Yarrow et al. 1988). In some cases, children may take on too much responsibility for their age.

> *My husband was my carer but now Janice (aged 10 years) looks after me. Janice helps me when I have fits and with my drugs ... I can do the washing and Janice helps. I could cook but mainly go out to McDonald's or to the fish and chip shop.*
>
> (Learning-disabled mother of four children, explaining how she will manage having left her violent husband, quoted in Cleaver and Nicholson 2007, p.100)

Reviewing the possible effects of mental illness, learning disability, substance misuse and domestic violence on mothers' relationships with their children suggests mothers may be less sensitive to their children's needs, less responsive to their cues, express more anger and be more critical of their children. Much research has shown that these traits are among the strongest and most reliable predictors of insecure parent–child attachment (see Bowlby 1973; Ainsworth et al. 1978; Egeland and Scroufe 1981).

Separation of children and parents

The introduction of medication such as anti-psychotic and anti-depressant drugs, the increased treatment facilities for drug addiction and support services for parents with learning disabilities has meant that in the majority of cases children are not separated from parents who are experiencing such difficulties. However, chronic and multiple parental problems can have a cumulative impact on children's development, safety and welfare. The effectiveness of services in addressing parents' and children's needs must be carefully monitored to prevent over-optimistic beliefs in parents' capacity for change (Cleaver and Nicholson 2007).

When parents' problems become extreme, they may result in children being separated from one or both parents. For example, drug dealing to sustain a 'habit' may lead to the parent's imprisonment, domestic violence to a mother's escape to a refuge, or an acute episode of mental illness to hospitalisation. If the other parent or a close relative can provide a stable environment and the time and attention the children require, the risk of negative outcomes is much reduced. However, the luxury of a second caring parent or relative is not always available. For these children the hospitalisation or imprisonment of one parent results in the child being 'looked after' by the local authority. Although professionals are reluctant to place children in local authority care because of the well-publicised difficulties surrounding placement, there is growing evidence to suggest that *foster care provides a positive service to many children. Often it is both valued and, as far as research has been able to assess, valuable'* (Wilson 2006).

Recurrent separations have the potential to disrupt the continuity of care provided to children and the formation of harmonious stable family relationships.

Approximately three-quarters of children (76%) living with domestic violence, a similar proportion (73%) of those living with parental substance misuse and half the children (48%) living with a parent with a learning disability were assessed as not having a stable family environment in which to develop and maintain a secure attachment to a parent figure[6] (Cleaver et al. 2007; Cleaver and Nicholson 2007).

Social consequences

Parental mental illness, learning disability, problematic alcohol and drug use or domestic violence are associated with a variety of social consequences which are similar to the majority of children and families receiving child-care social work support (Sheppard 1993 and 1997; Cleaver and Walker with Meadows 2004). Although these are explored from the starting point of parental problems, it is important to note that mental illness, problem drinking or drug use may be understandable reactions to intolerable life circumstances (Brown and Harris 1978).

Three issues are of particular significance for parenting:

- the impact on living standards

- the loss of friends and family

- the disruption of family relationships.

Impact on living standards

Parental mental illness, learning disability, excessive drinking and drug use and the consequences of domestic violence can have financial consequences. For example, the bizarre and unpredictable behaviour of the schizophrenic, the weariness and inactivity of the depressive, the fear and terror of the anxious, the lack of abstract thinking, literacy and numeracy of the learning disabled, the unstable lifestyle of the substance misuser and the desire to keep domestic violence private can make it difficult to sustain a job. Longstanding disability or illness is correlated with unemployment; only 20% of people with mental health problems are employed, and for people with learning disabilities the employment rate is 25% (Morris and Wates 2006). Similarly, the uncontrolled and exaggerated mood swings and irritability associated with problem drinking and drug misuse can affect the parent's ability to keep a job. Some 50% of people treated for problem drinking have been sacked because of their drinking (Velleman 1993). When jobs are lost family income is reduced. Canadian research suggests unemployment is high among parents using cocaine or crack – only 7% of families had salaries as the main source of income (Leslie 1993).

---

[6]   The statistics provided are the result of a re-analysis of data gathered for two research studies: Cleaver and Nicholson 2007 and Cleaver et al. 2007. The research did not cover children living with mentally ill parents and, consequently, such detailed information is not available.

Living standards can also be adversely affected because family income is used to sustain parents' excessive alcohol or drug use. Coleman and Cassell (1995) estimated that a 'reasonable income' can support alcohol or methadone habits but only the very rich can afford to fund the continued use of heroin or cocaine. However, over recent years the street price of heroin and cocaine has fallen considerably and average income has increased, even taking into account inflation. The price of alcohol, compared to income, has also come down. It is likely that a drug or alcohol habit today (i.e. in 2011) is 'more affordable' than 10 years ago, but only if we assume that the individual's consumption hasn't increased as well.

To sustain excessive drinking or an escalating drug problem, many parents seek an additional source of income; parents may engage in criminal activities such as shoplifting, drug dealing or prostitution (Hogan 1998; Barnard 2007). Shielding children from the criminality associated with problem drug use is difficult, and in some cases parents use children as a cover for their criminal activity. *'Cos I used to kind of use her as well, so that I wouldn't get pulled by the police and things like that if I had her with me'* (drug-misusing parent, quoted in Barnard 2007, p.74). The home may also be jeopardised because money for rent and essential household items such as food, heating, and clothing is used to satisfy parental needs, or bills are simply overlooked or regarded as irrelevant (Velleman 1996).

The impact of criminal activities may place children at risk of suffering significant harm in several ways. Drug dealing, which often takes place in the child's home, means children cannot easily escape exposure to drugs and other drug users. Drug dealing places families at risk of police raids, but of more concern is the likelihood of children witnessing their home raided by other drug users looking for money or drugs and using intimidation and violence to get what they want. *'Then, the house that I was staying in, the fella was selling heroin and we got robbed at knifepoint. Now the kids were there when this happened...'* (Barnard 2007, p.75). The impact on children may be indirect; exposure to criminal behaviour may affect children's attitudes to authority and crime (Hogan 1998). Prostitution, one way of sustaining an expensive drug habit, may result in even very young children observing or being drawn into inappropriate sexual activity (Cleaver and Freeman 1995; Barnard 2007).

Violent and aggressive outbursts are associated with domestic violence, problem drinking or drug use and the lifestyle associated with drug dealing. *'There was a lot of violence that Nicky* (aged 2 years) *was seeing. Andrew was drinking. He was verbally aggressive. It was after an England football match that he had been drinking and he lashed out at me and broke my arm ...'* (mother, quoted in Cleaver and Nicholson 2007, p.202). Such incidents can also result in adults deliberately damaging property. When this takes place within the home, the fabric of the house may be destroyed and the place becomes unsafe for children to live in.

Apart from children being exposed to such dangers, parental problems may also result in children being neglected or exposed to potentially harmful situations. Homes need to offer warmth, sanitation and shelter and to reach basic standards of hygiene. The effects of mental illness, learning disability, problem drinking and drug use or domestic violence on parents' consciousness and energy levels can result in the living space being littered with food scraps, or heavily polluted with human or animal faeces. Such circumstances can pose serious risks to children's health. *'It was reported by the health visitor that the house was incredibly dirty, including dog dirt in a number of the rooms. The family also have quite large snakes in the front room, kept in a box'* (social worker discussing a family where both parents had a learning disability, quoted in Cleaver and Nicholson 2007, p.99). Excessive alcohol or illicit drug use may also mean drugs and used needles and syringes are easily accessible to the child, and a lack of supervision may result in experimentation.

Such negative scenarios are not inevitable. Some families where there are mental health problems, learning disability, excessive alcohol and illicit drug use or domestic violence ensure the children are looked after, clean and fed and have all their needs met (Brisby et al. 1997). Parents may make adequate provision for their children and thus ensure that they are not exposed to environmental dangers. For example, parental forethought can ensure adequate substitute child care arrangements so that children are not privy to drinking binges or drug misuse. Careful attention to storage means that unsafe substances or equipment are not accessible to children. In fact local initiatives have been developed to keep children safe. For example, the Nottingham Crime and Drugs Partnership (www.nottinghamcdp.com) fund the provision of lockable storage boxes to give to drug users who are parents. These boxes can be used for medicine storage as well as for drug-using paraphernalia such as needles and syringes.

In addition, a caring partner, spouse or relative, particularly the children's grandparents, can make sure that essential household services are intact, check that the home is sanitary and safe for the child, act as an agent of social control or provide a safe refuge for children (Cox et al. 2003; Reupert and Maybery 2007; Barnard 2007). *'Me ma and da were very supportive with the kids and minding them, or if I was short of money'* (drug-using mother of 12-year-old girl, quoted in Hogan and Higgins 2001, p.25). However, relatives and especially grandparents who provide this important source of continuity and stability for children often experience hardship, not only incurring the costs of looking after their grandchildren but also providing continuing financial support to their adult children (Social Care Institute for Excellence 2005).

The involvement of the wider family may not always be welcomed. Although useful in assisting with household tasks and child care, relatives may also become a source of stress by taking over the role and tasks of parenting in ways that undermine parents' own parenting skills (Hogan and Higgins 2001; Cleaver and Walker with Meadows 2006; Tarleton et al. 2006). In some families, when grandparents assume the care of the children this can lead to conflicting loyalties and resentment. For example, other members of the family may feel strongly that the problem drug-using parent should not abrogate their responsibility to raise their own children and burden the grandparent (Cleaver 2000; Barnard 2007).

Finally, there are financial implications for children when parental difficulties result in families breaking up. It is widely acknowledged that separation and divorce have financial costs for both parties, with women generally at a disadvantage in the job and housing market (Hague and Malos 1994). But when families break up because of domestic violence this is exacerbated because, overwhelmingly, it is women and children who have to leave their home. Many will need somewhere safe and secret to go to in the short term and, later, more permanent accommodation. The imposed move and the increased child-care responsibilities often bring with them job losses for mothers and increased problems for securing alternative work. It is hardly surprising, therefore, to learn that a major reason many women remain with violent men is their lack of economic resources and having nowhere to go (Hague and Malos 1994; Office of the Tanaiste 1997).

Loss of friends and family

Parents with poor mental health, learning disabilities, problem substance use and domestic violence often have poor relationships with their own parents, siblings and other relatives. For example, research suggests that mothers with learning disabilities may be among the most socially isolated of parents and thus lack the networks of social support from extended family and friends that are often crucial to young families (McConnell et al. 2003). Social isolation was also a factor in the lives of many families referred to children's social care when there was evidence of domestic violence, parental substance misuse or parental learning disability. Social workers' initial assessments identified difficulties in the area of 'family history and functioning' in some 81-89% of cases where children were living with parents with learning disabilities, substance misuse or domestic violence[7] (Cleaver et al. 2007; Cleaver and Nicholson 2007). For some parents, childhood adversity and their own behaviour during adolescence can result in hostility and estrangement from relatives.

> *He's a hard person to be with ... he's very selfish, very ... I think when people, anybody, that starts using drugs, they totally lose all reality ... they become totally different people...*

(Sibling of a drug-using man, quoted in Barnard 2007, p.48)

Close family relationships and friendships are also placed under increasing strain when adults with mental health problems or problem alcohol or drug use start to withdraw from reality or become obsessed with self. Self-absorption bores even the most faithful of friends, and bizarre behaviour and incoherent conversation or violent outbursts generate unease and fear (Kandal et al. 2000).

---

[7] The statistics provided are the result of a re-analysis of data gathered for two research studies: Cleaver and Nicholson 2007 and Cleaver et al. 2007. The research did not cover children living with mentally ill parents and, consequently, such detailed information is not available.

Friendships may also be curtailed because mothers in violent relationships wish to hide their experience. *'I was ashamed', 'I was too embarrassed', 'No one would have believed me', 'I had no friends left I could tell'* were all reasons given by women for keeping their abuse secret (NCH Action for Children 1994, p.79). This NCH survey of mothers attending family centres found that few had told anyone about the violence when it first happened. Women subjected to domestic violence may also keep silent about their experiences through fear and a lack of opportunity to develop close and confiding relationships.

> *I was kept in one room for six years. Six years of my life was in one room and kitchen. He kept me there. He wouldn't let me go out except sometimes with him ... And if anything he didn't like about the cooking and the shopping, he'd start doing the beating. Just like I was his slave...*

(Asian woman who had three children, quoted in Malos and Hague 1997, p.403)

Parents with mental health problems, learning disabilities and problem substance use may also become estranged from family and friends, because they are ashamed or frightened or because they have stolen from them or do not wish to see their own or their abusive partner's family. They may also cut themselves off from their own family because the behaviour of close relatives places their children at risk of harm (Tarleton et al. 2006). As a result, families become isolated and may lack the support needed to ensure their children are safely parented.

When parents are drug users, research suggests that they often base their social activities around the procurement and use of the drug. For example, Canadian research on families where at least one parent was using cocaine or crack, found that in over a quarter of cases (28%) the family lived with others who also used crack. Children living in these circumstances have been found to be at increased risk of physical and sexual abuse, lack supervision and be exposed to unsafe strangers and violence (Leslie 1993).

A further critical factor is the likelihood that drug-misusing families will experience greater levels of community rejection and be less involved in religious, neighbourhood or cultural activities. Women appear to be particularly affected. Problem drug-using women reported higher levels of loneliness and social isolation than men in similar circumstances (Hogan 1998). The children of parents with drug or alcohol problems can soon become known to the community and neighbourhood schools and as a consequence they can suffer from the stigma of their parents' problems.

Children may also experience repeated separations from home, community and friends through moves to avoid drug and other related debts, irate neighbours, or the stigma resulting from bizarre behaviours. Moving into a new neighbourhood will disrupt a child's schooling, and new links with health and community services will have to be forged. Leaving home in an emergency means children have little time to plan and pack and may be forced to leave behind personal and precious things including well-loved pets (Stafford et al. 2007).

Disruption of family relationships

Parental mental illness, learning disability, substance misuse and domestic violence place considerable strain on relationships between spouses or intimate partners. For example, more than 30% of problem drinkers receiving treatment believed marital conflict was a result of their drinking. Furthermore, it has been estimated that 80% of cases of domestic violence are alcohol related (Velleman 1993).

Learning disability is also associated with domestic violence and substance misuse. Research on children living with a parent with a learning disability found that in 42% of cases receiving social work services there was also evidence of domestic violence, problem drinking or drug misuse[8] (Cleaver and Nicholson 2007).

Mental illness is associated with marital breakdown because coping on a day-to-day basis with a depressed partner can be very exhausting and dispiriting (Weissman and Paykel 1974). Moreover, the risk of marital breakdown is further increased when a depressed person marries someone with a psychiatric illness, a situation which is not uncommon (Merikangas and Spiker 1982). When this happens, the symptoms of depression become more severe and marital and family disruption more likely (Merikangas et al. 1998). The link between mental illness and marital discord is highest when parents suffer from a personality disorder.

The association between mental illness, learning disability or problem drinking and domestic violence is complex. For example, not only may the psychiatric disorder, problem drinking or drug use result in marital discord, but women may develop mental health problems, or turn to drugs and alcohol as a direct consequence of domestic violence (Velleman 1993; Farmer and Owen 1995).

> *I was drinking and there had been a lot of violence from my husband – he beat me up and caused me a miscarriage by sticking his fist up me. He also forced me into prostitution.*

(Mother of three children, quoted in Cleaver et al. 2007, p.87)

Alternatively, domestic violence, mental illness and problem alcohol or drug use may be related to a prior condition (such as childhood adversities). A quarter of parents with learning disabilities whose children were receiving social work services had experienced childhood abuse[9] (Cleaver and Nicholson 2007).

---

[8] The statistics provided are the result of a re-analysis of data gathered for two research studies: Cleaver and Nicholson 2007 and Cleaver et al. 2007. The research did not cover children living with mentally ill parents and, consequently, such detailed information is not available.

[9] See footnote 8.

To sum up

Physical and psychological impact

- Children do not necessarily experience behavioural or emotional problems when parents suffer a single disorder such as mental illness, learning disability, problem drinking or drug use or domestic violence. However, when these parental problems coexist, the risk of children's health or development being impaired increases considerably.

- Mental illness can seriously affect functioning. For example, the delusions and hallucinations suffered by the schizophrenic can result in a preoccupation with a private world. Depression results in feelings of gloom, worthlessness and hopelessness, which mean everyday activities are left undone. Regardless of its cause, mental illness can blunt parents' emotions and feelings, or cause them to behave towards their children in bizarre or violent ways.

- Learning disability affects parents' capacity to learn and retain the new skills that are necessary to parent a child. In addition, negative childhood experiences leave many parents with low self-esteem and a poor sense of self-worth. Consequently, parents with learning disabilities and their children are vulnerable to financial and sexual exploitation, domestic violence, harassment and bullying.

- The effects of alcohol and drugs vary according to the type of drug, the amounts taken and means of administration, the individual's physical make-up, experience and/or tolerance of the drug, the user's personality and current mental state. Excessive drinking and drug misuse can produce symptoms such as erratic mood swings, paranoia and hallucinations, or feelings of elation and calm, diminished concentration, memory impairment and a loss of consciousness. Withdrawal symptoms can induce nausea and vomiting, cramps, hallucinations and epileptic-type fits. Stable, but controlled, use of drugs or alcohol can minimise the above effects and this could be a reasonable medium-term goal of treatment.

- In situations of reported domestic violence women are the main victims. Domestic violence involves physical assaults and psychological abuse. Both can have a negative impact on women's ability to look after children. Many women have difficulty in ending the violence because they fear leaving a violent partner or asking for help from outsiders. For example, a partner may have threatened their own lives and those of their children. Some women believe they will not survive emotionally or financially without their partner. Furthermore, many women fear their children will be taken into care if their situation becomes public knowledge.

Impact on parenting

- To safeguard and promote the welfare of children, parents must provide basic care, safety, emotional warmth, appropriate stimulation, guidance and boundaries and stability. Mental illness, learning disability, substance misuse and domestic violence can affect parents' capacity to address adequately these issues.

- Parental problems can result in parents having difficulty organising their lives. This may result in inconsistent and ineffective parenting, and rituals and routines which cement family relationships not being sustained. A disorganised lifestyle will have a differential impact on children depending on their age, development and personality; but a lack of supervision leaves children, regardless of their age, vulnerable to abuse and neglect. When parents lose consciousness, children may be in unsafe physical situations. When mental illness results in parents losing contact with reality, children may be drawn into their parents' delusional world, which can have long-term consequences for the child's own mental health.

- Parental problems may mean parents have difficulty controlling their emotions. Violent, irrational or withdrawn behaviour can frighten children. Mental illness, learning disability, substance misuse and domestic violence can lead to feelings of apathy and disengagement, which result in parents not providing children with adequate emotional warmth.

- When parents experience feelings of depression or despair, when drink or drugs divorce them from reality, or when a learning disability hampers the acquisition of new skills, parents may neglect their own and their children's physical needs. Neglect can affect all children and young people and not just babies and toddlers.

- Children may be insecurely attached because mental illness, learning disability, excessive drinking, drug misuse or domestic violence has meant parents are insensitive, unresponsive, angry and critical of their children. Insecure patterns of attachment may mean that children develop unstable internal working models which affect later relationships.

- When parents' behaviour becomes extreme and results in hospitalisation or imprisonment, children will need to be cared for by someone else. If the other parent or a close relative can look after the child and provide the time and attention the child needs, negative effects are minimised. However, for some children shelter within the extended family is not possible and they will need to be looked after by the local authority. Other children may need to be looked after because their parents are unable to change their behaviour sufficiently to ensure the child is not exposed to significant harm. Although there are well-known concomitant difficulties surrounding local authority looked-after children, for some children this is necessary and it can offer them a new start. A reluctance to take children into care and the application of the 'rule of optimism' is resulting in some children being left in dangerous circumstances.

Social consequences

- Parental mental illness, learning disability, excessive drinking, drug misuse and domestic violence can impact on the family's standard of living because:

  - Family income may drop. Apathy, bizarre or unpredictable behaviour or a lack of literacy or numeracy makes jobs difficult to acquire or sustain.

  - Family income may be used to satisfy parental needs. Purchasing food and clothing or paying essential household bills may be sacrificed.

  - To sustain parental habits, alternative sources of income may draw families into criminal activities, exposing children to unsafe adults.

  - Parents' behaviour can result in basic standards of hygiene being neglected.

  - Violence may result in the fabric of the home and possessions being damaged or destroyed.

  - Separation, particularly as the result of domestic violence, can result in a parent and children having to move out of the family home. Separation has financial consequences for both parties, but women and children are generally at a greater disadvantage.

- Families can become isolated because relationships with wider family and friends are eschewed. This can have a number of causes: bizarre or unpredictable behaviour can alienate friends and family; families wish to hide their experiences; violent husbands or partners limit or terminate the mother's and child's contact with wider family; and friends and social activities are based around parents' current needs and circumstances.

- Relationships within families can be disrupted. Mental illness, learning disability, problem drinking and drug misuse are associated with marital breakdown. The association is complex. The parental disorder itself, or its consequences such as the loss of a job and reduced income, may strain family relationships. Alternatively, mental illness, excessive drinking or drug misuse may be a consequence of an unhappy or violent relationship. Finally, all may have a common cause, such as childhood adversity.

3 Which children are most at risk of significant harm?

Chapter 3 explores factors that increase children's vulnerability and those that protect children from suffering significant harm. Vulnerability factors include:

- co-morbidity of parental problems

- a cumulation of negative childhood experiences including abuse and neglect

- genetic transmission of parental disorders

- involvement in parental delusions

- exposure to illicit drugs and the paraphernalia of drug use.

Protective factors include:

- quick resolution of parental problems

- day-to-day presence of a caring, safe adult who parents the child

- the child's own temperament, coping strategies and resilience.

What constitutes significant harm?

The concept of significant harm was introduced by the Children Act 1989 as the threshold for compulsory intervention in family life in the best interests of children. The Act places a duty on local authorities to make enquiries to decide whether they should take action to safeguard and promote the welfare of a child who is suffering, or likely to suffer, significant harm. Statutory guidance (HM Government 2010a) discusses the issues that should be considered when judging what constitutes significant harm in individual cases.

> *There are no absolute criteria on which to rely when judging what constitutes significant harm. Consideration of the severity of ill-treatment may include the degree and the extent of physical harm, the duration and frequency of abuse and neglect, the extent of premeditation, and the presence or degree of threat, coercion, sadism and bizarre or unusual elements. Each of these elements has been associated with more severe effects on the child, and/or relatively greater difficulty in helping the child overcome the adverse impact of the maltreatment. Sometimes, a single traumatic event may constitute significant harm, for example, a violent*

assault, suffocation or poisoning, More often, significant harm is a compilation of significant events, both acute and long-standing, which interrupt, change or damage the child's physical and psychological development. Some children live in family and social circumstances where their health and development are neglected. For them, it is the corrosiveness of long-term emotional, physical or sexual abuse that causes impairment to the extent of constituting significant harm. In each case, it is necessary to consider any maltreatment alongside the child's own assessment of his or her safety and welfare, the family's strengths and supports, as well as an assessment of the likelihood and capacity for change and improvements in parenting and the care of children and young people.

(HM Government 2010a, p.36, paragraph 1.28)

Vulnerable children

The seriousness of parental problems is less relevant than the capacity of parents to provide protection and support for their developing child when parents experience personal, environmental and relationship stressors. *'Parents need to be sensitive and mindful of their children's needs, anxieties, joys and success'* (Brandon et al. 2008, p.57). Those who are most at risk of suffering significant harm are children whose parents face a combination of stressors (Daniel et al. 2009). Children in these circumstances are more likely than children living in families whose parents experience fewer problems to have severe developmental needs, and experience abuse and neglect (Falkov 2002; Cleaver et al. 2007; Cleaver and Nicholson 2007; Brandon et al. 2008). For example, the co-morbidity of maternal depression and alcohol problems increases the likelihood of children's exposure to physical violence (Berger 2005). Most relevant is the presence of domestic violence. There is much research to suggest that when domestic violence is present along with other issues such as parental mental illness, learning disability, drug or alcohol misuse, it increases the likelihood of children suffering significant harm (Velleman and Reuber 2007; Daniel et al. 2009; Brandon et al. 2010).

Research on adverse childhood experiences suggests that the more negative childhood events (such as emotional, physical and sexual abuse, parental substance misuse, mental illness and domestic violence) to which an individual is exposed, the more likely it is that as adults they will experience physical and mental illnesses (Bentovim et al. 2009). For example, experiencing domestic violence and child physical maltreatment not only has an immediate negative impact on children's health and development, but is also associated with increased trauma symptoms and behaviour problems in young adults (Shen 2009). The salience of psychological aggression during childhood has also been highlighted by Miller-Perrin and colleagues (2009). In fact, their work suggests that the negative messages children receive from psychological aggression may be more important in contributing to the psychological outcomes for the child than the actual occurrence of physical violence.

Genetic factors

Genetic factors also play a significant part. For example, children of parents with learning disabilities are more likely to be born with a learning disability and psychological and physical disorders (Rende and Plomin 1993; McGaw and Newman 2005). The risk of abuse for children with disabilities, regardless of their parents' intellectual capacity, is between four and ten times that of the generic population (Baladerian 1990). Research that has focused on parents with learning disabilities found that the risk of harm to children increased significantly when their child had special needs (Booth et al. 2005; McGaw et al. 2010).

Genetic transmission is also a factor in schizophrenia and major affective and personality disorders (Kidd 1978; International Schizophrenia Consortium 2008). However, it is increasingly accepted that the interaction between genetic factors and physical, psychological and psychosocial factors determines who develops schizophrenia (Kidd 1978; Portin and Alanen 1996). A more recently published longitudinal study examined the interaction of genetic risk for schizophrenia and the type of home environment. Exposure to high levels of stress and adversity was shown to increase the likelihood of children, born with a genetic predisposition, to develop the symptoms of schizophrenia at an early age (Rutter, Moffitt and Caspi 2006). Children have less chance of becoming schizophrenic when brought up in supportive environments (Tienari et al. 2004; Wynne et al. 2006). Similarly, twin and adoption studies have found that genetics also play a part in the heritability of problem substance misuse (Kendler et al. 2006). Finally, the large differences observed in individual tolerances to alcohol among certain ethnic groups also suggest genetic factors play an important role (Agarwal 1996).

Substance misuse and learning disability

A focus on particular parental disorders suggests that there are aspects which increase children's risk of suffering significant harm. For example, parental substance misuse and learning disability increase the likelihood of an absence of order and routine in family life (Vellman 2004; Cleaver and Nicholson 2007; Daniel et al. 2009). High levels of household chaos have been shown to accentuate the impact of negative parenting (Coldwell et al. 2006).

Parental substance misuse, particularly the injection of drugs, can place children at risk of harm from needles and syringes. Needle-stick injuries and the transmission of HIV and AIDS and hepatitis B and C are possible even though the risk is small (Foster 2008). When drugs are taken within the home, children may be present, and witnessing such parental behaviour can be confusing and frightening. In order to sustain the cost of chronic substance misuse, parents may allow their homes to be used by other drug users and dealers, exposing children to unsafe adults, and to witnessing prostitution and other forms of criminality (Velleman 2009a, 2009b).

Children of parents with learning disabilities are more likely to have a disability or to have a sibling with a disability. The challenge of caring for a disabled child is stressful for even very capable parents and can result in the needs of other children within the family being neglected (Butcher et al. 2008; Epstein et al. 2008).

Mental illness

In relation to mental illness, the risk of suffering significant harm increases when children become targets of their parents' delusions. A specific child within the family may become a scapegoat and be the focus of parental hostility and rejection (Stroud 1997; Reupert and Maybery 2007). Children of mentally ill parents may be forced to participate in parental rituals and compulsions; or parental illness can result in marked restrictions to the child's social activities (Rutter 1966). Although rare, a child may also come to share the same delusions as the parent as part of a *folie à deux* (madness shared by two). This can occur when the delusional beliefs formed by a parent during a psychotic episode are imposed on the child (Arnone et al. 2006; Erol et al. 2008).

Domestic violence

Simply witnessing parental distress can have adverse effects on children. Children are witnesses, to a greater or lesser extent, of every aspect of domestic violence against their mothers. The incidence of children actually witnessing or hearing the violence ranges from all children in a study based on children in refuges, to 45% of children based on anonymous interviews with mothers (Humphreys and Houghton 2008). Research that seeks the experiences of children reveals their distress at seeing their mother's physical and emotional suffering.

> *He would come in and rip my mother's clothes off. He tried to strangle her, just beat her up like ... We were always watching it...*

(Child, quoted in the NCH Action for Children 1994, p.31)

Children living with domestic violence are also at risk of physical injury during an incident, either by accident or because they attempt to intervene (Humphreys and Stanley 2006). In attempts to halt the violence and protect their mother from assault children may call the police, or urge their mother to separate (Hamner 1989). However, separation should not be viewed as a simple solution which will protect mothers and children. The British Crime Survey showed that although separation was the best way to escape domestic violence (Walby and Allen 2004), domestic violence murder reviews showed separation can increase the likelihood of extreme violence being perpetrated. Three-quarters of multi-agency domestic violence murder reviews involved separation (Richards and Baker 2003, quoted in Humphreys 2006) and at least 29 children were killed in the last decade by their fathers post-separation (Saunders 2004). Self-reports included in the British Crime Survey (Walby and Allen 2004) showed child contact arrangements place a significant proportion of women and children at risk of abuse; a third of women reported experiences of abuse and threats to themselves or their children during contact.

> *He's nasty, verbally abusive through the children. He'll say things to the children and they'll come back and tell me ... even though the contact centre is public, it is not public enough.*

(Mother whose children had supported contact with their father, quoted in Humphreys and Stanley 2006, p.144)

The following serve as illustrations of more tragic cases.

> *A man who is believed to have smothered his two young daughters while they were on a weekend custody visit telephoned their mother to say 'the children have gone to sleep forever' before killing himself, it emerged last night.*

(The Guardian, 23 September 2008)

> *A DAD going through a bitter custody battle killed himself and his children after telling friends he was barred from seeing them on Father's Day.*

(Daily Post, 17 June 2008)

The impact of domestic violence on children is aggravated by the following factors:

- severity of the violence

- child being directly abused or neglected

- combination with problem drinking, drug misuse, mental illness or learning disability

- witnessing the parent's sexual and physical abuse

- being drawn into participating in the abuse of a parent

- colluding in the secrecy and concealment of the assaults

- lack of wider family and community support.

(Hamner 1989; Jaffe et al. 1990; Humphreys and Houghton 2008)

Children trying to help

Children may place themselves at risk of suffering significant harm because they are active participants within their families and may try to intervene in order to improve the dynamics and protect their parents. Although most parents try to shield their children from the effects of parental mental illness, domestic violence or substance misuse, unless the children are very young, parents believe that their problems affect their children's behaviour (Cleaver et al. 2007). For example, children may try to protect and support their mothers by staying home from school in order to look after them, and in some cases with the specific aim of stopping them from taking drugs (Barnard 2007). Children of parents with learning disabilities or mental illness may also act as carers (Aldridge and Becker 2003; Cleaver and Nicholson 2007).

The weekends – she can't bath herself you see properly – so at weekends when the carer doesn't come ... I bath my mum yeah and I wash her hair as well sometimes if I remember to wash it ...

(Helen, 16, talking about her mother who has psychotic depression, quoted in Aldridge and Becker 2003, pp.70–71)

Protective factors

From a developmental perspective, deficits in early life would be expected to be more pervasive and severe in their effects than later parenting problems. The reason for this is because from this perspective, developmental competencies build up over time, each are dependent and reliant upon successful negotiation of previous stages.

(Jones 2009, p.289)

No one age group of childhood seems either particularly protected from or damaged by the impact of parental mental illness (see for example d'Orban 1979), alcohol or drug problems (see for example Velleman 1996; Velleman and Templeton 2007) or domestic violence (see Centre de liaison sur l'intervention et la prévention psychosociales 2007 for a review of the research). However, a re-analysis of data[10] suggests parental learning disabilities may affect children aged 5 to 9 years referred to children's social care more than other age groups (Cleaver et al. 2007). Although the numbers are small, the findings reveal that 9 of the 10 children aged 5–9 years had severe developmental needs compared to half of those aged 10 years and over and 40% of those under the age of 5 years. Nonetheless, regardless of the age of the child, or the difficulties parents are experiencing, there is strong evidence to suggest that family and social support can act as a protective factor (Ghate and Hazel 2002; Vranceanu et al. 2007).

Children's ability to cope with parental adversity is related to their gender and individual personality. With regard to gender, findings from the US suggest boys are more likely than girls to have a learning disability; 10% of boys and 6% of girls aged 3 to 17 had a learning disability (Child Trends 2004). There is also some evidence to suggest that children of the same sex as a mentally ill parent are at greater risk of developing the disorder. This is particularly so with the development of depression in girls (Goodyer et al. 1993). There is also some evidence to suggest

---

10 The data was gathered for a study of children referred to children's social care services who were living with parents with learning disabilities: Cleaver and Nicholson 2007.

that when exposed to domestic violence girls are more likely than boys to manifest internalising and externalising behaviour problems (Sternberg et al. 2006). A more widely applicable phenomenon is the finding that girls are less affected in the short term, but as parental problems continue they are just as likely to exhibit distress as boys (for domestic violence see Yates et al. 2003; with relation to problem alcohol and drug use see Werner 1986 and Tweed 1991; for parental mental illness see Rutter 1985 and Stewart et al. 1980). Finally, Moffitt and colleagues' (2007) prospective-longitudinal study found that genes moderated an individual's response to stressful life events (see also Caspi et al. 2003; Rutter et al. 2006).

Individual variations in how children respond are, in part, a function of the severity, characteristics and social and cultural context of their parents' problems. Children are less likely to be affected adversely from parental mental illness when:

- it is mild

- it is of short duration

- one parent does not suffer from mental illness

- it is unassociated with family discord, conflict and disorganisation

- it is unassociated with the family breaking up

- the children have good social networks, especially with adults.

(Rutter 1990; Smith 2004; Somers 2007)

In relation to parental alcohol and drug misuse, children are less likely to suffer significant harm when:

- one parent has no problems with alcohol or drug use

- treatment is being given to the parent(s)

- parents manage to maintain a cohesive relationship and present a united and caring front to the child

- other responsible adults are involved in child care

- family rituals and activities are maintained

- drugs, needles and syringes are out of reach of children

- the child is not present when drugs are taken

- substance misuse does not take place in the home

- the social environment does not expose children to contact with drug users or other criminal activity

- there is a stable home with adequate financial resources

- the child has a friend, relative or other responsible adult in whom they can confide

- the parents have the capacity to be effective

- there are strong bonds with the local community or there is community involvement.

(Hill et al. 1996; Kroll and Taylor 2003; Cleaver et al. 2007; Velleman and Reuber 2007; Velleman 2009a)

Many of these factors also apply to the impact of parental learning disabilities on children. For example, key to children's safety and the promotion of their welfare is:

- a lack of family violence

- the presence of a non-abusive partner in the household

- other responsible adults, such as grandparents, involved in child care

- on-going support and training to enable parents to react appropriately to their child's changing needs and circumstances as they grow up

- parents with the capacity to act effectively in relation to themselves and their children

- community support

- a stable home and adequate financial resources.

(Booth and Booth 1996; Cleaver and Nicholson 2007)

A child's ability to cope with adversity is not the result of a specific factor or coping mechanism (Little et al. 2004; Collishaw et al. 2007; Jaffee et al. 2007). What is of importance is that children have developed the necessary strengths, which will enable them to find ways to cope with different situations.

> *Key building blocks for developing resilience in children and parents come from a sense of security, a recognition of self-worth and the experience of control over one's immediate environment.*

(Parrott et al. 2008)

Velleman and Templeton (2007) raise a few notes of caution in relation to resilience. They argue that the processes that allow children and young people to become resilient to parental problem behaviour may not all be totally positive, either in the short or the long term. For example, strategies of detachment, avoidance and withdrawal used for coping with domestic violence or parental substance misuse can result in later relationship difficulties.

Research has highlighted a variety of mechanisms that may explain why some children who have experienced childhood maltreatment reported no mental health problems in adult life. Collishaw and colleagues (2007, p.213) report 'resilient functioning appears to arise from the interaction between heritable factors, individual characteristics and experiential factors over time'. The study identified that good-quality relationships in childhood, adolescence and adulthood were especially important for adult psychological well-being for those who had experienced childhood abuse.

Resilience is related to children having:

- a sense of self-esteem and self-confidence

- a belief in one's self-efficacy and ability to deal with change and adaptation

- a repertoire of social problem solving approaches.

Rutter (1985; 2007)

Protective factors which are likely to foster such a cognitive set include a secure, stable, affectionate relationship and experiences of success and achievement (Rutter 1985). See Collishaw et al. (2007) for a detailed discussion of resilience to adult psychopathology.

It is important that professionals do not pathologise all children who live in families where a parent suffers from mental illness or a learning disability, has problems with alcohol and drugs or is in a violent relationship. As we have already noted, although these issues serve to qualify children as 'in need' (HM Government 2006) a significant proportion show no long-term behavioural or emotional disturbance. Nonetheless, the health and development of a considerable number of children living in these circumstances are adversely affected and would benefit from services.

To sum up

Factors which increase vulnerability

- The potential for genetic transmission of mental illness, learning disability, substance misuse and alcohol problems.

- Children most at risk of suffering significant harm are those living in families exposed to a multiplicity of problems, such as a combination of one or more of the following: parental learning disability, mental illness, problem drinking or drug misuse and domestic violence.

- The risk of long-term harm, such as poor mental health when adult, increases when children are exposed to a multiplicity of adverse experiences.

UNIVERSITY
LIBRARY

- The risk of significant harm increases when children are involved in parental delusions, become targets for parental aggression or rejection, or are neglected for pathological reasons.

- Young children whose parents inject drugs are at risk of HIV/AIDS and hepatitis A, B and/or C from poorly stored used needles and syringes. Children may also be exposed to unsafe adults when their homes are used by other drug users and dealers.

- To witness parental distress and suffering can have an adverse psychological impact on children. Children are particularly vulnerable when exposed to domestic violence. Witnessing violence is extremely distressing to children and attempts to intervene can result in injuries.

- The negative impact of domestic violence is exacerbated when the violence is combined with drink or drug use or when children witness the abuse, are drawn into the abuse or collude in concealing the assaults.

- When parents separate as a consequence of domestic violence, children are at risk of being used as pawns in ongoing disputes between warring parents. In a few tragic cases this can result in the severe injury or death of a child.

Protective factors

- The adverse effects on children are less likely when parental problems are mild; of short duration; unassociated with family discord and disorganisation; and do not result in the family breaking up.

- Children may also be protected when the other parent or a family member responds to the child's developmental needs. The role of grandparents can be the key to children's safety and developmental progress when they live with parents with learning disabilities. In relation to problem drinking or drug use, children's safety also depends on drugs and alcohol, needles and syringes not being easily available.

- Children's ability to cope is related to their age, gender and individual personality. Children of the same gender as the parent experiencing difficulties may be at greater risk of developing emotional and behavioural problems. Children's ability to cope is related to a sense of self-esteem and self-confidence; feeling in control and capable of dealing with change; and having a range of approaches for solving problems. Such traits are fostered by secure, stable and affectionate relationships and experiences of success and achievement.

- A significant proportion of children show no long-term behavioural or emotional disorders when exposed to parental mental illness, learning disability, problem drinking or drug use, or domestic violence. However, a considerable number of children do exhibit symptoms of disturbance during their childhood and would benefit from services to prevent their health or development being impaired.

Moving on to explore the impact on children at different stages of development

Although there are, in general, factors that make children more or less vulnerable to the behaviours which result from their parents' problems, the impact on children will vary depending on their age and stage of development. Therefore, it seems appropriate to look in more detail at the different stages of development.

This review has been deliberately confined to the findings from research, which may mean that factors which are more readily identified from clinical and professional practice have been omitted. These are no less important as a source of evidence but are beyond the scope of this book.

In exploring the research findings, six stages of childhood are discussed in Part II. Chapter 4 looks at children under 5 years and includes pre-birth to 12 months, children aged 1 to 2 years and those aged 3 to 4 years. Chapter 5 focuses on middle childhood and explores the impact of parental problems on children aged 5 to 10 years. Chapter 6 looks at the adolescent years and includes teenagers aged 11 to 15 years and young people aged 16 and older.

To provide a context for the difficulties that children may experience as a result of their parents' problems, each chapter is prefaced with a discussion of expected development.

PART II: ISSUES AFFECTING CHILDREN OF DIFFERENT AGES

4 Child development and parents' responses – children under 5 years

This chapter includes three age bands: pre-birth to 12 months; 1 to 2 years; and 3 to 4 years. Pre-birth to 12 months has two sections, the first focuses on the unborn child and the second on infants from birth to 12 months. The section on the unborn child explores initially the conditions needed for optimal development before examining the possible impact of parental mental illness, learning disability, substance misuse and domestic violence.

The format for the section on infants from birth to 12 months follows the same style as is used for all other age groups. What might be expected for the child's health, education (cognitive and language development), emotional and behavioural development, and family and social relationships is described before identifying the possible impact of parental problems. For children aged one to two years and those aged three to four years the child's identity and social presentation is also included. Each age band ends with summary points of the key problems and the protective factors.

Pre-birth to 12 months

This section looks initially at the unborn child before focusing on children from birth to 12 months.

Pre-birth to 12 months – the unborn child

Clearly, it is not relevant in relation to the unborn child to explore the range of developmental dimensions for children once they are born. Instead, the focus is on the ways parental mental illness, learning disability, problem drinking or drug use and domestic violence affect the unborn child, through genetic transmission and environmental impact. Although there is considerable information concerning the effects on the unborn child of maternal alcohol and drug consumption, what is known about the impact of maternal mental illness, learning disability and domestic violence is more limited.

Conditions needed for optimal development of the unborn child

The unborn child needs nourishment and a safe environment in order to develop. Regular visits to the ante-natal clinic can help ensure that the health of the expectant mother and the developing child are monitored. To address the nutritional needs of the unborn baby the expectant mother needs an adequate diet. A safe environment requires that expectant mothers should avoid contact with viruses such as rubella and avoid unnecessary medication. The devastating effects on children of women who were prescribed thalidomide are still evident. In addition, there is increasing evidence that expectant mothers should not smoke tobacco excessively; smoking during pregnancy reduces babies' lung function. Babies born to heavy smokers are more likely than those born to non-smoking mothers to suffer a higher risk of spontaneous abortion, premature delivery, stillbirth, sudden infant death syndrome and the possibility of low birth weight with its consequent negative effects (Julien 1995; Surgeon General's Report 2004).

The environment in which the mother lives and works also has an impact on the growing foetus. Physical impacts, collisions, bumps or blows which may damage the placenta and harm the foetus need to be avoided. In addition, where the expectant mother lives may be important. Highly polluted cities, the routine discharge of dangerous chemicals or nuclear leaks may have adverse effects on the unborn child. Research shows that exposure to pollution during pregnancy affects the breathing of the newborn baby (Latzin et al 2008).

Finally, there is growing evidence to suggest that the mother's emotional condition may affect her unborn child, although the impact is moderated by the nature, duration and timing of the occurrence (Lou et al. 1994). Maternal anxiety can release stress hormones which pass through the placenta and have been shown to influence foetal brain development and functioning (Kinsella and Monk 2009). Severe stress can also increase the mother's blood pressure and by implication decrease uterine blood flow. The overall result can be lower birth weight (Wolkind 1981; Reading 1983). However, not all studies have consistently shown stress to be related to low birth weight (see Rondo 2007 for a review of the research findings).

Most women want the best for their unborn child and try to eat and drink healthily during pregnancy. However, modern Western society bombards women with ever more advice and guidance to ensure a healthy child, which may raise levels of anxiety as women try to comply.

> *The modern Western pregnant woman must not drink more than four cups of coffee a day, drink alcohol, smoke cigarettes, change cat litter trays, eat soft cheese, uncooked eggs or packaged salads or go into the lambing sheds. They should not work too hard or too long, nor at night or be ambivalent about their pregnancies. Now it seems they must not become anxious either.*

(Oats 2002, p.502)

Many pregnant women will not always be able to comply with this barrage of advice and will need to be reassured that, in general, women who, for example, smoke, drink and use drugs in moderation during pregnancy give birth to healthy infants.

A model of an intensive, nurse-led home-visiting programme for vulnerable, first-time young mothers was developed in the US. Controlled studies carried out over three decades showed improved outcomes in relation to ante-natal health and the outcome of pregnancies, the child's health and development and parents' economic self-sufficiency (Olds et al. 2007). In England a pilot of the *Family Nurse Partnership Programme* was started 2007. The Partnership aims to provide intensive support from highly trained nurses for vulnerable young, first time mothers. This is to be achieved through building *'close, supportive relationships with families and guide young first time parents so that they adopt healthier lifestyles for themselves and their babies, provide good care for their babies and plan their future life goals'* (Department for Health and Department for Children Schools and Families 2009a, p27, paragraph 3.23). The Government has made a commitment to increase the numbers of families reached by the Family Nurse Partnership Programme (Cm 7985 2010).

Impact of parental mental illness – genetics and the environment

Although issues affecting the unborn child relate to both genetics and environment, genetic transmission is shown to be a factor in cases of schizophrenia, major affective disorders and antisocial personality disorders.

However, recent research reveals the complex relationship between genetics and the environment. For example, as noted in Chapter 3, Rutter and colleagues (2006) found that exposure to high levels of stress and adversity increase the likelihood that a child born with a genetic predisposition to mental illness (for example a child with a close relative who suffers from schizophrenia) will develop symptoms at an early age. Similar conclusions come from a longitudinal Finnish study, which compared the adopted children of mothers with schizophrenia with adoptees without this genetic risk (Tienari et al. 2004; Wynne et al. 2006). This work found that children with a high genetic risk of schizophrenia adopted into families which were well-functioning were less likely to develop a psychotic illness than similar children adopted into families which had high levels of family difficulties. The results suggest that the risk of developing schizophrenia for children with a high genetic risk can be mediated by good-quality care.

Similarly, understanding how depression is transferred from parents to children must take account of both environmental and genetic factors. A discussion of recent research findings highlights the complexity and inter-relationship of environmental and genetic factors. The review concludes *'that maternal depression is a potent but malleable risk factor for child psychopathology, and there is reason to believe that early detection of depression in mothers, along with short-term support for their children, may prevent the development of disorders before they begin'* (Reiss 2008, p.1084).

A study by Wolkind (1981) found that babies born to mothers suffering a psychiatric illness during pregnancy were of a lower birth weight than babies born to mothers without a psychiatric illness during pregnancy. However, a direct causal link was difficult to establish because significantly more mothers in the psychiatric group smoked. Smoking rates among adults with depression are about twice as high as among adults without depression, and the rates for people with schizophrenia are three times those for people who are not affected. Moreover, smokers with mental health problems are more likely to smoke heavily than those without mental health problems (Mental Health Foundation 2007). A further complicating factor is that the effects of mental illness impact on the expectant mothers' attendance at ante-natal clinics. Mothers suffering from schizophrenia, anxiety and depression find it more difficult to keep medical appointments.

Impact of parental learning disability

Learning disability can affect parents in their decision making and preparation for the birth of their child. Many parents with learning disabilities are poorly informed about contraception and the significance of changes in their menstrual pattern, and as a result they may find it hard to take realistic and informed decisions about family planning; initially, they may fail to recognise their pregnancy (James 2004). Consequently, the quality of the woman's ante-natal care is often jeopardised by late presentation and poor attendance (McGaw and Sturmey 1993). When women with learning disabilities do attend ante-natal care, they may experience difficulty in understanding the information and advice they receive or have problems in putting it into practice.

Genetics and the environment

Genetics and the environment are both important factors in the understanding of how parental learning disability affects the unborn child. For example, the children of parents with learning disabilities have been found to be at increased risk from inherited learning disabilities, psychological and physical disorders (Rende and Plomin 1993; McGaw and Newman 2005). Research suggests that approximately 40% of children born to parents with learning disabilities experience developmental delay (Gath 1988). McConnell and Llewellyn, who examined the literature, conclude,

> '... there is a higher incidence of developmental delay in younger children, and learning difficulties and challenging behaviours in primary school aged children of parents with intellectual disability ... these difficulties cannot be attributed to poverty or parental intellectual disability per se, since these children are a heterogeneous group'.

(McConnell and Llewellyn 2002, pp.304–305)

Although a child may have inherited learning disabilities, the environment can still make a difference; children brought up in a warm and stimulating environment will have better outcomes than those who are not.

It can be argued that learning disability appears to run in families, because parents with learning disabilities experience difficulty in providing sufficient general stimulation for the child's development and learning. However, it would be dangerous to attribute this solely to parents' intellectual impairment. Parents with learning disabilities frequently experience a combination of stressors that will impact on their parenting, such as having a large number of offspring, marital disharmony and violence, poor mental health, childhood abuse, lack of social supports and poverty (Cleaver and Nicholson 2007).

Impact of parental substance misuse

There is little dispute that excessive parental drinking or drug use negatively affects the unborn child (see Royal College of Obstetricians and Gynaecologists 2006 for the impact of alcohol; Avis 1999; Juliana and Goodman 1997 for the impact of illicit drugs). What is in dispute is the degree and nature of that impact.

The effect of drinking or drugs on the developing foetus is dependent on three inter-related factors (Julien 1995; Gerada 1996):

- the pharmacological make-up of the drug

- the gestation of pregnancy

- the route/amount/duration of drug use.

The foetus is most susceptible to structural damage during 4–12 weeks of gestation; drugs taken later generally affect growth or cause neonatal addiction (Julien 1995).

Two further complicating factors in gauging the impact of maternal substance use on the unborn child are the combination of substances taken and the pattern of alcohol or drug misuse. For example, women who use heroin may also use tobacco, cannabis, stimulants and tranquillisers. Moreover, the quantity and pattern of alcohol or drug use can vary from day to day (Plant 1985).

There is considerable evidence to suggest that the more frequent the use and the larger the quantities of alcohol or drugs ingested, the greater the impact on the unborn child (Rivinus 1991; Julien 1995). Even this agreed evidence must be tempered by further factors, which suggest how complex it may be to predict outcomes for individuals.

Most of the difficulties associated with problem alcohol and drug use could be ameliorated to some extent by good ante-natal care. However, many pregnant drug users do not come for ante-natal care until late in pregnancy because opiates, such as heroin, often affect menstruation and women are uncertain of dates (Department of Health et al. 2007). Others may fear that revealing their drug use to ante-natal care staff will result in judgemental attitudes, the involvement of children's social care services and the possible loss of the baby once it is born (Dore and Dore 1995; Burns 1996; Powell and Hart 2001). A review of the literature on child neglect found that substance misuse may also result in neglect during pregnancy (Daniel et al. 2009).

Finally, while there is general agreement that alcohol and drug use can increase the risk of impairment to the unborn child's healthy development, it is also probable that most mothers who use alcohol or drugs will give birth to healthy, normal children who suffer from no long-term effects (Powell and Hart 2001).

Drugs

For pregnant drug users in general, irrespective of the substance used, especially where poor social conditions prevail, there is an increased risk of low birth weight, premature delivery, perinatal mortality and cot death (Standing Conference on Drug Misuse 1997). A meta-analysis, which included only studies which controlled for maternal smoking although not for other lifestyle factors, found cocaine use during pregnancy caused low birth weight. The effect was greater with heavier use (Hulse et al. 1997).

Cocaine also increases the risk of a premature birth or miscarriage because its use can restrict the blood flow to the placenta and foetus. Babies may also be born with neonatal abstinence syndrome, although those born to mothers receiving methadone under medical supervision tend to have fewer complications than babies born to heroin addicts or methadone users who are not receiving medical care and adequate nutrition (McNamara et al. 1995). Good ante-natal care can help the newborn baby regain their weight deficiency and increase the likelihood that they will achieve their milestones.

Tetrahydrocannabinol (THC), the chemical in marijuana that produces a 'high', can easily cross the placental barrier, and when this happens it reduces the amount of oxygen present within the foetal blood. Research suggests this probably does not increase risk of miscarriages and stillbirths, nor is there adequate evidence to suggest it causes low birth weight (McNamara et al. 1995). The effects on the unborn child of newer drugs such as Ecstasy are not well researched.

In 2009 the overall prevalence of HIV among injecting drug users in England, Wales and Northern Ireland was 1.5%; twice the rate found in 2000 (Health Protection Agency 2010). The transmission of HIV infection across the placenta to the unborn child is a serious complication of intravenous drug use. When the expectant mother does not receive drug therapy, research suggests 22% of babies are HIV positive (Ene et al. 2007). However, in developed countries where the administration of drugs such as zidovudine is provided, the transmission of infection can be largely prevented (Gottlieb 2002). Clinical guidelines on the management of drug misuse and dependence is that specialist advice should be sought on breastfeeding when the mother is HIV positive (Department of Health and the devolved administrations 2007).

Almost half of injecting drug users are infected with hepatitis C (Health Protection Agency 2010). Vertical transmission rates of the virus from mother to infant have been reported to be about 4%. However, multiple virus infection can dramatically increase the risk of vertical transmission (Roberts and Latifa 2002; McMenamin et al. 2008).

Alcohol

Excessive drinking during pregnancy is associated with an increased rate of miscarriage and can cause Foetal Alcohol Syndrome, now often referred to as Foetal Alcohol Spectrum Disorder. Foetal Alcohol Spectrum Disorder describes a pattern of physical, behavioural, and intellectual characteristics children may display when prenatally exposed to alcohol. The foetus is most vulnerable to damage during the first three months. There are three categories of symptoms:

- growth deficiently for height and weight

- distinct pattern of facial features and physical characteristics

- central nervous system dysfunction.

Alcohol-related changes in brain structure can be identified by modern imaging techniques (Royal College of Obstetricians and Gynaecologists 2006).

Research into Foetal Alcohol Spectrum Disorder is difficult because much of the data rely upon women being able to remember how much they had to drink months or even years previously and even before they became pregnant. Some women may underestimate their drinking because of the stigma attached to drinking while pregnant (Alvik et al. 2006).

The impact on the unborn child is related to the amount and pattern of alcohol consumed by the mother. For example, research carried out in the United Kingdom found women who were light drinkers (defined as 1 to 2 drinks per week) during pregnancy did not have a higher risk of producing children (aged up to 5 years) with cognitive or behavioural problems compared to abstinent mothers (Kelly et al. 2010). There is growing evidence to suggest that moderate, regular alcohol consumption may be less harmful than binge drinking (Plant 1997). A small South African study on the drinking habits of women who had a diagnosed Foetal Alcohol Spectrum Disorder child also suggests that heavy-drinking episodes may be a better predictor of Foetal Alcohol Spectrum Disorder than average weekly consumption (Khaole et al. 2004). However, research on the impact of binge drinking on the unborn baby is inconclusive in relation to the risk of miscarriage, stillbirth, intrauterine restricted growth, prematurity and birth weight, and is minimal for gestational age at birth and birth defects including Foetal Alcohol Spectrum Disorder (Henderson et al. 2007).

While there is little doubt that Foetal Alcohol Spectrum Disorder exists, it is becoming more apparent that exposure to high levels of alcohol may not be sufficient to explain the inconsistent data on the incidence and prevalence across countries and over time (Abel 1998). Abel also suggests that average national alcohol consumption is a poor predictor of Foetal Alcohol Spectrum Disorder, and he goes further by estimating that only 4% of heavy-drinking mothers give birth to a Foetal Alcohol Spectrum Disorder child.

Adverse effects on the unborn child are not confined to maternal drinking. There is some evidence to suggest that fathers who are heavy drinkers produce children with lower birth weight and increased risk of heart defects (Plant 1997). Furthermore, spontaneous abortion and neonatal deaths are associated with the excessive drinking of either parent (Royal College of Obstetricians and Gynaecologists 2006).

Research conducted in the US identifies a less severe manifestation of Foetal Alcohol Syndrome, labelled Foetal Alcohol Effect. Symptoms are fewer or less apparent, particularly physical characteristics. Typical symptoms include poor feeding, tremors, irritability, occasional seizures and increased risk of sudden death syndrome (Julien 1995; Avis 1999). Research from North America also suggests a link between any alcohol use in pregnancy and spontaneous abortion, but this evidence is refuted by European and Australian research (Abel and Sokol 1991).

Guidance to pregnant women in the United Kingdom, produced by the Department of Health (2009b) and the National Institute for Health and Clinical Excellence (2008) has erred on the side of safety by providing strong messages about alcohol consumption. The advice is that pregnant women and women planning a pregnancy should avoid drinking alcohol during the first three months of pregnancy or restrict their intake to no more than one or two United Kingdom units once or twice a week. The guidance also stresses the possible danger to the unborn baby of getting drunk or binge drinking during pregnancy. However, it is important not to alarm pregnant women who may have consumed more than the recommended limit because the evidence is still developing and the role of other risk factors is still not clear.

Impact of domestic violence

Domestic violence can have a negative impact on the unborn child in three ways: through inherited traits, physical damage to the foetus and the effects of maternal stress.

Unlike for mental illness, there is no direct evidence to show that genetics play a role in the transmission of domestic violence. However, it might be argued that the evidence of an association between parental personality disorder, which may manifest itself in domestic violence, and conduct disturbance in boys stems from a single source (Rutter and Quinton 1984).

Domestic violence also poses a danger to the foetus; in fact the state of pregnancy can increase both the severity and frequency of abuse for women living in a violent relationship. The Confidential Maternal and Child Health Enquiry in England and Wales indicates that 30% of domestic abuse began during pregnancy (Humphreys and Houghton 2008).

> *I was in a bad relationship, my partner was battering me black and blue; it started when I was pregnant.*
>
> (Mother, quoted in Cleaver et al. 2007, p.216)

Women abused during pregnancy are more at risk of moderate to severe violence and homicide, including assaults such as beatings, choking, attacks with weapons and sexual assault (Humphreys 2006). Domestic violence threatens the unborn child because domestic assaults on pregnant women frequently include punches or kicks directed at the abdomen; there is more extensive injury to breasts and abdomen for women who are pregnant (BMA 2007). Research on domestic violence from both America (McFarlane quoted in Morley and Mullender 1994) and Northern Ireland (McWilliams and McKiernan 1993) suggests this was the experience of 40–60% of battered women during pregnancy. Such assaults can result in an increased rate of miscarriage, stillbirth, premature birth, foetal brain injury and fractures, placental separation, rupture of the mother's spleen, liver or uterus (Bewley et al. 1997; Mezey and Bewley 1997).

Studies of the effects on the unborn child of mother's stress suggest that marital disharmony is associated with increased childhood morbidity such as physical illness, developmental lag, neurological dysfunction and behavioural disturbance (Lou et al. 1994). The association may be indirect because domestic violence may lead mothers to become so depressed that they fail to look after their physical needs during pregnancy. *'I just didn't care. He was so cruel that I didn't take any pride in myself ... I lost the baby ... I was only seven stone'* (NCH Action for Children 1994, p.47). Domestic violence may place the unborn child at risk because women tend to be late or poor attendees for ante-natal care. Poor attendance may be the result of low self-esteem and maternal depression or due to abusive men controlling and restricting women's use of medical services (McFarlane et al. 1992; Hester and Radford 1995; Peckover 2001).

To sum up

Key problems for the unborn child

- Genetic transmission of some forms of mental illness, learning disability, psychological and physical disorders.

- Foetal damage brought about by high levels of environmental pollution.

- Foetal damage through maternal intake of harmful substances. The impact will depend on which, and in what combination, substances are taken; the stage of the pregnancy when drugs and or alcohol are ingested; and the route, amount and duration of drug and alcohol use.

- Foetal damage as a result of physical violence directed at the expectant mother. This may include foetal fracture, brain injury and organ damage.

- Transmission from mother to the unborn baby of HIV and hepatitis C.

- Spontaneous abortion, premature birth, low birth weight and stillbirth.

Protective factors

- Good, regular ante-natal care.

- Adequate nutrition, income support and housing for the expectant mother.

- The avoidance of viruses, unnecessary medication, smoking and severe stress.

- Robust legislation to control dangerous environmental pollution.

- Support for the expectant mother of at least one caring adult.

- An alternative, safe and supportive residence for expectant mothers subject to violence and the threat of violence.

Pre-birth to 12 months – from birth to 12 months

Health

Expected health

During the first few weeks of life, babies are expected to achieve a balanced state with regard to feeding, sleeping and elimination. Parents or carers need to take babies regularly to clinics for immunisations and developmental reviews.

A baby's development follows a recognised pattern and they generally achieve their milestones within the anticipated time frame. During the first year of life babies begin to gain control over their bodies. By 2 months they can lift their heads and shoulders off the mattress and by 4 months they can hold their heads up for an extended time. At 6 months most babies can roll from their back to their tummy and can sit in an adult's lap. Babies start to pull themselves up to stand by 7 to 9 months but getting down from standing takes rather longer. Many walk when led or held by 11 months. Babies develop motor skills by repetitively performing a limited range of movements. They kick, rock, wave, bounce, bang, rub, scratch or sway repeatedly and rhythmically. These repeated patterns are particularly prominent at about 6 or 7 months.

Fine motor control also begins to develop during the first few months of life. By 3 to 4 months babies play with their fingers and can grasp objects by 6 months. By 11 months most babies are able to feed themselves with their thumb and finger.

Babies with health problems, or with learning or physical disabilities, for example sight or hearing problems should receive appropriate and prompt professional attention.

The home should be suitable for the baby and offer adequate safety and protection. Babies who are ill or injured should get the attention they need, and periodic bouts of illness should generally have a recognised medical source.

Possible impact on health

Babies are vulnerable to injury, illness and neglect through living in a violent household, or because parental apathy, a lack of knowledge or interest means hygiene is neglected, illness and accidents are not promptly dealt with and routine health checks are missed.

Domestic violence places babies at risk of injury. For example, the baby may be in his or her mother's arms when an assault occurs (Mullender et al. 2002). Babies may also be harmed when parents' concentration is impaired because of mental illness, learning disability, excessive alcohol intake and drug misuse. When this happens parents may be less attentive to the baby's health needs (see Duncan and Reder 2000 for impact of mental illness). For example, the mother may not be able to concentrate for long enough to complete breastfeeding, nappy changing or bathing (Cassin 1996). However, there is little evidence to link babies who fail to thrive with poor mental health of the parent.

> *...child growth was not found to be associated with mental health measures in the mother including parenting stress, depression, self-esteem, parenting competence, somatic symptoms, anxiety/insomnia or severe depression.*

(Dunne et al. 2007, p.290)

When alcohol or drugs become the prime focus of a parent's attention, mental illness blunts perceptions or learning disability impacts on parental awareness, the baby may be dressed inappropriately and hygiene grossly neglected. The baby may not be given adequate nutrition because mothers with learning disabilities may not know what appropriate food for a baby is. Ongoing support and advice from health workers are essential because these parents may experience difficulties in adapting what they learn to the baby's changing needs (Cleaver and Nicholson 2007).

Furthermore, the disabling effects of mental illness, learning disability, problem drinking or drug use or domestic violence may result in routine health checks being missed and inadequate intervention being sought when the baby is unwell. Black families and those from minority ethnic communities may have less access to preventative and support services than white families.

Finally, it is important to remember the effects of social deprivation. There is a well-established association between poor material conditions and illness in small children (see Bradshaw 1990). The poor material conditions may not necessarily be the result of parental problems, but may have contributed significantly to parental stress (Brown and Harris 1978; Ghate and Hazel 2002).

Education – cognitive and language development

Expected ability

Newborn babies are able to see well close up (approximately the distance between the baby's eyes and the mother's face during nursing) and by 1 month can discriminate colour.

Soon after birth, babies respond to sound and voices. The baby hears best in the range of the human voice, and can discriminate the mother (or regular carer) from others on the basis of smell, sight, or sound almost immediately. At approximately 1 month the baby will start to coo and gurgle – sounds which stem from pleasurable social interactions. At this time babies with a hearing loss will vocalise in a reflexive way, but if very deaf will not show a startle reflex to sudden noises. By 3 months coos and gurgles will be used as a form of interaction with a familiar person and they begin to respond to stimuli, such as hearing a familiar voice or seeing a familiar smiling face, with a full social smile. By 4 months babies begin to laugh, and at around 6 months many engage in social play such as 'peek-a-boo'. Babbling starts spontaneously at around 6 months. This is also the time when words such as 'bye-bye'; 'mama' and 'dada' are understood. By 9 months the baby will enjoy communicating with sounds and can shout for attention or scream with rage. They can now also understand the command 'no' (Smith and Cowie 1993). Interest in their surroundings starts at around 3 months. By 9 months babies look in the correct direction for fallen toys.

Possible impact on cognitive and language development

The main impact of parental problems on babies' cognitive and language development results from inconsistent or neglectful behaviour rather than any direct impact.

Babies may be at risk of suffering significant harm when parents are preoccupied with their own feelings and emotions, find it difficult to notice the baby's feelings or wishes and fail to respond to them appropriately. In addition, feelings of exhaustion, physical illness, depression and a lack of self-confidence and self-worth – all factors associated with domestic violence, parental mental illness, learning disability and parental substance misuse – may result in limiting the mother's capacity to engage with and stimulate her baby.

> *Parents* (both with learning disability) *have received advice and guidance in respect of stimulation from both health visitors and the family centre. Their ability to demonstrate and continue to offer appropriate stimulation is questionable.*
>
> (Health visitor discussing parenting of an 8-month-old boy, quoted in Cleaver and Nicholson 2007, p.78)

Longitudinal studies have found no evidence to suggest that prenatal exposure to cocaine is associated with physical growth, cognitive development or the development of language skills (Frank et al. 2001; Messinger et al. 2004). However, there is some tentative evidence to suggest that premature exposure to alcohol is negatively associated with mental development among 12- to 13-month-old infants (Testa et al. 2003).

In relation to mental illness, the impact on cognitive development tends to result from parents' behaviour. For example, mothers who experience psychotic symptoms after giving birth are more likely to regard their babies as passive creatures and perceive their gestures and facial expressions negatively (Murray et al. 2001). When the mother suffers from depression the baby's cognitive development may be affected because interaction between mother and baby is reduced. Depressed mothers are also less likely to modify their behaviour according to the behaviour of their baby (Murray et al. 2001).

Depressed mothers, mothers with learning disabilities, or those with alcohol or drug problems have been shown to respond less frequently to their baby's cues, and when they did respond, were more likely to do so in a controlling rather than facilitative manner, *'it appears to be the manner or quality of this intrusive form of relatedness, that is most important for infant development'* (Hobson et al. 2005, p.342). For further information see: Cox et al. 1987, Murray et al. 2001 for mental health; Cleaver and Nicholson 2007 for parental learning disability; Hill et al. 1996 and Juliana and Goodman 1997 for alcohol and drugs.

Emotional and behavioural development

Expected development

'Babies are like the raw material for a self' (Gerhardt 2004, p.18). During the first year and a half of life, the baby's brain is growing at its most rapid rate and requires the right conditions to develop adequately. At birth, emotions and feelings are at a very basic level and the baby relies on adults *'to reduce discomfort and distress and increase comfort and contentment'* (Gerhardt 2004, p.18).

'*The primary task to be accomplished during the first year of life is for the baby to develop trust in others*' (Fahlberg 1991, p.64). This is achieved when a baby's needs are regularly satisfied by a familiar carer. A baby's temperament, which may become apparent soon after birth, will affect the parents' or carers' reactions, but regardless of temperament, the key to good outcomes is the parents' capacity to adapt and respond appropriately to their baby's emotional and developmental needs (Belsky et al. 1998).

Attachment begins during the first year of life, and the major characteristic of this relationship is the presence of a consistent person who is able to reduce the baby's anxiety in stressful situations. Babies who become securely attached feel sufficiently confident to explore their world (Bowlby 1973). The process of attachment is not confined to a single adult. Babies can develop secure attachments to more than one adult as long as they are constant figures in the baby's life (Bowlby 1973; Rutter 1995; Thoburn 1996).

Possible impact on emotional and behavioural development

There are two main ways in which parents' problems may impact on babies' emotional and behavioural development. Attachment may be affected by the treatment babies need to counteract the effects of maternal drug and alcohol consumption during pregnancy, and by parental moods and displays of anger.

The effects of drugs and alcohol on the mother and the newborn baby can impact on the immediate bonding process in a number of ways. Babies may need to be placed in special care units, thus separating them from the immediate presence of their mother. The treatment for withdrawal symptoms in hospital may result in babies being sleepy and unresponsive to their mothers. These babies are at greater risk of attachment problems than other babies (Fahlberg 1991). Similarly, women who decide to undergo a process of rapid drug reduction or abstinence may find it difficult to respond appropriately to their baby. Over the last 10 years, the care for newborn babies suffering from opiate withdrawals has improved, due in part to more accurate withdrawal-symptom control with fewer side effects. In some parts of the United Kingdom foetal withdrawal syndrome is now mainly treated by enhanced close physical contact rather than the use of psychoactive drugs.

Because babies have little sense of self, they are very dependent on their parents or key carers for their psychological well-being (Fahlberg 1991). To a great extent the baby's emotions and subsequent behaviours are related to the moods and actions of those who are looking after them. Consequently, the depressed affect, emotional withdrawal and unpredictable mood swings that frequently accompany problem drinking or drug use, mental illness, learning disability or domestic violence may be mirrored by the baby. Babies and infants who are regularly rejected come to see themselves as unloved and unlovable (Fahlberg 1991).

Parental apathy and despair, which can result from mental illness, learning disability, alcohol and drug use, or domestic violence may hamper the ability of parents to empathise with and appropriately respond to their children's needs. For example, depending on the mother's state of mind, the baby's cries may be met with a smiling face and soothing words or a blank, unfocused or grimacing visage. A consistent lack of warmth and negative responses, even at this early stage, may result in the infant becoming insecurely attached. A study of 19 parents who were observed to be emotionally neglecting found that practically half the infants whose cries and pleas for warmth and comforting were ignored were anxiously attached at 12 months, and by 18 months of age this applied to all the infants (Egeland 2009).

Research which looked at the babies of depressed mothers found they had higher rates of insecure attachment (Hobson et al. 2005) and showed more emotional and behavioural disturbances than infants of well mothers (Cox et al. 1987). Domestic violence can also affect the attachment process through undermining the mother's capacity to provide her baby with a sense of safety and security, which may be demonstrated by the baby crying and resisting comfort, excessive irritability, sleep disturbances, despondence and anxiety (Humphreys and Houghton 2008).

Family and social relationships

Expected relationships

From birth onwards babies start signalling their feelings, and parents can distinguish a variety of emotions in their infants in the first few months of life (Smith and Cowie 1993). During these months babies begin to distinguish important figures in their life and after about the age of 7 months, when the fear response increases, the infant becomes wary and fearful of unfamiliar persons and objects. Nonetheless, this is a time when most adults, even strangers, are able to comfort a distressed infant.

The early attachment or care-giving relationship between the baby and parent or carer, which begins during the first year of life, serves a number of functions including physical care, and soothing and stimulating emotions. It provides a secure base for the infant and child to explore his or her environment.

The process of attachment suggests a cognitive model, based on early attachment experiences, which influences the child's approach to all new relationships. What starts as the inter-relationship between mother (or other main carer) and infant becomes a characteristic of the child.

> *...starting during his first months in his relation with both parents, he builds up working models of how attachment figures are likely to behave towards him in any of a variety of situations, and on those models are based all his expectations, and therefore all his plans, for the rest of his life.*

(Bowlby 1973, pp.78–79)

The relationship between parent and child is usually reciprocal and works in a circular way, each player affecting the response of the other. There are, however some circumstances where reciprocity is not present; for example although the parent may be bonded to the child, severe autism or brain damage may result in the baby failing to attach to the parent (see Aldgate and Jones 2006 for a useful discussion on attachment and children's development).

Possible impact on relationships

There are a number of ways in which the relationship between parents and babies may be affected. Parents' behaviour may be inconsistent or disorganised, they may be emotionally detached or their commitment to their children may be reduced.

Mental illness, learning disability, problem alcohol or drug use or the psychological consequences of being a victim of domestic violence can all affect the ability of a parent to maintain consistency, predictability and a physical presence in relation to the child. In addition, parents with learning disabilities may experience difficulty identifying and interpreting their baby's cues (Cleaver and Nicholson 2007).

Research suggests that parents who experience these disorders display less aptitude in providing for the baby's needs for bodily contact and loving care. For example, research has found that many drug-using parents are often emotionally unavailable to their children when using heroin, particularly in the morning when parents feel physically ill and are worried about securing more drugs for that day (Hogan and Higgins 2001). Mothers who are alcohol dependent and suffer from depression can become overwhelmed by their own needs and find it difficult to bond with their children, often being disinterested and highly critical of them (Woodcock and Sheppard 2002). Domestic violence can lead to maternal stress and depression, and result in the mother being emotionally distant from her baby. Depression can cause mothers to be more disorganised, unhappy, tense and irritable than non-depressed mothers. They may be less effective, show more anger, be less playful with their infants and less emotionally available (Field et al. 1990; Reupert and Maybery 2007). There is evidence that mothers who remained depressed by 6 months post-delivery felt more overwhelmed by the care of their infant and saw their infant as more difficult (Campbell 1999). When parents have a psychotic illness, attachment may be affected because the ill parent is guided by hallucinations which may include the baby (Cassin 1996). It must, however, be remembered that it is difficult to distinguish the impact of parental disorders from other factors which may influence the mother/baby relationship such as poverty, unemployment and social deprivation (Marcenko et al. 2000).

Maternal insensitivity to the infant's signals and emotional unavailability are issues key to the attachment process. This point is reinforced by Murray's (1992) research on postnatal depression, which found those infants to be less securely attached to their mothers than children of well mothers, despite the fact that in most cases the depression had remitted by 3 or 4 months after the child was born.

Key to the well-being of the child when a parent suffers from mental illness, learning disability or substance misuse is the presence of a safe caring adult. However, the detrimental impact on attachment will be compounded if the mother is living in a violent relationship. Rather than being able to compensate, violent men often emotionally distance themselves from their children (Holden and Ritchie 1991).

When parents put their own needs above those of the infant, which may happen when parents have a learning disability, alcohol or drug problems or are mentally ill, this reduces their commitment and may interfere with the attachment process. However, this is not necessarily the case and many parents who experience such difficulties in fact prioritise their children's needs (Ackerson 2003).

Some parents with drug problems (as well as parents without drug or alcohol problems) may be tempted to use non-prescription drugs to calm their baby, especially when the baby is not sleeping or is agitated. Annually there are a few deaths of young babies attributed to problem drug-using parents giving them illicit drugs. While this is not common, it must be kept in mind that it is possible, and parents need to be given clear instructions on not medicating their babies without the close involvement of medical staff.

To sum up

Key problems for children aged 0–1 year

- Drug and alcohol use and violence during pregnancy may have caused neurological and physical damage to the baby.

- Babies suffering neonatal abstinence syndrome or foetal withdrawal symptoms may be difficult to manage.

- Babies may be born with the HIV or hepatitis B or C virus.

- Babies may be injured during incidents of domestic violence.

- Babies' health needs may not be recognised and they may be neglected physically and emotionally.

- Cognitive development and learning may be delayed through parents' inconsistent, under-stimulating and hostile behaviour.

- A lack of commitment and increased unhappiness, tension and irritability, insensitivity and emotional unavailability in parents may result in inappropriate responses which causes poor bonding and insecure attachment.

- Problems in relation to the baby's health and development may be exacerbated by living in an impoverished physical environment.

Protective factors

- The input of specialist medical practitioners when babies are born with the HIV or hepatitis B or C virus.

- Attendance at clinic for immunisations and developmental reviews.

- The presence of an alternative or supplementary caring adult who can respond to the developmental needs of the baby.

- Wider family support and good community facilities.

- Sufficient income support and good physical standards in the home.

- The relevant parent acknowledges the difficulties and is able to access and accept treatment.

- Regular supportive help from primary health care team and social services, including consistent day care.

- An alternative, safe and supportive residence for mothers subject to violence and the threat of violence.

Children aged 1–2 years

Health

Expected health

It is expected that, taking into consideration any disability or chronic sickness, most children will be healthy and parents and carers will recognise and seek appropriate medical help for any sickness or injury. To ensure the child's long-term health, parents need to keep immunisations up to date.

Most infants achieve their milestones within the anticipated time frame. By 15 months many infants will be able to walk unassisted and by 18 months many can run. By 24 months infants have sufficient gross motor control to be able to climb onto furniture; fine motor control also continues to develop. By 15 months infants are generally able to manipulate small objects and can scribble with a pencil or crayon onto paper. By 18 months infants can use a spoon to feed themselves, and by 24 months, for many, the fine pincer grasp has developed sufficiently to allow tiny objects to be picked up. Physical or learning disability, sensory or auditory impairment may mean some or all of these milestones are not reached within the time frame. If the infant has not reached an expected developmental milestone, professional advice should be sought.

Children of this age are curious and will have a natural desire to explore their immediate surroundings. To prevent accidents from occurring parents must ensure that the home is suitable for the infant and offers adequate safety and protection.

Possible impact on health

Infants of this age are vulnerable to injuries, inadvertently eating or drinking harmful substances, having illnesses or injuries which are not attended to promptly and being given an inadequate or inappropriate diet.

Parental mental illness, learning disability, the effects of domestic violence and excessive alcohol intake or drug misuse can affect parents' concentration and result in parents being less attentive to their infants. Children of this age are very mobile and curious, and parents must be vigilant to ensure bath times are safely supervised, that harmful substances, including alcohol and drugs, are stored securely, that stoves and fires do not present a danger and in general that the home provides a safe environment. Children of substance misusers are in more danger of inadvertently ingesting drugs because these substances are present in the home; methadone and cocaine are extremely dangerous to children. Newly mobile babies may be exposed to injecting equipment if insufficient care has not been taken. If infants are difficult to soothe, parents who use drugs may give the drug to their children to quieten them or make them sleep (Alison 2000).

Parents with a learning disability may not be fully aware of the potential dangers facing their mobile infants or how to put in place the necessary safety measures. The effects of mental illness, domestic violence and substance misuse may result in periods of unconsciousness, feelings of deep despair, or a preoccupation with drugs or alcohol.

> *Charles* (father) *had been drinking and the home conditions weren't improving at all.* Adam (aged 2 years) *looked dirty and poorly. I asked Charles to pick up the dog excrement from the garden as the children were playing in it. Again asked them to start making some improvements to the children's rooms.*
>
> (Information contained on the initial assessment: both parents had learning disabilities and the father had an alcohol problem, quoted in Cleaver and Nicholson 2007, p.32)

Infants need a well-balanced diet and may not be given adequate nutrition because mothers with learning disabilities may not know what appropriate food for a baby is and mental illness and substance misuse may result in parents neglecting their own and their children's need for a nourishing diet.

> *See as long as your wean's got something to eat, you think that's the thing, whether it be a Mars bar or cereal or something, like, 'they're all right.'*
>
> (Mother with a drug problem, quoted in Barnard 2007, p.64)

Parents with learning disabilities are likely to be provided with considerable support from health visitors when their baby is very young; however, ongoing support and advice from wider family and/or professionals are essential because these parents may experience difficulties in adapting and coping with children as they grow up and require different types of food (Cleaver and Nicholson 2007).

Furthermore, the disabling effects of mental illness, learning disability, problem drinking or drug use or domestic violence may result in parents not recognising or not responding appropriately when the infant is unwell (Daniel et al. 2009). For example, all parents are stressed when their children are ill or injured and find it difficult to take in what medical practitioners say to them. When parents have the additional stress of mental illness, learning disability, domestic violence or substance misuse, information may be difficult to remember and hard to recall.

> *Patrick* (aged two years) *has recently been in hospital as Sally* (mother) *felt he had a fever. However, the staff in the refuge felt concern as Sally had been giving Patrick too much medication and they felt his welfare was at risk.*
>
> (Mother with a learning disability who had recently left her violent husband, quoted in Cleaver and Nicholson 2007, p.77)

Children are also placed at risk of injury when serious parental addiction to drugs results in children, including the very young, being left alone at home while the parent is out buying drugs, as the report by this mother shows.

> *One morning I got up – Sam was sleeping right, and I was rattling. And I was like 'Oh no, I've got to wake him up and get through all this getting dressed carry on, get the clothes on and into the buggy … he was sleeping by the time I got back and I was like 'that's alright then'. So the next morning, same thing happened.*
>
> (Mother, quoted in Barnard 2007, p.72)

The effects of social deprivation exacerbate parental problems, and the link between poor material conditions and illness in small children is well established.

> *Shortage of money, debt, unemployment, chronic housing problems, fraught relationships, the hardships of single parenthood, personal harassment, victimisation and skill deficits all contribute to their vulnerability.*
>
> (Booth and Booth 1996, p.15)

Education: cognitive and language development

Expected ability

Typically by about 12 to 13 months, infants start to say their first words. Early word learning is very slow and requires much repetition. Between the ages of 12 to 18 months the infant may learn no more than 30 words. After this slow start, however, most children begin to add new words rapidly although the majority of new words are names for things or people; verbs tend to be learnt later. Thus, children of this age frequently use a sentence made up of two nouns such as 'mummy sock'. By two years, infants are able to follow simple instructions and are always asking questions. At about the age of two and a half years children's vocabulary has grown to some 600 words, a quarter of which are verbs (Fenson et al. 1994).

Children of 12 months are curious about their environment and spend much time exploring and manipulating objects, shaking them, moving them along the floor or putting them in and out of containers. By 18 months, infants are able to start to play matching and sorting games. By 24 months, physical games and pretend play are enjoyed.

Possible impact on cognitive and language development

Parental disorders may impact on children's cognitive and language development due to a lack of adequate stimulation, parental encouragement and support, or parents' inability to recognise and respond to their infants' cues.

The child's cognitive and language development may be negatively affected when parents are preoccupied with their own feelings and emotions and find it difficult to focus on their infants and prioritise their needs.

> *I want to be able to ... just be like a normal young mother and be able to get up in the morning, get her ready first thing in the morning, take her up the park and feed the ducks and all that with her instead of getting up and thinking 'oh no', where am I going to get my next hit from before I can change her or do anything like that?'*

(Drug-abusing mother, quoted in Barnard 2007, p.67)

The effects of some drugs or mental illness can cause hyperactivity and make parents impatient with their children. *'You want people to hurry up ... kids can't and you can't be bothered sitting down and talking to them, like you are supposed to'* (Klee et al. 1998, p.14 quoted in Kroll and Taylor 2003, p.123). In contrast, feelings of exhaustion, physical illness, depression and a lack of self-confidence and self-worth may limit the parents' capacity to engage with their child, listen to what they say and offer praise and encouragement and foster learning. In such circumstances, instead of responding with interest and enjoyment to the infant's efforts to communicate, the impact of parental disorders may result in parents reacting with hostility and negativity; thus establishing difficult cycles of relating and longer-term conflictual interactions (in relation to depression see Murray et al. 2001; see Barnard 2007 in relation to drug addiction).

Parents with a learning disability may find it difficult to support the child's learning. For example, illiteracy curtails parents' ability to read simple stories to their children, and problems in learning and recalling information means the repertoire of nursery rhymes and other children's songs will be restricted. Parents with learning disabilities may not understand how to play and stimulate their child and will need considerable support from wider family, friends and professionals to ensure their child receives adequate stimulation.

The evidence on how maternal depression may impact on children's cognitive development is not clear. On the one hand, some research suggests that depression is associated with negative consequences for infants. Expressive language is delayed (Cox et al. 1987) and the child's ability to concentrate and complete simple tasks is worse than for children of well mothers (Breznitz and Friedman 1988). On the other hand, an observational study of 2- to 3-year-old infants of depressed and non-depressed mothers found no overall differences in terms of the child's temperament, language or mental state (Pound et al. 1988).

The 'ecological model' of parenting (Bronfenbrenner 1977, 1979; Belsky 1980) helps to set some of these seemingly inconsistent findings within a broader perspective. The model takes a systems perspective on family functioning and provides a framework for understanding how critical factors relate one to another within a hierarchy of four levels: the socio-cultural level; the community; the family; and the level of the individual parent or child. Thus, for example, stressors that impact on a mother and baby, such as learning disability, mental illness, substance misuse or domestic violence, may be ameliorated by the support of wider family and good community facilities.

Emotional and behavioural development and self-care skills

Expected development

During the second year of life, attachment experiences will continue to influence the development of the infants' working model of how people are likely to behave towards them. Young children need to gain a sense of security and the confidence to explore their environment.

During this period of life infants' moods can fluctuate greatly and learning how to manage them depends upon the parent–infant relationship.

> To optimise the infant's capacity to manage his or her emotions it is essential that the infant has the experience of an attuned, responsive parent who can engage themselves in a detailed process of interaction with them.

(Bentovim et al. 2009, p.43)

Although at 12 months the child is still the centre of his or her own world, by 2 years children have developed an awareness of others and the capacity to empathise.

Difficulties in communication and in fine motor control can be a frustrating experience, which may result in occasional temper tantrums. Two-year-olds often become insistently independent, and can appear contrary.

In relation to self-care skills children of this age are beginning to learn to dress and feed themselves, and meal times are generally hassle free.

Possible impact on emotional and behavioural development

Parents' preoccupation with their own problems to the exclusion of other priorities, the need to get and use drugs or alcohol, feelings of apathy and despair, and a sense of worthlessness will impact on children's sense of emotional security. Parents who are unavailable emotionally will evoke feelings of separation anxiety. Inconsistency and a lack of routine increase a child's sense of insecurity and fearfulness and may result in infants being extremely clingy.

Children may be separated from their parents when, for example, parents go for residential treatment, are arrested because of violence or drug-related crimes or detained under the Mental Health Act 2007. When partings are unplanned, or parents fail to return or return in a confused state, children may become extremely anxious. Planning the separation and ensuring the presence of a caring and familiar adult can ensure continuity of care and reduce the impact of separation on infants.

Parental mental illness, learning disability, substance misuse and domestic violence can result in parents behaving in unpredictable and frightening ways.

> *...One minute Mammy's wanting to play with you all happy and the next minute she's 'GRRR', screaming at you, running you up the hall and throwing you in your room, know what I mean, and shut the door, 'STAY THERE'...*

(Mother, quoted in Barnard 2007, p.77)

Very young children find it difficult to express fears and anxieties in words and may display aberrant behaviours such as rocking, disturbed sleep patterns and bed wetting.

Identity and social presentation

Expected development

A sense of identity starts around the age of 1 year and is demonstrated by children's ability to recognise their own reflection in a mirror and to respond to their own name. By the age of 2 years children are able to give their full name and gender, and identify their own image in a photograph.

This is the stage when children gain a sense of ownership, an understanding of 'me' and 'mine'. The ability to differentiate self from others is also reflected in children becoming aware of physical differences between themselves and others. An independent sense of self-differentiation is thought to be gained half way through a baby's second year of life (Bee 2000).

Infants who receive sufficient love and attention develop a positive sense of self, and at 2 years are relatively confident in themselves and take a pride in their achievements. Children of this age expect to be liked by adults, and see adults as dependable and trustworthy (Smith and Cowie 1993). In relation to social presentation, most mothers will take a pride in ensuring their child is clean and dressed appropriately.

Possible impact on identity and social presentation

When alcohol or drugs become the prime focus of a parent's attention, or mental illness blunts perceptions, or a learning disability impacts on parental awareness, the infant may be dressed inappropriately and hygiene grossly neglected. Parental disorders may inhibit the ability to care about themselves or their infants.

Parents with learning disabilities may need support to learn how to keep their infant clean, and what constitutes appropriate clothing to suit the weather or the occasion. Children who grow up in families which experience many stresses and problems will need positive messages to avoid developing a negative self-image and poor self-esteem.

Parental mental illness or other parenting problems can result in a child being shown little warmth, being physically and emotionally rejected or held responsible for the difficulties within the family. Children need to be respected, valued for themselves and included in family gatherings and outings. Identity problems can develop if parents or carers call the child by a different name or if they are highly critical of the child and show little warmth. Infants who are regularly rejected come to see themselves as unloved and unlovable (Fahlberg 1991).

Family and social relationships

Expected relationships

The fear of strangers and separation anxiety, which began during the latter end of the first year of life, continues to rise until approximately the age of 16 months. Practically all infants show at least mild forms of these two types of distress, regardless of whether they have been looked after by their parents or have attended regularly a day-care facility (Bee 2000).

Infants from 14 months onwards start to show interest in one another, gazing at or making noises at each other. Although infants will play side by side at the age of 2 years, co-operative play and pro-social behaviour tends to start between the ages of 2 and 3 years.

After 2 years, children start to show signs of favouring a particular child as a playmate. There is some evidence that children as young as 2 years are more likely to choose friends of the same sex (Bee 2000).

Possible impact on relationships

Of central importance to all children is a loving and protective relationship with a consistent and safe parent or carer. Parents or carers need to spend sufficient time with their child to reinforce emotional bonds.

Mental illness, learning disability, substance misuse and domestic violence can all affect the attachment process. Inconsistent parenting, unplanned separations, erratic and frightening behaviour or emotional unavailability – all possible characteristics of such parental disorders – can result in disrupting the attachment process and leave children insecurely attached (see Ainsworth et al. 1978 for details on attachment).

Exposure to domestic violence may result in infants displaying excessive irritability, regression in terms of language and toilet training, sleep disturbances, emotional distress and fear of being left alone. Children's inability to verbalise the powerful emotions they are experiencing may manifest itself in temper tantrums and aggression, crying and resisting comfort, or despondency and anxiety (Holt et al. 2008). Parents in these circumstances are not always able to provide the comfort and reassurance that children need to cope adequately with such experiences.

When parents place their own needs above those of the children they may leave them unattended, thus putting them at risk of injury, illness or fire. Children may also be left in the care of unsuitable and unsafe people. For example, some children will be at risk of abuse and neglect because their home is used as a base for selling drugs, as a place for other drug users to ingest drugs, or for prostitution to fund a severe drug or alcohol habit. Children of parents with learning disabilities may be similarly at risk from unsafe adults because parents may not recognise the threat they pose, or lack the self-confidence to prevent them having access to their children.

Witnessing domestic violence and cruelty to animals (a feature frequently found in violent homes) may cause children to suffer feelings of helplessness through their inability to protect their mother or their much-loved pet, or they may come to see such cruelty as acceptable behaviour (Lipinski 2001). While some children of this age may cause pain to an animal through innocent exploration, calculated animal cruelty is rare and may be the result of witnessing domestic violence or threats to, or abuse of, family pets (Hackett and Uprichard 2007).

Children may be isolated because parents who experience mental illness, learning disabilities, substance misuse and domestic violence frequently distance themselves from family and friends. There is a danger that children within such households are rarely taken out of the house, do not visit relatives and friends or get taken with parents to shops and playgrounds; as a result they may lead very restricted and isolated lives.

> *I used to take the children to the park and feed the ducks, but I can't do that now because I might have a fit. I can't let them play on swings and things like that because I might have a fit. I have a hard time with them and keeping them from doing things.*

(Mother with a learning disability with four children the youngest being two years, quoted in Cleaver and Nicholson 2007, p.100)

To sum up

Key problems for children aged 1–2 years

- Health may be affected because illness and injury are not recognised and adequate and timely medical help not sought.

- Risk of accidents, injuries and abuse may be increased because parental awareness and supervision is inadequate.

- Diet may be inadequate and unsuitable.

- Health problems can be exacerbated by living in impoverished physical environments.

- Cognitive and language development may be delayed because of a lack of parental encouragement and praise, or because parents react negatively and with hostility.

- Insecure attachment and longer-term emotional and behavioural problems may arise as a result of unpredictable and frightening parental behaviour. This may be exacerbated by unplanned separations or when parents are emotionally unavailable.

- Development of a positive identity could be difficult because children are rejected and uncertain of who they are.

- Witnessing violence and frightening behaviour may result in children feeling helpless and in some cases coming to view cruelty and aggression as acceptable.

Protective factors

- The presence of an alternative or supplementary caring adult who can respond to the child's developmental needs and provide continuity of care.

- Wider family support and good community facilities.

- Sufficient income support and good physical standards in the home.

- The relevant parent acknowledging the difficulties and being able to access and accept treatment.

- Regular supportive help from primary health care team and social services.

- Regular attendance at nursery or similar day care facility.

- An alternative, safe and supportive residence for mothers subject to violence and the threat of violence.

Children aged 3–4 years

Health

Expected health

Children of this age should be generally well and illnesses should have a medically recognised cause. Parents and carers need to ensure immunisations are up to date and the child's weight and height are within the expected range. Children who do not have learning or physical disabilities should be achieving their developmental milestones. In terms of gross motor development children around the age of 3 years are able to ride a tricycle or stabilised bicycle using pedals and climb stairs with one foot on each step. By 4 years they can generally catch, kick, throw and bounce a ball and enjoy climbing on frames. In terms of fine motor control children of 3 years can control a pencil using their thumb and first two fingers, and are able to draw a person as a head with legs and arms coming out of it. By 4 years they can thread small beads on a lace and copy some letters.

When children have not reached their expected developmental milestones parents should seek professional advice. Children with learning or physical disabilities should get continued professional attention. Illnesses and injuries should be given appropriate and prompt treatment.

UNIVERSITY OF WINCHESTER
LIBRARY

Possible impact on health

Parents need to understand what constitutes a danger to children of this age and be able to protect the child. Children should not be left alone; their physical needs should be met and they need to be protected from physical or sexual abuse.

In order to protect children from harm, parents of pre-school children need to be able to anticipate danger. The paraphernalia of drug use, as well as more mundane poisonous household substances and medicines, must be stored safely out of the reach of enquiring and inquisitive young hands. Similarly, to prevent accidents it is important to ensure young children are supervised while playing in the home and not allowed to leave the house or play on the street unattended (Alison 2000). Substance misuse, mental illness, learning disability or domestic violence may make parents reluctant to take their child for medical treatment for minor injuries if these resulted from a lack of supervision.

Living with domestic violence may necessitate mothers spending considerable time placating and forestalling potential violence to themselves and their children. Most children of this age are aware of the violence and some may become injured in the crossfire or be deliberately targeted (Cleaver et al. 2007).

Serious alcohol or drug use may lead parents to leave children with multiple and unsuitable carers in order to raise the necessary money or to buy alcohol or drugs (Barnard 2007).

> ...B was 3 years old. One night, S was arrested by the police for soliciting. At the station she told the police that she had left B on her own at home ... S was financing her habit through prostitution. She said that her craving for crack cocaine was so overwhelming that she did not care what she did to raise the money ... B was seriously underweight and had marked developmental problems, especially in language.
>
> (Case example, quoted in Swadi 1994, p.241)

This example also suggests that when parents are taken up with their own needs, ensuring that young children are adequately fed and kept clean may not always be a priority. Drug taking and high levels of alcohol consumption, or the medication needed to stabilise mental illness, can depress appetite and parents may fail to respond to their child's need for food. Alternatively, children may not be adequately fed because too much of the family's income is used to buy alcohol or drugs. Moreover, meals may be missed because parents oversleep due to the effects of drugs or alcohol, mental illness or the aftermath of violence. Finally, parents with learning disabilities who do not have adequate support or training may not understand what constitutes adequate nutrition for a child of this age.

Education – cognitive and language development

Expected ability

Most children of 3 and 4 years can concentrate well and benefit from a variety of play, drawing and writing materials. Although children enjoy playing by themselves, they are beginning to be able to 'take turns'. Pretend play is developing and it is not unusual for pre-school children to have an imaginary friend (Smith and Cowie 1993; Bee 2000).

During the infant years a child's vocabulary increases significantly. However, children need encouragement to continue in the development of their language skills and they should be listened to and helped to take part in conversations. Reading to children helps them increase their knowledge and understanding of words and language. When children's development is delayed a parent or carer should seek relevant information and professional advice. If children have little or no speech, with help they may learn to communicate non-verbally.

By this age many children benefit from regular attendance at some form of pre-school facility. Attendance enables the child to play with other children and interact with a variety of adults. It is with this type of interaction that children learn about other people's feelings and reactions, a process which is considered key to cognitive development (Bee 2000). As Fahlberg aptly notes *'Play is the work of the pre school child'* (Fahlberg 1991, p.73). Research found parents whose children attended nursery reported emotional and interpersonal gains for them (Kelly 1995). *'Those who have been to nursery or play group start school with several advantages: they find it easier to settle and to make friends and they are better prepared to cope with academic work'* (Department of Health 1995b). Early learning is promoted in England and Wales through the Early Years Foundation Stage www.standards.dfes.gov.uk/eyfs/site/about/index.htm.

Possible impact on cognitive and language development

The effects of parental mental illness, learning disability, substance misuse and domestic violence may result in parents not having the practical or emotional reserves to engage with their children or provide the stimulation needed to support their cognitive development (Barnard 2007). Key to a child's learning is the praise and encouragement of a loved adult.

Learning disability may mean parents do not know how best to encourage their child's learning, particularly in relation to early literacy and numeracy. Although only 15% of children of parents with learning disabilities are similarly affected, a lack of stimulation and encouragement can, nonetheless, mean children fall behind their peers in acquiring new skills.

The conflicting findings around the impact of maternal depression on children's education and cognitive development, discussed in the section for children aged 1 to 2 years, remains unresolved in studies which focus on older infants. For example, Sharp and colleagues' (1995) findings suggest that postnatal depression is associated with poorer intellectual development in boys at the age of 3 years 10 months, while the work of Hammen (1988) found no such relationship.

Children's cognitive development may also be affected by parental problem drinking. Research using developmental tests shows educational deficits in pre-school children (Royal College of Physicians 1995). *'Children of problem drinkers studied both in childhood and adulthood reveal cognitive deficits when compared with children of non drinkers'* (Royal College of Physicians 1995, p.18).

Domestic violence has also been shown to be associated with children showing a lack of interest in their environment and poorer intellectual development (Humphreys and Mullender 1999). A possible explanation may be that growing up in violent households results in children being too frightened to show inquisitiveness or to attempt to explore their environment. A further interpretation of apathy and disinterest in young children is that it indicates insecure attachments (see section on family and social relationships for this age group).

Children's experiences of their parents' problems may also interfere with children's ability to concentrate.

> *Some days she is obviously upset coming to school and does very little work those days. She is an able, bright child who is not realising her full potential. She is bringing a lot of 'baggage' to school with her, which is causing concentration problems.*
>
> (Teacher of a 4-year-old girl with a drug-using mother, quoted in Hogan and Higgins 2001, p.19)

Children's learning may also be affected because the disorganisation and torpor resulting from mental illness, learning disability or problem alcohol or drug use (or the psychological consequences of domestic violence) may mean parents fail to regularly take children to nursery or other pre-school facilities (Hogan and Higgins 2001). Attendance may also be curtailed because a mother may not wish to go out in public, hoping to conceal the evidence of domestic violence or her drinking or drug taking.

Emotional and behavioural development and self-care skills

Expected development

At the age of 3 and 4 years children are gradually gaining greater control over their behaviour. Although at this age children are usually friendly and helpful, outbursts of temper are not unusual and can include both verbal expressions of anger and frustration, as well as physical ones such as biting, hitting and scratching (Fahlberg 1991).

This is an age when children are plagued with irrational fears. For example, many are frightened of the dark or of loud noises (Fahlberg 1991). However, as mentioned earlier, the main fear of young children is that of abandonment, perhaps not so irrational in today's world (Owusu-Bempah 2006).

Children are pleased to be able to do some things for themselves, and by 4 years many are able to dress and undress themselves although they generally enjoy being helped. With maturation children normally learn to have control over bladder and bowels (Smith and Cowie 1993).

Possible impact on emotional and behavioural development

This age group is very vulnerable to the development of emotional and behavioural disturbance. The extent of their distress may be missed because young children cannot easily articulate their feelings, and their observable reactions may not tally with their emotional state.

Parental mental illness places children at significantly greater risk of behavioural and emotional problems when compared with the general community (Oyserman et al. 2000; Covell and Howe 2009). Some observational studies of depressed mothers, however, suggest this may reflect the mother's negative perceptions of her child rather than real differences in behaviour (Lang et al. 1996).

Alcohol or drug addiction, domestic violence and mental illness may result in parents showing little warmth towards their children, leaving them feeling unloved and rejected (VanDeMark et al. 2005). Alternatively, the use of substances may enable some parents to more easily demonstrate their emotions.

> *In many cases parents may only express emotions when they have been drinking, which leaves children deprived of affection and afraid that their parents don't love them.*

(Turning Point 2006, p.9)

Drug or alcohol addiction or mental illness may result in parents being inconsistent in expressing emotions to their children. As a result children learn to alter their behaviour according to their parents' state of mind.

> *She knew not to go near me in the morning 'till I had me foil, then Mammy would play. In the mornings the sickness was the worst ... I'd just be telling her to get away. Once I had the gear into me I'd be the best mother on the earth.*

(Drug-using mother of 4-year-old girl, quoted in Hogan and Higgins 2001, p.22)

Problem drug-using parents also felt that they were not as available to their children (aged 4–12 years) as other parents who did not have drug problems. They recognised that their lifestyle – time spent obtaining money for drugs, time in treatment and custodial sentences – had a negative impact on their children (Hogan and Higgins 2001).

When parents' behaviour is unpredictable and frightening, research suggests children react with symptoms similar to those identified in post-traumatic stress disorder. These include sleep disturbance, bed-wetting and rocking (Holt et al. 2008; Humphreys and Houghton 2008). Children who witness domestic violence have generally been found to have more frequent behavioural and emotional problems than children who do not (Humphreys and Mullender 1999). Extreme anxiety and fear may result from children seeing their parents as powerless or untrustworthy. They may react by withdrawing or, alternatively, by always trying to please (Fahlberg 1991). These symptoms are noted in the NCH Action for Children study of children who experience domestic violence (NCH Action for Children 1994). Many mothers talked about their children's fear, *'They would wake up screaming and crying'* (p.35). Other children showed their fear by being unnaturally quiet or withdrawn, while over a third developed bed-wetting problems. Practically two-thirds of mothers mentioned other disturbing reactions, particularly children's fear of any type of separation.

> *My daughter used to like walking in the street by herself. But now, I have to be holding her hand constantly or pick her up. Even on the bus, she sits on me, she do not want to sit by herself. Inside the house, she sitting on me all the time. It's like she's just scared.*

> (Mother subjected to domestic violence, quoted in DeVoe and Smith 2002, p.1088)

Finally, research suggests that those children who had both witnessed violence directed towards their mother and been the direct victims of violence experienced significantly more behavioural problems than those who had only witnessed the violence or those who had neither witnessed nor been a victim (Hughes 1988; Hughes et al. 2001).

Identity and social presentation

Expected identity and social presentation

Children of 3 and 4 years are clear about their gender and have some understanding of their race and culture, depending on their family's approach and attitude (Bee 2000). Most children know who their parents and siblings are and have a sense of who belongs to their immediate family. Children can generally give their first name and last name and know how old they are.

Definitions of self tend to focus on concrete, visible characteristics: whether they are boys or girls, what colour hair they have or what they are good at doing, rather than more enduring inner qualities (Bee 2000). The children's perceptions of themselves tend to be tied to specific settings or tasks and they have yet to develop a more global sense of self (Quinton 2006).

Pre-school children are at the stage of integrating the 'good' and 'bad' aspects of self. Through adults telling them about the way they behave, children can learn that sometimes their behaviour is good, while at other times it is not. The expectation is that by integrating these two aspects of themselves they will come to believe that *they are good people who sometimes do "not good" things* (Fahlberg 1991, p.74).

Possible impact on identity and social presentation

The impact of adverse parenting for this age group is more damaging in some areas than in others. The most likely damage will result from children blaming themselves for parents' problems, taking on too much responsibility, and being emotionally and physically neglected.

As will be shown for older children, even children of this age can learn to act beyond their years. For example, a 4-year-old may attempt to make a cup of tea for a parent who is drowsy or irritable as a result of drugs or alcohol, or for a parent with learning disabilities who does not understand that such activity has inherent dangers for a child of this age.

There are also surprising examples of how even very young children see themselves as responsible for their parents' behaviour and make attempts to put things right. Reports from mothers who are victims of domestic violence suggest that infants who witness the violence try to protect their mother.

> *He smashed my head against the wall because (the baby) was making a mess ... I just collapsed on the floor. (The baby) was trying to pull me across the floor crying ... saying 'Mummy get up'.*

(Mother, quoted in NCH Action for Children 1994, p.32)

Parents may neglect their own and their children's physical care because of a lack of knowledge and understanding or as a result of the effects of drugs or alcohol, or because they are depressed. In some extreme cases the impact of parents' problems may be such that basic hygiene is neglected and children are unwashed, hair is infested and clothing dirty and unkempt. At this age few children are sufficiently skilled to see to their own needs.

Children living with a parent who is suffering hallucinations may be vulnerable to physical harm or emotional damage. Quinton and Rutter (1985) have suggested that drawing children into parents' fantasies may place them at risk in all areas of development, and in extreme cases this may result in the child's death (see Falkov 1996; Brandon et al. 2008).

Family and social relationships

Expected relationships

Between the ages of 3 and 4 years, the fear of strangers gradually diminishes and the need to be physically near a parent is no longer so urgent. After the age of 3 years children begin to more easily understand why a parent or carer has to leave them and are less distressed by short separations. The child no longer requires the constant presence of their parent and understands that the parent continues to exist when absent, as does their relationship (Bee 2000). This enables the child and parent to plan for separation (such as attending nursery school), agree on when and how they will be reunited, what the child should do if frightened and who to turn to for comfort.

It is generally accepted that children can cope well with having more than one adult look after them, provided that they are the same care givers over time and that child and carers have a secure attachment relationship (Aldgate and Jones 2006). However, this is a fearful age: the greatest of which is a fear that parents will abandon them (Fahlberg 1991).

Pre-school children start to establish relationships with peers and develop social skills. By the age of 3 or 4, over half of children have at least one mutual friendship, more often than not with a child of the same sex (Bee 2000). Research has shown that children of this age show pro-social behaviour such as sharing, helping or comforting. The development of pro-social behaviour is thought to be influenced by parental reinforcement or punishment for not being helpful, modelling of altruistic behaviour, and moral exhortation (Smith and Cowie 1993).

Possible impact on relationships

The impact of parental mental illness, learning disability, problem alcohol or drug use or domestic violence on children of this age results from inconsistent parenting, emotional unavailability, fear of violence and parental conflict, unexpected and unplanned for separations, exposure to unsafe carers, and learning to imitate inappropriate behaviour.

Young children living in families where at least one parent has a mood disorder, learning disability, a problem with drink or drugs, or where there is domestic violence, are more likely to experience inconsistent parenting, which can be frightening. As a result, children never know what will happen or whether their needs will be met. In such situations children may become fearful and unnaturally vigilant believing they are in continual danger (Stallard et al. 2004).

A problem already discussed in relation to younger infants is that parents may become unavailable emotionally, causing children to develop insecure attachments. Children of 3 and 4 years may respond by showing apathy and disinterest in their environment. Alternatively, they may exhibit controlling behaviour, which is often accompanied by a good deal of inner turmoil. Children who cope with disturbing parental behaviours by apparently not responding can appear more competent in dealing with adverse parental behaviours, but in reality they are attempting to prevent further frightening responses from the parent (Jones et al. 1991).

The further problem is that young children model their parents' behaviour. Research indicates that children as young as 3 and 4 years who are exposed to domestic violence are more likely to display significantly more anger, peer aggression and behaviour problems than non-exposed children (Covell and Howe 2009). Aggressive and acting-out behaviour may result both from children learning to resolve conflict through violence and from mirroring what they see. *'Like my son, he had this thing with hitting little girls, I would just see him hitting on little girls'* (DeVoe and Smith 2002, p.1086). Research also found that mothers in violent relationships worried that their children would grow up to be violent in their adult relationships.

> *I discipline him every time he needs to be disciplined. Cause he's 4 years old, and I feel at this point that – he told me once, 'When I get bigger, I'm gonna hit you like my dad.' So I feel if I don't stop it now, he'll walk all over me by the time he's 13 'cause I'm a single parent.*

(Mother, quoted in DeVoe and Smith 2002, p.1086)

When parents' problems require hospitalisation or are so extreme that children need to be looked after full-time by others, children of this age will find separation bewildering and frightening. This is because of their inability to think beyond the immediate and the concrete. Unlike older children, the cognitive ability of children aged 3–4 years is less developed, which makes it difficult for them to grasp explanations for the long-term absence of a parent (see Aldgate 1992). In situations of domestic violence which has resulted in family separation, some children may have conflicting feelings of relief and a sense of greater safety, mixed with sadness and a sense of loss (McGee 2000).

Many parents with learning disabilities have the additional challenge of parenting a disabled child. The challenge is enormous for even the most skilful of parents, but can overwhelm parents with learning disabilities.

> *It was about Sammie, how to cope with him. We needed help with him. They said he had autism. I had never heard of it, they said it was some form of brain damage. I was very upset, it would go on forever.*

(Mother, from unpublished material gathered for the Cleaver and Nicholson 2007 study)

Parents who are preoccupied with their own needs may leave children in the care of inappropriate adults, thus exposing them to the possibility of abuse. For example, parents with learning disabilities who experienced familial sexual abuse as children may find it difficult to protect their own children; grandparents and other relatives frequently provide much valuable practical support including looking after the children.

> *The children should not have any unsupervised contact with their maternal grandfather due to a history of sexual abuse. Mum has allowed her father and Jade's step father to influence her, allowing Jade to have contact with them. Mum is confused by her feelings for her father who abused her in the past.*

(Social worker's notes, from unpublished material for Cleaver and Nicholson 2007)

In addition, some mothers with learning disabilities may be targeted by men who wish to gain sexual access to the children.

To sum up

Key problems for children aged 3–4 years

- Physical needs may be neglected. For example, children may be not adequately fed or kept clean.

- Risk of direct physical violence may be increased.

- Cognitive development and learning may be delayed because fear and anxiety prevents children from exploring their environment.

- Cognitive and language development may also suffer due to a lack of stimulation and encouragement; and parental disorganisation may mean children fail to regularly attend pre-school facilities.

- Trauma and stress may result in children regressing in their behavioural and emotional development.

- Attachment relationships may be insecure due to inconsistent parenting.

- Inappropriate behavioural responses may be learnt through witnessing domestic violence.

- When parents' behaviour is unpredictable and frightening, children may display emotional symptoms similar to those of post-traumatic stress disorder.

- Children may assume responsibilities beyond their years because of parental incapacity.

- Children could be left in the care of unsuitable and unsafe people, including relatives.

Protective factors

- The presence of an alternative, consistent caring adult who can respond to the cognitive and emotional needs of the child.

- Sufficient income support and good physical standards in the home.

- Regular attendance at pre-school facilities.

- A safe adult who listens to the child, observes their behaviour and acts appropriately to ensure the child's safety and welfare.

- Regular, long-term support for the family from the primary health care team, adult social services and children's social care, and community-based services.

- A long-term package of services to meet the diverse and enduring, complex and multiple needs of some families.

- An alternative, safe and supportive residence for mothers subject to violence and the threat of violence.

- Parent(s) receiving treatment for their drug, alcohol or mental health problem.

Identified unmet developmental needs in children under 5 years

The information shown in Table 4.1 is the result of a re-analysis of data gathered for two research studies carried out by Hedy Cleaver, one of the authors. The first explored parental substance misuse and domestic violence (Cleaver et al. 2007) and the other looked at parental learning disability (Cleaver and Nicholson 2007); neither included parental mental illness. Both studies involved children who had been referred to children's social care, and social workers identified children's developmental needs at the initial assessment stage.

In the majority of cases families were experiencing a multitude of difficulties such as the co-existence of domestic violence and learning disability, poor mental health, poverty, and deprivation. It should, therefore, not be assumed that children's needs were solely the result of a single parental disorder.

Moreover, because the sample size for the age group is not large (particularly for the group of children living with parents with learning disabilities) caution should be used before making any extrapolations.

Table 4.1: **Proportion of children with identified unmet needs – children under 5 years**

Dimension	Parental substance misuse n=66	Parental learning disability n=24	Domestic violence n=70
Health	46%	51%	65%
Education	23%	53%	18%
Emotional and behavioural development	35%	38%	32%
Identity	21%	38%	18%
Family and social relationships	58%	73%	61%

These findings suggest that young children are more likely to experience unmet needs in relation to their health and with regard to family and social relationships. It is also of concern that over half the children living with parents with learning disabilities had educational needs, which suggests that many of these parents experienced difficulty in supporting and stimulating their children's learning.

In the original two studies, children were classified as having severe unmet needs when social workers identified developmental needs in three or more of the five dimensions – for example, severe need in relation to the child's health, education, and family and social relationships. A re-analysis of the original data suggests that a quarter (25%) of children under five years who were living with parental substance misuse or domestic violence (24%) had severe developmental needs, whereas 42% of those living with a parent with learning disabilities met the criteria.

5 Child development and parents' responses – middle childhood

Chapter 5 focuses on children aged 5 to 10 years. The format is consistent with the younger age groups. The following developmental dimensions: health; education; emotional and behavioural development; identity; family and social relationships; social presentation; and self-care skills are prefaced by what might be expected for this age group, based on research findings. This is followed by the possible consequences of living with a parent experiencing mental illness, learning disability, problem substance use and domestic violence. Summary points at the end of the chapter identify the key problems and the protective factors.

Children aged 5–10 years

Health

Expected health

Children aged 5–10 years should have regular medical and dental examinations, either as part of routine school medical checks or with the family doctor and dentist. These check-ups should ensure that the child's height and weight are within normal limits, and that problems with hearing and sight, physical dexterity and mobility are identified and addressed. Although children's co-ordination is improving, at 5 and 6 years they frequently overestimate their ability and injure themselves during normal play. Convulsions are rare at this age unless associated with high fevers or a recognised physical condition.

During these years boys are more likely than girls to have some form of mental disorder; 10% of boys and 5% of girls aged 5 to 10 years were found to have a mental disorder in 2004 (Green et al 2005).

Some health problems for this age group are on the increase. For example, a large-scale study of 8- to 9-year-old children found the prevalence of ever having experienced asthma rose from 19.9% of children in 1991 to 29.7% in 1999 (Ng Man Kwong et al. 2001). Eating disorders have also increased. Obesity among children aged 2 to 10 years rose from 9.9% in 1995 to 13.7% in 2003, and the proportion of children of this age group being overweight rose from 22.7% in 1995 to 27.7% in 2003. Obesity and being overweight was greatest for children aged 8 to 10 years; 16.5% were found to be obese in 2003 (Jotangia et al. 2006). However, more recent research comparing data from 2006/7 to 2008/9 suggests this upward trend in childhood obesity appears to have flattening out (Dinsdale et al 2010).

At this age children who do not have speech or hearing problems or a learning disability should have a well-developed vocabulary and communicate easily with adults and children. When there is a permanent hearing loss or physical disability which interferes with verbal communication, children should be communicating using a form of signing. Children with physical disabilities are more able to understand their condition and talk about it. Many children with disabilities take part in specialised group activities.

Children 10 years and younger rarely smoke cigarettes and, although some children will experiment with smoking, regular smoking is negligible (Scottish Executive Department of Health 1998).

Possible impact on health

There are two issues with relation to the impact of parental disorders on children's health: an increased risk of physical injury and extreme anxiety and fear.

The increased risk of physical injury can result from the well-established link between domestic violence and physical child abuse (Humphreys and Mullender 1999; Onyskiw 2003; Covell and Howe 2009).

> *Among parents who engaged in serious spouse abuse, half of the fathers and a quarter of the mothers said they had also engaged in serious child abuse.*
>
> (Moffitt and Caspi 1998, p.142)

> *I have seen him hit all the members of the family at least once.*
>
> (Ten-year-old boy, quoted in Humphreys and Mullender 1999, p.9)

Children may also be injured because they are caught in the cross-fire or have tried to intervene to protect their mothers.

> *Me and my sister would jump on his back (to stop him hurting Mum), but he would just hit you off ... Then you would go flying because he was so big.*
>
> (Child, quoted in Abrahams 1994, p.33)

There is gathering evidence to show a link between domestic violence and elevated levels of child sexual abuse, with research suggesting approximately half of children who have been sexually abused were living with domestic violence (Humphreys and Stanley 2006; Hester et al. 2007).

In a large study, Macleod and colleagues (2008) found that children's smoking at age 10 years was related to family adversity, parental smoking, manual parental social class and material disadvantage. Maternal drinking was associated with an increased risk of children aged 10 drinking alcohol, but paternal drinking was associated with a lower risk of children drinking. Overall though, even in families experiencing adversity, smoking, drinking or drug use was not common among children aged 10 years.

Children whose parents suffer from mental illness, learning disability, parental drug or alcohol problems or who are in a violent relationship have an increased risk of medical problems, including injuries, convulsive disorders and increased frequency of hospitalisation. For example, children living with domestic violence or with parental substance misuse are more likely than children who do not live in such circumstances to experience allergies and respiratory tract infections, psychosomatic complaints such as headaches and stomach aches, stomach disorders such as nausea and diarrhoea, and sleep disturbances such as insomnia, nightmares and sleepwalking (Lewis and Bucholz 1991; Onyskiw 2003).

Children of parents suffering mental health problems have an increased risk of experiencing depression and anxiety disorders (Tunnard 2004), although there is no evidence to suggest children's physical health is affected (Somers 2007). A study by Dave and colleagues (2008) found that when fathers suffered major depression their children aged 4–6 years were more likely to demonstrate pro-social behavioural difficulties.

The health of children of parents with learning disabilities may suffer because of a lack of hygiene. In addition, health problems may not be recognised or adequately dealt with.

> *The school said that Steven [a boy aged 10 years] was coming into school very smelly, dirty and that he had lice. He was also having dental problems and dental appointments were not being kept.*

(Social worker, quoted in Cleaver and Nicholson 2007, p.61)

Children may also be likely to suffer harm because when they have severe health problems, parental mental illness, learning disabilities, substance misuse and the effects of domestic violence may result in parents not fully understanding the importance of attending medical appointments and ensuring that instructions are systematically carried out.

> *There was a downward slide in her caring for the child – she was missing important appointments and I was not getting access to the home. I was concerned about Danielle not getting the regular treatment she needed.*

(Health visitor's report on Danielle aged 8 years living with her mother who was depressed and had a serious drug problem, quoted in Cleaver et al. 2007, p.86)

Finally, children's health problems may go unrecognised because school absenteeism as a result of parenting disorders may mean routine school medicals are missed.

Education and cognitive ability

Expected ability

Children in this age group typically attend school regularly and on the whole enjoy the experience. Teachers are generally liked and most children have at least one friend. However, bullying is not uncommon among primary school children. The findings from a survey of schools in England found 28% of primary school children reported having been bullied during the previous term (Oliver and Candappa 2003).

Children of 5 and 6 years frequently aspire to do more than they can achieve and easily become frustrated. There is an increasing ability to concentrate, as children are able to screen out distractions and focus on a single issue. By 9 years, children are capable of long periods of concentration; they should be proficient in school subjects, able to read, use basic maths and write.

Notions of truth and fairness are increasingly understood.

Possible impact on education and cognitive ability

The issues for children of this age relate to academic attainment and learning and behaviour in school.

Research findings on the impact of parental learning disability suggest that delays in a child's cognitive development and learning may arise because genetic factors affect the child's capacity to learn, or because of inadequate stimulation and poor school attendance (Cleaver and Nicholson 2007). Parents with literacy and numeracy problems will have difficulty in reading stories to children, helping with their school work and encouraging learning in general. A caring adult, for example a relative, friend or sympathetic teacher, can provide additional support for learning, and children's education need not be negatively affected.

Maternal depression early in a child's life has been shown to be a strong predictor of behaviour problems; the more chronic the maternal depression the greater the child's behavioural problems (Covell and Howe 2009). A comparison of 5- to 6-year-old children of hospitalised schizophrenic and depressed women with a control group found the children whose mothers were depressed showed most failures on tests of attention and greatest impairment in intellectual ability (Cohler et al. 1977). Further evidence comes from Weissman and colleagues (1986) who noted that teachers reported children of depressed mothers to be more likely to require special educational classes than those whose mothers were not depressed.

A review of the research on the impact of domestic violence on children's school performance for this age group shows conflicting results (Onyskiw 2003). To counteract previous methodological limitations Koenen and colleagues (2003) carried out a large-scale study of twins aged 5 years who were exposed to domestic violence in England. They found strong evidence that domestic violence was associated with children's delayed intellectual development, independent of genetic effects. A further key finding was the relationship between delays in cognitive development and the level of domestic violence; children exposed to high levels of domestic violence had IQs that were, on average, 8 points lower than unexposed children.

Research also suggests that parental substance misuse negatively affects children's cognitive development and education. Children of parents with chronic alcohol problems are likely to experience learning difficulties, reading problems, poor concentration and low performance (Velleman and Orford 2001; Cleaver et al. 2007). Other research focuses on academic performance in school and out of six studies, five reported the children of alcoholics to have a significantly lower performance than children of parents who did not have alcohol problems (reviewed in West and Prinz 1987). Similar results have been found for the children of drug-misusing parents (see Hogan 1998; Hogan and Higgins 2001; Cleaver et al. 2007). When parents are intoxicated or suffering withdrawals they may not be able to provide sufficient support with schooling. For example, parents may fail to attend school open days, or meet regularly with teachers. A reluctance to become involved in their child's school may be compounded by the stigma of being known to the school as problem drug or alcohol users.

Children's education may also suffer because their parents' problems and their home circumstances may dominate the child's thoughts and affect his or her ability to concentrate, which will have negative consequences for learning. *'His work is suffering at school ... his reading is suffering ... he can't concentrate'* (child experiencing domestic violence, quoted in NCH Action for Children 1994, p.57).

Parental problems can also affect children's cognitive development and learning due to poor school attendance.

> *At the time of the referral concerns expressed at lack of attendance at school and poor time-keeping, signs of neglect, dirty clothes, hungry and smelling of body odour ... Lynn's speech is a matter of concern...*
>
> (Social worker's recorded notes about Lynn, aged 8 years, whose parents had a learning disability, quoted in Cleaver and Nicholson 2007, p.74)

Children may also experience difficulties in attending school regularly or on time because parental disorders mean they must often take care of themselves, including getting to school.

> *Danielle* (aged 8 years) *had to do a lot of her own care, her schooling was affected as Danielle had to get herself up and ready for school which made her late a lot...*
>
> (Mother who used heroin and cocaine, suffered depression and was exposed to domestic violence, quoted in Cleaver et al. 2007, p.212)

Schooling may also be disrupted because families have unplanned moves which necessitate a change of school. As a result, children may miss out on coursework and lose touch with friends. Children may also stay away from school or miss classes because they are worried about their parents; for example they may be concerned about their mother's mental health and wish to be there to help (Maybery et al. 2005) or anxious over their mother's safety (NCH Action for Children 1994). When parental problems result in parents needing residential treatment, children report that this affects their school attendance (Maybery et al. 2005).

The other issue in relation to education is the child's behaviour in school. Emery and colleagues (1982) found that parental schizophrenia was associated with problematic school behaviour in children. The same direct relationship was not obtained in cases of maternal depression unless marital discord was also present. Children of parents with alcohol or drug problems, compared with children whose parents did not abuse substances, have been shown to experience higher levels of *'fighting, teasing, irritability, and anger, and of interpersonal difficulties at school'* (Covell and Howe 2009, p.117). Similarly, there is evidence that children exposed to domestic violence are more likely to be aggressive and have difficulty in adhering to school rules (Holt et al. 2008). However, it is important not to pathologise all children of parents with problems. Research by VanDeMark and colleagues (2005) found that in a study of children of women entering treatment for drug abuse, most did not evidence behavioural problems. Cleaver and colleagues (2007) found education was not a cause for concern for two-thirds of children aged 5 to 9 years who were living with domestic violence. Research suggests that it is the co-morbidity of child abuse and exposure to domestic violence that accounts for behavioural problems amongst children of substance abusers (Nicholas and Rasmussen 2006; Cleaver et al. 2007).

Research also shows that not only do the majority of children whose parents have problems not evidence any behavioural problems at school, but for some children school offers respite and a safe haven from troubled home circumstances. Children can use school as an escape and gain a sense of accomplishment through sport or academic achievement (Joseph et al. 2006).

Emotional and behavioural development

Expected development

Children trust and confide in adults and seek comfort from them when distressed. In most situations children are able to manage their emotions when upset through drawing on an internal working model that represents them as loved and effective (Schofield 2006).

Children aged 5–6 years are frequently very active with a poor ability to modulate their behaviour. Concepts of ownership are not yet fully established and it is not unusual for 6-year-olds to take things that belong to others. For example, children in infant school may come home having 'found' pencils or small toys.

When stressed, children of 5 and 6 years may revert to behaviours normal for earlier years, for example sucking a thumb, or communicating through baby talk. When children are frustrated, temper tantrums involve name calling which often is lavatorial in nature.

By the age of 8 and 9 years family values become incorporated and the child increasingly relies on internal, as opposed to external, controls. For example, the child's behaviour is no longer entirely dependent upon the immediate presence of an adult. Nonetheless, children in middle childhood frequently test out the boundaries which, for most, results in confirming their core knowledge of the rules and their ability to manage their behaviour under the circumstances (Schofield 2006). When they are frustrated or angry, boys in particular may talk of fighting and 'beating up' other children. Actual aggression though is more likely to be verbal rather than physical. Swearing shifts from elimination-related words to a vocabulary associated with sex.

Possible impact on emotional and behavioural development

There are several ways in which parental problems can have an adverse affect on the emotions and behaviour of children aged 5–10 years. Children show their distress through conduct disorders and emotional distress, uncontrolled behaviour and fear.

When parents suffer mental illness, learning disabilities, misuse alcohol or drugs or are violent to one another, children may become extremely fearful. The accounts of children of this age provide clear evidence of the fear and anxiety which these parental disorders can generate:

> *I was scared that mummy would kill herself with the drink.*
>
> (Quoted from Brisby et al. 1997, p.14)

> *If anything happened to daddy where would we be ... who would mind us?*
>
> (Child whose father had poor mental health, quoted in Somers 2007, p.1327)

Research suggests that school-aged children of depressed parents generally show higher levels of problem behaviours than control children (Downey and Coyne 1990). There is considerable dispute, however, over how children manifest their problems. Work by Hammen et al. (1978), Beardsley et al. (1987) and Klein et al. (1988) all found a significantly higher rate of conduct disorder in children of depressed parents. In contrast, Lee and Gotlib (1989) found maternal depression was related to emotional disorders in children aged 7–12, such as greater fear and mood disturbances, which were likely to continue after the mother's depression had abated, but failed to show an association between maternal depression and conduct disorders in children.

Children whose parents misuse substances or are violent towards one another are found to show higher levels of aggressive, non-compliant, disruptive, destructive and antisocial behaviours compared with children from non-violent homes and those whose parents do not misuse drugs (Covell and Howe 2009).

> *[He] can be very aggressive in school. The slightest offence can lead to an argument. He can't control his temper.*
>
> (Teacher of 9-year-old boy with a drug-misusing mother, quoted in Hogan and Higgins 2001, p.21)

Non-compliant behaviour may result in law breaking.

> *I went to live with my foster-carer because my mum didn't look after us properly and she didn't have a house and she didn't know what we were doing at night and things ... me and my young brother we were stealing out the Asda 'em, smashing windows and not listening to what my mum was saying...*
>
> (Ten-year-old boy of problem drug-using parent, quoted in Barnard 2007 p.93)

Children living with parents with learning disabilities, who have been referred to children's social care have higher levels of emotional and behavioural problems than comparable children whose parents do not have a learning disability (Cleaver and Nicholson 2007). Behaviour problems may be exacerbated because when faced with the emotional demands of middle childhood, parents with learning disabilities may find it difficult to assert their authority.

> *Roger says he doesn't like school and sometimes will not go. I tell him I don't want to go to prison because he will not go to school. Julian [stepfather] can be a bit hard on him and shouts and sends him to bed early if he will not go to school.*
>
> (Mother with a learning disability discussing her son, quoted in Cleaver and Nicholson 2007, p.88)

Moreover, when children demonstrate emotional and behavioural problems, parents with learning disabilities are less likely to seek and use professional help than parents of average ability (Dowdney and Skuse 1993).

Exposure to domestic violence is also found to be associated with children being more anxious, sad, worried, fearful and withdrawn than children not exposed (Onyskiw 2003; Hogan and Higgins 2001). Research suggests also that children who witness anger or violence have problems in controlling their emotions and behaviour (Cicchetti and Toth 1995). Exposure to male-to-female domestic violence has also been shown to be correlated with animal cruelty by children (Currie 2006). Temper tantrums, aggression or extreme passivity with sudden outbursts are the frequently recorded behaviours of children living in situations of domestic violence (Brandon and Lewis 1996). For example, these authors quote a paediatric nurse's comments about a 6-year-old,

> *I've seen her very upset on the ward literally running up the curtains when her father got violent on the ward.*

(Brandon and Lewis 1996, p.61)

However, it is important to stress that not all children whose parents are experiencing mental illness, learning disability, substance misuse or domestic violence display emotional and behavioural problems (VanDeMark et al. 2005). What is identified in much research is that children are more at risk of experiencing difficulties when parental substance misuse, mental illness or learning disability co-exist or when children are also exposed to domestic violence (Velleman and Orford 2001; Cleaver et al. 2007; Covell and Howe 2009). Time and again, it seems that the combination of problems is much more likely to have a detrimental impact on children than a parental disorder which exists in isolation.

Children cope with parents' frightening and unpredictable behaviour in different ways depending on their personality, age, gender, level of self-esteem and the opportunities open to them (Gorin 2004). For example, although boys and girls are thought to be equally affected by their parents' problems, their response tends to differ. It is widely accepted that boys are more likely to act out their distress with antisocial and aggressive behaviours such as stealing, lying, attention seeking and attacks on peers. In contrast, girls tend to respond by internalising their worries, showing symptoms of depression, anxiety and withdrawal (Bentovim and Williams 1998; Velleman and Orford 2001).

> *We didn't notice Kylie's [aged 8 years] difficulties at first. We noticed with her brother – he was aggressive with her, copying his dad.*

(Disabled mother experiencing domestic violence quoted in Cleaver et al. 2007 p.89)

Temperament of the child is also an issue. When parents became irritable, aggressive and quarrelsome this does not impinge equally on all children in the family. For example, parental annoyance may be directed towards the child who is regarded by their parents as being temperamentally 'difficult' (Rutter and Quinton 1984).

Some children may cope with the stress produced by unpredictable, unexpected and irrational parental behaviour by seeking to escape. They may do this through fantasy and make-believe, where the frightening behaviour of their parents is reinterpreted in acceptable ways.

> *Sometimes, when my parents were raging at each other in the kitchen, Lecia and I would talk about finding a shack on the beach to live in. We'd sit cross-legged under the blue cotton quilt with a flashlight, doing parodies of their fights. 'Reel Six, Tape Fifty One. Let her roll,' Lecia would say ... as if what we were listening to was only one more take in a long movie we were shooting.*

(Karr 1995, p.38)

Other children may cope by withdrawing into themselves. In Maybery and colleagues' study (2005) of children of parents with a mental illness, one child described how she coped when her mother was unwell, *'My dog is the closest thing I have to human contact for days when mum is in hospital'* (p.6). For other children a vivid sense of fear for their own safety was the overarching response and children withdrew to a place of safety. *'I thought that he was going to hit me too ... I ran into the other room and shut the door'* (child, quoted in Joseph et al. 2006, p.34).

Identity

Expected identity

Children are developing a more global sense of self and self-worth. For example, by 6 years instead of giving a concrete and discrete description of themselves such as 'I am good at drawing' children may use more global terms to describe themselves such as 'I'm a clever girl'. By 10 years of age children are able to compare themselves to other children: 'I'm better at drawing than most of my friends' (Bee 2000). Comparisons with others make it possible for children to develop views of themselves as good, adequate or failing in one thing or another, which is the grounding for developing the child's self-esteem (Quinton 2006). *'With proper help and encouragement, they can make sense of these comparisons and learn to see themselves as good at some things and not so good at others at the moment rather than forever'* (Quinton 2006, p.103). Self-esteem usually refers to the global evaluation of one's own worth. A child's level of self-esteem is the discrepancy between the child's ideal self and what the child perceives to be his real self (Bee 2000).

Children in middle childhood see themselves as autonomous and separate individuals from their parents. In general they are at ease with themselves and accept their gender, race and physical attributes. They expect to be liked by both peers and adults, and see adults as dependable and trustworthy (Smith and Cowie 1993). The family is valued and the child knows important members. Their own history intrigues them and there is an interest in photos and stories from earlier years (Fahlberg 1991).

Magical and egocentric thinking characterise this age. Children believe that wishes and ritualised behaviour can make things happen (Fahlberg 1991).

Possible impact on identity

For this age group there are three issues with regard to the impact of parental problems on the child's developing identity: gender, self-esteem and guilt.

> *If parents are unavailable to provide positive reinforcement of who and what their children are, celebrate their skills and express confidence in their potential, or are inconsistent in their responses, it is easy for children to feel rejected, uncertain and undermined.*

(Kroll and Taylor 2003, p.210)

There is some evidence to suggest that the child's relationship to the parent with problems affects the child's self-esteem. Being of the same gender as a parent with a disorder appears to be more traumatising and psychologically distressing than for children of the opposite sex (for domestic violence see Fantuzzo and Lindquist 1989; for mental illness see Rutter and Quinton 1984).

In cases of domestic violence the abusers' relationship to the child may also be pertinent. Qualitative research (Sullivan et al. 2000) suggests children are more affected when domestic violence was perpetrated by the child's biological fathers or stepfathers rather than by a more recent partner. The authors suggest that there *'may be something especially painful in the experience of witnessing one's own father abuse one's own mother'* (p.598).

Children's self-esteem and sense of identity can suffer when parents have a mental illness, learning disability, problems with substance misuse or domestic violence. For example, children living with domestic violence are shown to have lower self-esteem than children who do not (Onyskiw 2003). Other research suggests children of this age who live with a mentally ill parent have a more negative self-image and poorer self-esteem than their peers. Svedin and colleagues' (1996) longitudinal study of 156 pregnant women in Sweden found that by the age of 8 years, children of mothers categorised as 'mentally insufficient' (this included both psychiatric illness and learning disabilities) were faring less well than children in the reference group. More recent research showed similar findings; social workers reported problems in relation to identity for the majority of children aged 5 to 9 years who were living with a parent with a learning disability (Cleaver and Nicholson 2007).

There is considerable evidence which suggests that when parental problems coincide with other stressors, parents' capacity to value a child's inherent differences is much greater (Aldridge and Becker 2003; Cleaver and Walker with Meadows 2004). In the following case it was clear that a number of issues were affecting the parents' capacity to help their children develop a sense of self. Seven-year-old Paul lived with two sisters and a brother, his depressed and learning-disabled mother and his stepfather who had an alcohol problem. The social worker described the difficulties.

> *Parents do not appear to understand the importance of recognising the individuality of their children nor the extra effort they should be making due to mother's special needs, lack of birth father, poor relationship with step dad and the arrival of a new baby girl.*

(Cleaver and Nicholson 2007, p.75)

Experiencing domestic violence or seeing parents who appear unable to control themselves or their circumstances may leave children of this age group feeling helpless and confused.

> *I was really scared when I first heard my Mum and Dad shouting. I was afraid to go downstairs, and when I realised it was a fight I didn't know what to do. I tried to forget all about it and go to sleep, but I couldn't because of all the things in my head. I didn't know what to do – should I say something, stand up and speak out, or lay here and let it unfold? One night I went downstairs but they told me to go back to my room, and when I woke up the next morning it was all back to normal again. I didn't know what to do...*

(Silas aged 11 years, quoted in Barron 2007, p.13)

Children's sense of helplessness and low self-esteem is compounded when the perpetrator of the violence and controlling behaviour also targets them.

> *My father did not let me sit on the sofa with my brother, I had to sit on the floor. When he got angry he held my head in the toilet.*

(Seven-year-old boy, quoted in Greenwich Asian Women's Project 1996)

A third problem is that children may assume they are responsible for their parents' actions. It is commonly reported that children of substance-misusing parents, or whose parents are violent to each other, feel that they are somehow at fault for what is happening. Children may believe that what they do triggers their parents' drinking, drug use or violence, or that they should be able to find a way of stopping it. Children's ways of coping included attempts to shut out the exposure to the traumatic episode and wishful thinking (Joseph et al. 2006). *'I wished this horrible situation would go away'* (young girl, quoted in Joseph et al. 2006, p.32). To try and stop their parents' drinking, drug use or violence children may use *'methods containing a magical element, for example finding exactly the right words'* (Brisby et al. 1997, p.11).

Doyle illustrates well the belief in the magical quality of words.

> *People were talking, kind of shouting. I stopped. It was cold...*
>
> *The television was on; that meant my Ma and Da weren't in bed. They were still downstairs. It wasn't burglars in the kitchen...*
>
> *– Stop.*
>
> *I only whispered it.*
>
> *For a while I thought it was only Da, shouting in the way people did when they were trying not to, but sometimes forgot; a bit like screamed whispers...*
>
> *But Ma was shouting as well...*
>
> *I did it again.*
>
> *– Stop.*
>
> *There was a gap. It had worked; I'd forced them to stop.*

(Doyle 1994, p.42)

Children may also feel inadequate and guilty when they are unable to prevent or stop their parents' violence, drinking or drug abuse. *'One time, I tried to stop him from hitting her, and he nearly hit me ... so I never tried after that...'* (child, quoted in Joseph et al. 2006, p.37).

The extent to which children blame themselves for their parents' problems seems to depend on parents' ability to help children recognise that the problems lie with themselves rather than with the child. For example, Christensen (1997) found that children were more likely to feel guilty about parents' problem drinking if parents denied the problem. But difficulties can arise because parents may find it hard to know how to talk to children and feel too upset themselves to talk about their problems (Gorin 2004). However, not all studies found evidence of children blaming themselves for their parents' problems (Hill et al. 1996; Laybourn et al. 1996).

The notion that children sometimes feel responsible for their parent's drinking is not surprising, as the partners of adults with drink or drug problems often say the same thing.

> *Many family members, and especially parents, ask themselves if something they have done has caused drug/alcohol use, and commonly experience guilt. Many regret past actions or reactions.*

(ADFAM 2010)

Family and social relationships

Expected relationships

Children in middle childhood enjoy physical closeness and generally have a confiding relationship with a parent. They may have difficulty talking about their feelings and find it easier to discuss them in retrospect.

Children in this age group have developed the ability to understand time, which means they can cope well with short separations from a parent.

Peers are increasingly important and friends are valued for their physical attributes. At this age children develop the ability to put themselves in the shoes of others and understand the impact their behaviour may have on other people. As a result, children are able to sustain friendships and to function within a group. School-age children gradually develop a collection of reciprocal friendships – pairs in which each child names the other as a friend (Bee 2000).

Possible impact on relationships

The main problems for children are inconsistent parental behaviour which may cause anxiety and faulty attachments, fear of hostility and feelings of helplessness, and unplanned separation. In some cases children assume a role beyond their years.

A major problem for children is that mental illness, learning disability, problem alcohol or drug use or the psychological consequences of domestic violence can cause parents to behave in inconsistent and unexpected ways. This is difficult for children to understand, and as one 9-year-old boy said to his problem-drinking mother *'I didn't know whether you loved me'* (quoted in Brisby et al. 1997, p.14).

A second issue for children is the fear and helplessness in the face of parental violence.

> *(My daughter) would just sit there frozen, I mean, she didn't know what to do because if she got up to move ... he would maybe have gone for her. So she was just, like, sitting there, trembling and crying and stuff.*
>
> (Mother, quoted in NCH Action for Children 1994, p.36)

The child's fear may also be the result of anticipated hostility. In situations of domestic violence or parental substance misuse, children may find that the everyday aspects of their lives are subjected to a frightening and pervasive control.

A third issue is the undermining of the parent–child relationship. Children's expectations of their parents for care and protection are not always met, and they can feel betrayed, let down and angry.

> *I used to feel angry like when my mum was on drugs 'cos I used to think how could this have happened to me, it was just sad all the time and then I would get angry ... and we would have arguments all the time...*
>
> (Eleven-year-old child of drug-using parents, quoted in Barnard 2007, p.91)

The parent–child relationship can also be undermined when, in cases of domestic violence, male perpetrators insist that children witness their mothers' abuse; 10% of women interviewed in McGee's (2000) study reported that they had been raped with their children present. Many mothers exposed to domestic violence reported that it had eroded their self-esteem and left them with little confidence in their own parenting abilities.

> *He (my partner) always used to say I was a bad mother ... my way of coping was to start drinking, not to the level of an alcoholic, but it wasn't very good ... he used to tell everyone how awful I was.*
>
> (Mother, quoted in NCH Action for Children 1994, pp.45–46)

To see their mother sexually assaulted and humiliated undermines the relationship between mother and child, not to mention the impact on fathering (Humphreys 2006).

I am mad with my daddy for hurting my mummy and me and my sisters and brother...

(Tara 8 years, quoted in Barron 2007, p.14)

Sometimes, y'know, I get really angry with my father ... I just want him to go and never come back.

(Child, quoted in Joseph et al. 2006, p.36)

Children, even at this young age, may try to protect or look after the parent. For example, they may call the police or doctor, adopt a caring role or mediate between warring parents (Dobash and Dobash 1984; Hamner 1989; Cleaver and Nicholson 2007). *'At the age of eight I became like my daddy's wife, not in a sexual way but in all the other things'* (quoted in Brisby et al. 1997, p.14). Children of parents who are having problems with mental health, drugs or alcohol use, domestic violence and learning disability may assume many adult responsibilities and consequently miss out on their childhood, neglect school work, have erratic school attendance and be prevented from making friends with children of their own age.

Parental mental illness, particularly depression, is also associated with increased levels of hostility directed at children. Panaccione and Wahler (1986) found a strong association between the mothers' depressive symptoms and hostile child-directed behaviour which included shouting and slapping.

Siblings can be an enormous support for children when parents have problems. In particular, children identify brothers and sisters as key sources of support and comfort, the people they could rely on when things are not going well (McGee 2000; Velleman and Orford 2001; Maybery et al. 2005).

Relatives, particularly grandparents, can also provide children and families with emotional and practical support (McGee 2000). The help and support of the extended family has been identified as an important factor in ensuring the welfare of children, particularly those who live with parents with learning disabilities (Booth and Booth 1997; McGee 2000; Cleaver and Nicholson 2007; Cleaver et al. 2007).

The grandmother has a primary role, and with the children of school going age, in a lot of cases they are responsible for the child going to school ... They also make sure that the child has a good meal, that it's not just a packet of crisps.

(Child care worker in a drug treatment clinic, quoted in Hogan and Higgins 2001, p.25)

Children value greatly their friends, and play is used as an escape from the pressures of home. *'...I wouldn't say anything [about the domestic violence], but when we're playing I forget all of this [the abuse] for a while'* (child, quoted in Joseph et al. 2006, p.32). Research has shown the value of same-age friendships for vulnerable children; they can play a key supportive role and children with a friend suffer less loneliness than those without (Cleaver 2000; Dunn 2004).

But not all children have this opportunity for friendships. Research suggests children who grow up with domestic violence have poorer peer relationships and often suffer peer rejection. Bullying is also a feature identified by many children of parents with learning disabilities, mental illness and domestic violence (Aldridge and Becker 2003; Department of Health and Department for Education and Skills 2007; Holt et al. 2008). This may be the result of an impaired ability to handle frustration and regulate emotions. These children appear more likely to lack effective problem-solving skills and conflict resolution strategies (Onyskiw 2003; Holt et al. 2008).

Few children of this age discuss family problems with friends or relatives because they fear disbelief, separation, or negative repercussions for themselves and/or their parents. Boys in particular may find it harder than girls to talk about parental problems and difficulties within the home. *'If Daddy finds out that I told anyone, he might hit me too … I was scared he would hurt me too'* (girl, quoted in Joseph et al. 2006, p.35).

Moreover, children are acutely aware of social stigma and sense that mental illness, learning disability, alcohol or drug misuse and domestic violence should not be talked about, even when parents have not explicitly told them not to do so (Humphreys and Mullender 1999; Aldridge and Becker 2003; Gorin 2004). For example, Karr (1995) describes the shame experienced by a 6-year-old girl whose parents were violent towards one another.

> *I felt like the neighbours' stares had bored so many imaginary holes in our walls that the whole house was rotten as wormy wood. I never quite got over thinking that folks looked at us funny on mornings after Mother and Daddy had fought.*
> (Karr 1995, p.39)

A fear of ridicule keeps many children from discussing their family with friends. For example, when one little girl was asked if she ever talked about what was happening at home her response was *'No! My friends will think my family is screwed up. I wouldn't be able to face them if they knew'* (quoted in Joseph et al. 2006, p.35).

Although children tend to protect their parents by erecting a wall of silence, they are more likely to open up and talk about difficulties at home when they perceive an adult, such as their teacher or school nurse, to be approachable, trustworthy, non-judgemental and willing to listen to what they have to say (Daniel et al. 2009).

Unfortunately, childhood friendships and the support of wider family and professionals may be disrupted because families flee their home and neighbourhood as a result of unpaid drug-related debts, evictions, or to escape a violent partner; unplanned moves were also a common feature in the lives of children who live with parents with learning disabilities (Cleaver and Nicholson 2007). *'He made me leave my home. He made me leave all my best friends. He made me leave all my things behind'* (9-year-old girl, quoted in Mullender et al. 2002, p.108).

Finally, there is the impact on children when separation from an attachment figure is unavoidable. Because children of this age have a greater understanding of time, they are less likely to show the high levels of distress expected from younger children. *'Nonetheless, if parents' departure seems capricious, unexplained, unacceptable or frightening in context, separation anxiety will be manifest'* (Rutter and Rutter 1992, p.113).

Social presentation

Expected presentation

Children of this age generally appear well cared for and are appropriately dressed. Children can make themselves understood by people outside the family and many of those without verbal ability have begun to use a form of non-verbal communication.

In general, children have learnt appropriate social skills and can adjust their behaviour and conversation to suit an increasingly wide range of situations including with peers, teachers and family.

Possible impact on social presentation

The main impact of parental problems confronting children of this age group is feelings of shame, embarrassment, fear of ridicule and social isolation.

Mental illness, learning disability, problem drinking or drug use or the effects of domestic violence may cause apathy and low self-esteem, which may result in parents struggling to exert sufficient authority to ensure that children behave appropriately and their appearance is acceptable. *'Jade's (aged 10 years) hygiene continues to be poor and in the home bath nights are Tuesdays, Thursdays and Sundays, but Jade will not co-operate'* (social worker's report, quoted in Cleaver and Nicholson 2007, p.74).

Parents' problems can cause children shame and embarrassment (McGee 2000; Mullender et al. 2002). For example, some caring responsibilities, particularly undertaking intimate care tasks, can embarrass children.

> *Sometimes I help her to get dressed and undressed to go to bed, if she goes to bed before me … it's slightly embarrassing helping your mum when she hasn't exactly got clothes on.*

(Dearden and Becker 1996, p.22)

Children want to belong to ordinary families. When parents' problems lead them to behave in unpredictable or embarrassing ways, children want to keep it secret. The description in Deane's book of his early childhood experiences of living with a mentally ill mother offers a touching description of such childhood anxiety.

> *We were all frightened. Also, I was ashamed. When I saw her wandering around the house, touching the walls, tracing out the scrolls of varnish on the sitting-room door with her finger, or climbing wearily up the stairs to gaze out of the window,*

*my cheeks burnt and the semi-darkness seemed to be full of eyes. She was going
out from us, becoming strange, becoming possessed, and I didn't want anyone else
outside the family to know or notice.*

(Deane 1997, pp.140–141)

A consequence of this wish to keep the family's distress and disintegration hidden
is that children are less willing to risk social encounters. Friendships and social
interaction are restricted. Often families, including children, adopt roles to try to
control and deal with the difficult behaviour of the drug- or alcohol-using parent.
These roles may seem to be a way of coping but can be destructive.

Keeping information about parents' difficulties contained within the family is not
always possible, or indeed wise. Sadly, when information leaks out children's fear of
discrimination and stigma can become a reality.

*...They were picking on me because they just thought, I think they thought that
I was different and that's it. Sometimes like they start saying 'Look at your mum
she's got bad problems and she...', stuff I can't repeat, it gets me really upset. They
kept on saying that she was a tramp.*

(Girl aged 11 years, quoted in Aldridge and Becker 2003, p.81)

Self-care skills

Expected self-care skills

Children of this age will be able to help adults or older siblings with household
chores. Similarly, children are able to help look after younger siblings or assist in
the care of sick or disabled parents. However, children between the ages of 5 and 10
years are still too young to adequately shoulder the parental role and an adult should
always retain responsibility for their own and their children's care.

Possible impact on self-care skills

While all children help their parents in a range of ways, when parents' problems are
severe children may be expected to assume too much responsibility for themselves
and others within the family.

Charles (aged 10 years) *is a resilient boy, but he was having to behave like a much
older child: he had to look after himself, take responsibility for getting to school
and to generally care for himself because of his dad's serious drinking. Dad was
unable to offer reasonable parenting ... The son and father had in effect changed
roles – Charles had become the carer, with Dad the dependent person.*

(Social worker, quoted in Cleaver et al. 2007, p.205)

Parental problems may mean that children have to grow up quickly and take
responsibility for a parent who may often be unwell, incapacitated or in danger

(Kroll and Taylor 2003; Maybery et al. 2005). For example, in cases of domestic violence children may assume the role of protector.

> *Sam (9 years) took responsibility for protecting their mother from assaults by telephoning the police from a public call box, or by shouting until the neighbours came to help.*

(A case study of domestic violence, quoted in Brandon and Lewis 1996)

When children grow up with parents with learning disabilities, the eldest child may assume a major caring role.

> *Three of the four children in this family are severely disabled and the older child [James aged 10 years] is acting as carer. Mother has learning disabilities. There has been a long history of domestic violence and mum has been assaulted by dad. There is also a history of dad's misuse of alcohol, which is associated with the domestic violence.*

(Social worker, quoted in Cleaver and Nicholson 2007, p.52)

Although children may find caring for parents and young siblings burdensome and wish for help and support, many do not wish to relinquish this role, and describe their relationship with their parents in very positive terms. As Gorin (2004) points out, *'The strength of children's love and loyalty to their parent comes across in many children's accounts. Children and young people often want to be able to help their parents in any way they can'* (p.29).

To sum up

Key problems for children aged 5–10 years

- An increased risk of physical injury; children may show symptoms of extreme anxiety and fear.

- Academic attainment may be negatively affected and children's behaviour in school can become problematic.

- Identity, age and gender may affect outcomes. Boys more quickly exhibit problematic behaviour but girls are also affected if parental problems endure.

- Poor self-esteem; children may blame themselves for their parents' problems.

- Inconsistent parental behaviour may cause anxiety and faulty attachments.

- Unplanned separation can cause distress and disrupt education and friendship patterns.

- Embarrassment and shame over parents' behaviour. As a consequence children may curtail friendships and social interaction.

- The assumption of too much responsibility for themselves, their parents and younger siblings.

Protective factors

- The cognitive ability to rationalise drug and alcohol problems in terms of illness. This enables children to accept and cope with parents' behaviour more easily.

- The presence of an alternative, consistent caring adult who can respond to the cognitive and emotional needs of children.

- Sufficient income support and good physical standards in the home.

- Regular supportive help from a primary health care team and social services and community-based resources, including respite care and accommodation.

- Regular attendance at school.

- Positive school climate and sympathetic, empathic and vigilant teachers.

- Attendance at school medicals.

- An alternative, safe and supportive residence for mothers and children subject to violence and the threat of violence.

- Peer acceptance and friendship.

- A supportive older sibling.

- An effective anti-bullying policy within schools.

- Social networks outside the family, especially with a sympathetic adult of the same sex.

- Belonging to organised, out-of-school activities, including homework clubs.

- Being taught different ways of coping and being sufficiently confident to know what to do when parents are incapacitated.

- An ability to separate, either psychologically or physically, from the stressful situation.

Identified unmet developmental needs in middle childhood

Finally, a re-analysis of data on children referred to children's social care (Cleaver et al. 2007 and Cleaver and Nicholson 2007) was undertaken for children aged 5 to 9 years.[11]

Table 5.1: **Proportion of children with identified unmet needs – middle childhood**

Dimension	Parental substance misuse n=40	Parental learning disability n=10	Domestic violence n=43
Health	27%	89%	27%
Education	57%	78%	33%
Emotional and behavioural development	56%	67%	55%
Identity and social presentation	39%	89%	35%
Family and social relationships	69%	100%	63%

The findings, shown in Table 5.1, show that a greater proportion of children living with domestic violence or parental substance misuse experience unmet needs in relation to their emotional and behavioural development and with regard to family and social relationships. It is also of concern that over half the children (57%) living with parental substance misuse also had unmet needs with regard to their education. Although numbers are very small, the pattern is not replicated for children living with parents with learning disabilities, indeed the figures suggested they are more likely to have unmet needs in relation to every aspect of their development. The extent of their vulnerability is also highlighted when considering severe needs.

Children were classified as having severe unmet needs when social workers identified developmental needs in three or more of the five dimensions. The data show a similar but more extreme pattern to that found for younger children. A smaller proportion of children living with parental substance misuse or domestic violence had severe developmental needs compared with those living with a parent

---

[11] All information given in this section on the impact of parental disorders on children's developmental needs is the result of a re-analysis of data: Cleaver and Nicholson 2007 and Cleaver et al. 2007. The research did not cover children living with mentally ill parents and, consequently, such detailed information is not available.

UNIVERSITY OF WINCHESTER
LIBRARY

with learning disabilities. Forty-one per cent of children aged 5 to 9 years living with parental substance misuse had severe developmental needs and 35% of children living with domestic violence. However, practically all children in middle childhood (90%) met the criteria for severe developmental needs when living with a parent with learning disabilities.

6 Child development and parents' responses – adolescence

Chapter 6 focuses on adolescence and includes two sections. The first looks at children aged 11 to 15 years and the second young people aged 16 years and over, and as for all age groups the information is research-based. Although there is considerable information for children up to the age of 15 years, less is known about the needs and experiences of older adolescents.

The same format used for younger children is followed here. The expected development for the age group is covered prior to exploring the possible consequences of parental mental illness, learning disability, problem substance use and domestic violence. Summary points at the end of each age group identify the key problems and the protective factors.

Children aged 11–15 years

Health

Expected health

Children and young people should have regular medical and dental checks. Immunisations need to be up to date: BCG for all those at risk of tuberculosis and immunisation against rubella for girls.

The body changes which take place at this age can confuse and distress children. The main health concerns for teenagers are those related to appearance such as skin and weight issues, and those linked to sexual health including contraception (Gleeson, Robinson and Neal 2002). For example, some girls dislike the changes puberty brings and seek to reverse them through dieting. One in every 150 fifteen year old girls in the United Kingdom is affected by anorexia nervosa (Royal College of Psychiatrists 2008). The rate is negligible among teenage boys. However, most adolescents generally eat a sufficiently balanced diet to ensure their physical development. Of greater concern are the rising levels of obesity among this age group. Around one in four 11- to 15-year-olds is considered obese. This is an increase for the period 1995 to 2004 from 14% to 24% for boys and from 15% to 26% for girls (NHS Information Centre 2006).

Health needs for this age group are mainly due to chronic illness and mental health problems. A survey of children's mental health suggested 11% of children aged 11–16 years have a mental disorder, with boys (13%) being more at risk of experiencing poor mental health than girls (10%) (Green et al. 2005).

Between the ages of 11 and 14 years some children experiment with their first sexual encounter. Children need accurate factual knowledge about puberty, sex and contraception. The conception rate for girls aged 13–15 in 2009 was 7.5 per thousand girls (Department for Education 2011). Although the rate of teenage pregnancy in England is on the decline, it remains one of the highest in Europe. Teenage pregnancy is associated with higher rates of infant mortality and increased low birth weight. Moreover, teenage mothers are three times more likely to suffer from postnatal depression, and teen parents and their children are at greater risk of living in poverty. The Government's strategy for public health aims to strengthen young people's ability to *'take control of their lives, within clear boundaries, and help reduce their susceptibility to harmful influences, in areas such as sexual health, teenage pregnancy, drugs and alcohol'* (Cm 7985 2010, p.35, paragraph 3.17).

Teenagers are also likely to experiment in other ways. For example, a survey in 2009 of 7674 secondary-school pupils (11 to 15 years) in 247 schools in England found that 6% were regular cigarette smokers (defined as smoking at least one cigarette a week). A lower proportion than at any time since pupil smoking was first surveyed in 1982. The likelihood of smoking was strongly related to age. At 11 years, less than 0.5% of children were regular smokers, but this figure steadily increased and by 15 years 15% of youngsters admitted to being regular smokers. In comparison with the early 1980s, when boys and girls were equally likely to smoke, a higher proportion of girls now smoke than boys. In 2009, 7% of girls were regular smokers, compared with 5% of boys. Compared to white pupils, those of mixed ethnicity and black pupils were less likely to be regular smokers (Fuller and Sanchez 2010).

The proportion of young people drinking or using drugs shows a similar decline. The 2009 survey (Fuller and Sanchez 2010) found 51% of pupils admitted to having ever drunk alcohol, a fall from the 61% noted in the 2003 survey. A decline was also recorded in the number of pupils who admitted having had an alcoholic drink in the previous week – 18% as opposed to 26% found in the 2001 survey. The likelihood of alcohol consumption was related to age; only 3% of 11-year-olds had drunk alcohol in the previous week compared to 38% of 15 year olds. There is no significant difference overall in the proportion of boys and girls who drink. White pupils were more likely to have drunk alcohol recently than those from minority ethnic groups (Fuller and Sanchez 2010).

The 2009 survey also showed drug use among this age group was on the decline. In 2009, 22% of pupils aged 11–15 admitted ever using drugs (compared to 29% in 2001) and 15% to having taken any drugs in the last year (again a fall from the 20% in 2001). More problematic use, i.e. drugs used in the previous month, had also fallen in the same period, from 12% to 8%. Boys are more likely to have taken drugs than girls, (16% and 14% in the last year respectively). Drug use increases with age; for example in the year prior to the survey 4% of children aged 11 years had taken drugs compared to 30% of 15 year olds. Sniffing volatile substances was more popular among 11- and 12-year-old pupils than taking cannabis, whereas the reverse was true for older pupils (Fuller and Sanchez 2010).

Accidental physical injuries among this age group are commonplace because many children participate in sports and physical activities.

Children with permanent hearing loss or physical disability which interferes with verbal communication should be using a form of signing. Those who have a health condition need information about it and opportunities to talk about how it affects them.

Possible impact on health

There are several ways in which children's health may be affected by their parents' problems. The first is that youngsters have to cope with puberty without support. Second, there is an increased risk of psychological problems. Third, there is a risk of physical abuse and neglect: a risk of actually being hurt, the fear of being hurt or anxiety about how to compensate for physical neglect.

The first issue is that youngsters may be left to cope alone with the physical changes which accompany the onset of puberty. The emotional unavailability which can accompany parental mental illness, learning disability, problem drinking and drug use or domestic violence may mean that parents are unaware of children's worries about their changing bodies (Advisory Council on the Misuse of Drugs 2003). Moreover, parents may be so absorbed in their own problems that little attention is given to ensuring that children attend routine medical and dental appointments.

Parents with learning disabilities may not understand the physical changes that result from puberty and fail to educate, support or protect their children.

> *Cathy (15 years) has little knowledge of sex and contraception. Has previously received treatment for two sexually transmitted diseases. Cathy's understanding of her own health and safety is limited and her mother appears to have a similar low understanding.*
>
> (Social work case notes on Cathy whose mother has a learning disability, quoted in Cleaver and Nicholson 2007, p.89)

Parental mental illness does not appear to affect children's physical health (Somers 2007). However, research which focused on the mental health of children and young people found that approximately a quarter of parents of children with conduct or emotional disorder had a serious mental illness, compared to 7% of parents whose children did not (Green et al. 2005). This is in line with earlier research which found an association between parental depression and psychological symptoms in adolescents. The risk of major depression at this age was found to increase linearly if both parents were psychiatrically ill compared to only one or neither parent having a psychiatric illness (Weissman et al. 1984).

Research suggests that parental drug and alcohol misuse increases the likelihood of children having a problem with alcohol and drugs. For example, children aged 11–12 years used more alcohol, cannabis and tobacco if their parents had drug or alcohol problems. Parental problem drug and alcohol use also made children more susceptible to peer influence; if parents were abstinent it decreased the influence of peers (Li et al. 2002). A similar relationship was found in a large-scale Finnish study which focused on 15-year-old children (Seljamo et al. 2006). Finally, research would suggest that mothers' prenatal cannabis and tobacco use increased the chance of their children using cannabis at age 14 years (Day et al. 2006). A longitudinal Canadian study reported similar findings in relation to prenatal cannabis use but also showed this was more strongly associated with male rather than female offspring (Porath and Fried 2005). But the relationship is complex, and most children of parents with substance misuse problems do not themselves become problem drinkers or drug users (Velleman 1993). For some children, growing up observing the devastating impact that problematic drugs or alcohol use had on their family was a sufficient deterrent.

> *Never, never in my life, no ... no way, after what happened with my mum and dad, no way, nothing, I'd never touch nothing. I know a lot of folk just say that, but from experience, like what's happened; never ever.*

(Child of problem drug-using parents, quoted in Barnard 2007, p.131)

Adolescents may be at risk of physical assaults when parental problems result in violence and unpredictable behaviour. Children report *'the fear of constant arguments, actual physical violence or the threat of it, either to a parent (usually the mother) or to themselves and, at times, fear of sexual abuse'* (Kroll and Taylor 2003, p.169). Three out of five children with a problem-drinking father and two out of five with a problem-drinking mother spoke of their own physical abuse (ChildLine 1997). A non-drinking parent may not always be able to protect the child because the parent with the alcohol problem may assault both the child and the non-drinking parent. *'Dad gets drunk every day, he hits me and Mum ... we don't provoke him ... he broke my arm once'* (Tracy aged 12, quoted in ChildLine 1997, p.23). When parents fail to protect the child it may undermine the child's confidence in, and respect for, the parent concerned.

Adolescents may also be at risk of physical harm if they are routinely left in the care of the drinking or drug-misusing parent. This can engender feelings of betrayal and not being cared about.

> *Mum works at night. Dad comes home drunk and beats me up. I dread the nights.*

(Jane aged 12, quoted in ChildLine 1997, p31)

In situations of domestic violence children may get injured when they try to protect one parent from the other.

> *Joanne (13) said that her mum's partner hits her mum all the time. The last time it happened Joanne went to help her mum but she was also beaten.*
> (Quoted in ChildLine 1997, p.35)

Finally, adolescents may feel anxious about how to compensate for the physical neglect they are experiencing. Research shows that when parents' problem drinking or drug use absorbs most of the family's income, children are fearful that they will go without basic necessities such as food and clothing (ChildLine 1997).

Parental neglect, in the form of inadequate supervision, is related to an increased likelihood that young people will engage in risky behaviour outside the home, such as drug taking, which will endanger their health. This is exacerbated if the young people are also living in poor neighbourhoods where the availability of alcohol and drugs is higher than average (Stein et al. 2009).

Education and cognitive ability

Expected education

Most parents recognise the importance of education and school attendance and their commitment to their child's education is reflected in attending school events such as parents' evenings and meetings. The majority of adolescents go to school regularly and absence is unusual for this age group. Schagen and colleagues' (2004) study for the National Audit Office, based on data obtained from 3,078 secondary schools in England, showed that for the year 2002/3 the average attendance rate was 91.6%; a similar rate was found in Scotland (Scottish Government 2009). Absence from school can be for a variety of reasons with illness being the most common. Less than 1% (0.7%) of non-attendance in English schools was unauthorised, and although overall attendance is improving, the rate of unauthorised absence remains steady (National Audit Office 2005). The 2009 practice guidance for schools on setting educational targets included targeting absenteeism in secondary schools (Department for Children, Schools and Families 2009).

GCSE options are generally chosen during year group 9 (when children are aged 13 years) and course work started the next year. Homework is the norm and children need encouragement, relative quiet and a suitable place to study. When the children's school work is not commensurate with their ability or there are other school-related problems, most parents or carers take appropriate action. Parents and teachers are usually aware if a child has special educational needs and ensure the relevant resources are available.

Bullying is not uncommon at this age. A survey of 12 English schools found 28% of secondary-school pupils in year 8 reported *'that they had been bullied during the term'* (Oliver and Candappa, 2003, p.6). Occasional bullying of others was reported by 8% of children of this age and 1.7% admitted to regular bullying (Smith and Thompson 1991).

Learning does not only take place at school. Many children are involved in out-of-school activities such as football, boxing, swimming or playing music.

Possible impact on educational and cognitive ability

The negative impact of parental mental illness, learning disability, problem alcohol or drug use, or domestic violence on youngsters' education results from a lack of parental support; an inability to concentrate; performing below expected ability; and missing school because of the need to look after parents or siblings.

Parental problems can result in parents not attending meetings and other school events or failing to support and encourage learning at home. Parental involvement in the form of interest in the child, particularly parent–child discussions, has been shown to have a positive effect on children's behaviour and achievement, irrespective of factors such as social class or family size (Desforges with Abouchaar 2003). The opposite is also true and an overview of the available research suggests that parental neglect is associated with adolescents and young people having poorer educational engagement, conduct and achievement in school (Stein et al. 2009).

The impact on children's education and academic competence is varied. Children of parents with learning disabilities, mental illness, alcohol or drug problems and domestic violence are more likely to develop problems at school, including learning difficulties, loss of concentration and general poor performance (for parental alcohol misuse, see Velleman and Orford 2001; Girling et al. 2002; for learning disability, see Cleaver and Nicholson 2007; for parental substance misuse and domestic violence, see Cleaver et al. 2007 and Barnard 2007; for parental mental illness, see Downey and Coyne 1990). Education and learning may also be impaired because family problems preoccupy the child's thinking.

> *I can't get on with my work at school because I'm always thinking about what's going on at home ... Mum drinks and Dad left.*
>
> (Sam 11 years, quoted in ChildLine 1997, p.37)

In contrast, other children and some parents see school as a source of help and a sanctuary from problems at home (Joseph et al. 2006). For this group school is the one area of their lives which is 'normal' and academic or sports achievement and school friends are viewed as an escape route. Indeed, one US study of the children of opiate users found practically three-quarters of the children participated in after-school activities and a similar proportion received academic awards (Kolar et al. 1994).

I always remember thinking like she's got to get to school, she's got to get to school because I knew she'd get her dinner there and she'd be away, she wouldn't really see anything during the day.

(Parent, quoted in Barnard 2007, p.69)

Although teenagers may value school and learning, their education may be interrupted because they feel impelled to stay at home to look after a sick or incapable parent or younger siblings (Aldridge and Becker 2003).

Anthony said that he is left to look after his baby brother. He hasn't been to school all week.

(Quoted in ChildLine 1997, p.24)

Others were frightened for the safety of their parent and stayed at home or missed classes.

Because I was scared in case, like, he battered her and she went away and then I went home and she wasnae there and it was just me left and him. Ye ken what I mean? So I was scared.

(Girl, quoted in Stafford et al. 2007, p.13)

In recent years awareness of the roles and responsibilities of young carers has been raised within schools and as a result there has been an overall decrease in the incidence of educational difficulties. A national survey of young carers shows missing school or experiencing educational difficulties fell from 42% of young carers of secondary-school age in 1995 to 27% in 2003 (Dearden and Becker 2004). The survey also revealed that young carers who were looking after a relative with drug or alcohol problems were more likely to experience educational difficulties; 40% were missing school or had other indicators of educational difficulties. Many young carers believe that looking after a parent meant they lost opportunities for learning which subsequently limited their horizons (Edwards and Smith 1997). The majority of young carers don't want to relinquish their role but do want support to enable them to attend school regularly and participate in extra-curricular activities. Targeted Youth Support provided practice guidance and a toolkit aimed at ensuring that the needs of vulnerable teenagers were identified early and met by agencies working together effectively in ways shaped by the views and experiences of young people (Department for Children, Schools and Families 2008). Finally, parental problems can result in families having to move to a new neighbourhood, resulting in a change of school. This can cause an interruption in learning, missed course work, and loss of friends, familiar teachers and community.

[I've moved] about eight times ... went to eight different schools. Whenever I went into a school, they'd either be like behind me or ahead of me, so I'd either have to wait for them or catch up or stuff like that, em, with my work but I found it hard

having to make new pals all the time, really, I couldn't handle that, it was just pure nerve-wracking every time I went to a new school.

(Child of problem drug-using parent, quoted in Barnard 2007, p.86)

Emotional and behavioural development

Expected development

Adolescence is a period when children are striving for independence, which may involve them in conflicts with parents. To be able to experiment and stretch themselves, children of this age need the secure base of close, stable attachments (Daniel et al. 2000).

In early adolescence emotions are frequently unstable and poorly controlled. *'They can fly into a rage at short notice and burst out laughing with little provocation'* (Fahlberg 1991, p.102). There may be considerable strife with parents but on the whole children are loved and trusted, and adults in general are viewed as trustworthy.

Children may assert themselves by talking back to parents, or striking out physically or by throwing things. As children get older, verbal responses become more frequent; as teenagers gain greater control over their emotions they can appear undemonstrative. Physical responses to anger are less common, and increasingly the child resorts to swearing, name calling and sarcasm. Although the teenage years are assumed to be a period of heightened stress, a survey carried out in 1999 found only 11.5% of young people aged 11-15 years had any mental disorder (Meltzer et al 2000).

Scottish-based research suggests 13.8% of young people aged 15–16 years in Scotland admitted to self-harm – a rate in line with that identified for England. Girls were approximately 3.4 times more likely to self-harm than boys. In addition, almost one in four of those who reported self-harm also said they wanted to die (O'Connor et al. 2009).

Leaving children of any age in the sole care of adolescents under the age of 16 is strongly discouraged in Britain. Nonetheless, in many families older siblings occasionally look after younger brothers and sisters. Research from Scandinavian countries suggests some 70% of young children with older siblings have been looked after by them. Although caretaking by older siblings is shown to lack the quality of parental care, both the looked-after child and the caretaker can benefit from the occasional experience (Kosonen 1996).

Adolescent worries and fears tend to centre on school and social issues. Concerns about appearance, friends, exams and performing in public are commonplace. Teenagers may also worry about their health, and minor ailments or blemishes can be interpreted as a crisis.

In addition many teenagers worry about becoming the victims of crime. Around half of 11- to 16-year-olds are victims of crime every year. A school-based survey of secondary-school pupils found that this age group were most likely to be victims of threats (26%), bullying (23%), theft (15%), destruction of property (14%) and physical attacks (13%) (MORI 2004).

Research suggests that teenage males are the most likely group to have been involved in crime (Self and Zealey 2007). A quarter of secondary-school pupils in mainstream schools (26%) said they had committed a criminal offence in the last 12 months: 31% of teenage boys compared with 20% of girls. Offending peaks at 14 years (MORI 2004). Most adolescent offending was minor and carried out in the company of friends.

Possible impact on emotional and behavioural development

There are five major issues for this age group: emotional disturbances, conduct disorders including bullying, sexual abuse, caring responsibilities and denial of own needs and feelings.

The volatility of this age group means that the impact of parental problems, while similar to that at a younger age group, is more intense. Mothers' mental health problems (and in particular depression) may result in teenagers showing more behaviour problems than those whose mothers are well (Downey and Coyne 1990). Parents with poor mental health reported more behavioural problems in their adolescent children than well parents, in particular anger and strange behaviours (Somers 2007). Other research suggests that problems do not only exhibit themselves in terms of conduct disorders (see for example Beardsley et al. 1987; Klein et al. 1988) but can also be manifest in emotional disturbances (see for example Lee and Gotlib 1989).

Domestic violence may also lead to both emotional and behavioural problems for adolescents. The reports of children illustrate the emotional impact of experiencing domestic violence. Alexander and colleagues' (2005) survey of 254 secondary pupils found that of those experiencing domestic abuse, a fifth (21%) reported feelings of fear, 15% sadness, 10% felt lonely and isolated and 9% suicidal. Others reported different feelings including anger, worthlessness and depression, 'like they're going mad', worry or helplessness.

Although girls are more likely to turn their feelings of anger onto themselves, boys are more likely to express anger outwardly. For example, when having witnessed domestic violence boys may wish to carry out retaliatory acts of violence towards the perpetrator. *'I want to catch him alone ... and I want to hit him hard ... break all his teeth...'* (12-year-old boy, quoted in Joseph et al. 2006, p.31).

When children feel things are out of control, their aberrant behaviour is frequently a cry for help. Booth and Booth's (1997) study of the adult children of parents with learning disabilities found widespread experience of social isolation, victimisation and problems at school, including being suspended, truancy, frequent punishment, being bullied and having few friends. Children want adults to recognise the difficulties they are experiencing and help them sort things out, as the following illustration shows.

> *Did go through a time when I was cutting myself when I was about 13 or 14. At the time mum was struggling and getting annoyed with the social worker – someone telling her how to run her life. I helped out more than I should. I was getting bullied at school. Had no one to talk to. Was getting really aggressive. Talked to grandma who helped said I must go to school as I was getting mum into trouble. Now I've got friends. Best mate also had trouble with social services – we're now dead close. I now do less around the house Mum does more than she used to.*

> (Girl aged 16 years living with parents with learning disabilities, unpublished interview Cleaver and Nicholson 2007)

A similar experience is reported by Jane (aged 16 years) who lived with her mentally ill father. *'I felt ashamed ... and when someone who was supposed to be my friend told others at school about dad, I then started to get bullied'* (Barnardo's 2005, p.16). As the bullying got worse Jane started to self-harm. An attempt at suicide brought her to the attention of professionals and also introduced her to the Barnardo's Young Carers project, which she valued greatly. Since 1995 when the first national survey of young carers was carried out, the number of young carers' projects has grown rapidly from 36 in 1995 to more than 200 in 2004 enabling many more young people who are looking after a relative to gain the support they need (Dearden and Becker 2004).

Family violence may also result in children exhibiting behavioural problems. Wolfe et al. (1985) found serious behavioural problems were 17 times higher for boys and 10 times higher for girls who witnessed the abuse of their mother than a comparative group who did not. Some children from violent homes may react to frustration with aggression and force. In school and at home this may take the form of bullying, which the child sees as an effective and acceptable way of solving problems.

> *Roger (13 years) and Lucy (6 years) have a poor relationship. His mother explains that he was 'lashing out at her (Lucy), and jumping on top of her, sometimes until she can't breathe, and has to be pulled off'. Mum also said that Lucy is very vulnerable outside the home as she will approach men in cars and talk to them.*

> (Mother and stepfather both with learning disabilities and four children, quoted in Cleaver and Nicholson 2007, p.93)

In addition to findings on bullying, there is evidence from clinical studies of an association between young perpetrators of sexual abuse and childhood experiences of family violence (Monck and New 1996; Bentovim and Williams 1998; Skuse et al. 1998). Research by Skuse and colleagues (1998) found the experience of physical violence, both as victim and as witness, was common among sexually abusing adolescent boys, irrespective of whether or not they had been victims of sexual abuse. But caution must be attached to making simple causal links between being brought up in violent and abusive homes and becoming an abuser (see Morley and Mullender 1994).

The adolescent years are a challenge to most parents, but those with learning disabilities may experience greater difficulty in empathising with their children and understanding the emotional changes they are undergoing. *'When children are more intellectually able than their parents, it can become increasingly difficult for parents to act effectively in making decisions and setting boundaries for the child'* (James 2004, p.34). This can be made much worse when children need support and understanding because they have been exposed to childhood abuse and neglect; parents may have difficulty in managing their child's behaviour and providing the necessary support.

> *My stepfather was sexually assaulting me. He touched me up from 6 years to 14 years. He raped me up the back passage. My mother would not believe me. I reported him to the police but nothing happened. He was also touching up my sister. My mum would not believe us. I wanted my mum to believe me but she loved him that much that she wouldn't.*
>
> (Eighteen-year-old girl, reflecting on her childhood; mother had a learning disability and was herself abused during her childhood, quoted in Cleaver and Nicholson 2007, p.89)

A further problem for children whose parents are unable to look after them adequately is that the normal pace of emotional maturity can be accelerated. For some young carers this results in a loss of childhood. As well as having to take on practical household tasks which are normally carried out by an adult, some adolescents have to assume emotional responsibility for a parent or younger siblings. The national survey of young carers shows 82% provide emotional support (Dearden and Becker 2004).

> *The worst thing about my childhood? I think the fact it was as if she was the child and I was the mum, it was the way it was kind of reversed.*
>
> (Child of drug-using parent, quoted in Barnard 2007, p.93)

Marie (14) describes to ChildLine how she had to look after her mother who was a problem drinker.

> *I have to tell her when to go to bed, I have to undress her. She is covered in cuts and bruises and never knows where she gets them ... She used to be pretty but now she is bloated and lined and looks terrible.*
>
> (Quoted in ChildLine 1997, p.38)

Conflict between the caring role and the child's own needs can lead to feelings of guilt and resentment (Edwards and Smith 1997; Barnett and Parker 1998). Children may be so wrapped up in the needs and feelings of a parent that they find it hard to think or talk about themselves. This preoccupation with their parents can mean that they deny their own needs and feelings (ChildLine 1997). The needs of young carers can be assessed under the Children Act 1989, the Carers (Recognition and Services) Act 1995 or under the Carers and Disabled Children Act 2000. There should, however, be no cause for complacency. A survey of young carers carried out by Dearden and Becker (2004) found only 18% of young carers had received an assessment, with the majority of these having been carried out under the Children Act 1989. The Government's Carers' Strategy acknowledges the role of young carers and the difficulties they may have in identifying themselves *'because of family fears that they will be taken into care or because the young people themselves are concerned about the reaction of others and bullying by their peers'* (HM Government 2010d, p.8, paragraph 103)

Identity

Expected identity

As children reach adolescence they define themselves less and less by what they look like and more and more by what they believe or feel (Bee 2000). For most young people, self-esteem has been shown to change gradually, both on a daily and on a yearly basis. However, a small number of teenagers experience very fluctuating feelings (Smith and Cowie 1993).

As children enter adolescence they frequently question the belief system with which they were brought up. Although, in general, teenagers remain strongly identified with the values of the family, new models provided by a more diverse group such as teachers and peers become increasingly important. With the psychological separation from parents it is likely that family rules, values and expectations will be temporarily opposed. Although at times teenagers can be rebellious and moody they still have a strong need to belong to the family and to be taken seriously (Fahlberg 1991).

Most teenagers remain integrated within the family culture and participate in important family events. Key relatives are generally known and the child understands the make-up of their family and their place in it.

Children of different ethnic origins and cultural groups have an important additional identity task in their adolescent years. Those who have migrated from a country with very dissimilar cultural values face the challenge of reconciling the expectations of their parents' cultural beliefs and their own wish to fit in with the resident teenage culture (Bailey 2006). Generally, adolescents are aware of, and feel comfortable about, their race and ethnic background.

Young people's anxiety about being racially targeted differs depending on their ethnic group. Over half (53%) of Asian young people said they worried about racism compared with 42% of black young people and a quarter of white young people. Fear of racism was greatest among 11-year-olds and declined as children grew older (MORI 2004).

Possible impact on identity

Children's attitudes and behaviours are shaped by their families. Problems for adolescents result from them being rejected by their families and from low self-esteem.

Parents and close relatives act as role models and their values and beliefs are absorbed. This is an age when children begin to question their parents' values and beliefs. Rigid family thinking, which can accompany parental learning disability, or extreme behaviours such as domestic violence or problem drug or alcohol use, may lead to wholesale rejection. Although there is strong evidence to show that problem drinking causes family disharmony which has negative outcomes for children, whether parental drinking causes early drinking problems in children is not clear cut (Velleman and Orford 2001).

Parents with learning disabilities may have greater difficulty in presenting positive role models because illiteracy means they are dependent on their children for sorting out everyday issues.

> *Geoff (social worker) describes mother as a very independent lady, but one who needs considerable support. She is learning disabled with an IQ of about 60, unable to read or write or tell the time, had absolutely no education and when her children were at home she was dependent on them reading letters and other communications.*

(Unpublished interview Cleaver and Nicholson 2007)

The lifestyle of many teenagers of parents with learning disabilities suggests that early negative childhood experiences have left them with very low self-esteem.

> *She had a pregnancy terminated at 14 and after that her school attendance dropped off. She is under educated, has low self confidence and low self esteem. After the termination she was taken to a gynaecologist and was given a contraceptive implant which lasted three years and then Joanne wanted it removed.*

(Unpublished interview Cleaver and Nicholson 2007)

It would be wrong to assume that parental learning disability in itself is the issue. In the majority of cases teenagers of parents with learning disabilities who exhibit problems grew up in families where there were a multitude of difficulties.

When parental problems take precedence within the family, children are more likely to have a poor self-image and low self-esteem.

You feel like you're always put on the second shelf. You feel like you're not number one in your parents' life and that makes you feel horrible ... When you see 'em do drugs long enough you know you're not number one; you know you're always put second. And the drugs are put first...

(Howard Thompson 1998, p.34 – quoted in Kroll and Taylor 2003, p.165)

As with younger children, teenagers may blame themselves for their parents' alcohol or drug use, domestic violence or mental illness.

Sometimes it is [scary] yeah because you think what is really happening in her head? And you know, is it my fault that this is, that she is like this you know, have I done something bad?

(Eleven-year-old Leilah, quoted in Aldridge and Becker 2003, p.91)

Finally, the problems of being a young carer may affect children's self-esteem. Those who take on the role of looking after and supporting a relative often feel stigmatised. They believe they get little recognition, praise or respect for their contribution either from parents or other adults outside the family (Aldridge and Becker 1993). This is supported by research which found that young carers' views rarely informed assessments of their disabled parents (Ofsted 2009) However, many young people who have to care for a parent value the support offered by young carers' projects, particularly the opportunity to share their experiences.

When we thought my mum was the only one, we did all that [caring] you know we was really, really depressed and everything and then we went to Barnardos [young carers project] and, you know, [caring is] very common isn't it?

(Fifteen-year-old Julia, quoted in Aldridge and Becker 2003, p.91)

Family and social relationships

Expected relationships

Early adolescence is a stage when the child starts to gain a degree of autonomy and independence. Time is increasingly spent with friends and most children have at least one 'best friend'. Children of this age have the ability to empathise with others and friends are valued for their personal characteristics rather than solely for their physical attributes.

But independence takes time to accomplish and the self-assured young teenager may quickly dissolve into childish tears and temper tantrums when things don't go according to plan. This see-sawing of emotions can take its toll on relationships with parents. At times these may be turbulent, but regardless of the stage of independence, young teenagers need a caring parent who understands them, offers unqualified love and allows them to retreat into childhood when necessary.

Samantha (quoted by Fahlberg 1991) provides a good illustration of the stresses which are frequently involved in parent–child relationships at this stage.

> *Fourteen-year-old Samantha and her mum have a fairly normal relationship. Occasionally, when Sam's mother has been very supportive of her daughter's feelings, the teenager comments, 'You are the best mum in the world. You understand everything'. Mum replies, 'I'm glad I'm doing a good job, Mums of fourteen-year-olds are supposed to be understanding'. However, just as frequently, when Mum sets limits that her daughter does not like, Sam will scream, 'you don't understand anything'. Calmly Mum responds, 'I'm glad I'm doing a good job. Mothers of fourteen-year-olds aren't supposed to understand everything.*

(Fahlberg 1991, p.111)

Possible impact on relationships

Parental problems can affect every aspect of family and social relationships. Relationships with parents may be poor and parents may be unreliable. Teenagers are cautious of exposing family life to outside scrutiny, fearing ridicule and the possible breakup of the family; as a result friendships are restricted and teenagers can become very isolated.

Relationships between parents and children are affected by their parents' own childhood experiences; positive experiences provide a secure base for good future parent–child relationships. However, a common feature in the lives of parents with learning disabilities is being brought up in care, and/or being the victim of emotional, physical or sexual abuse (James 2004). Moreover, parents with learning disabilities can experience more difficulty in reflecting on these experiences and dealing with them, which as a result may continue to affect their capacity to relate to others, including their own children.

Substance misuse and mental illness may result in episodic or intermittent loss of parenting function. However, it could be argued that the wider social and educational networks of older children and teenagers and their greater experience of their parents' problems may act as protective factors. *'In general older children will be better equipped to cope with their parents' mental illness'* (Falkov 1998, p.57).

In many cases, although parents may want to put their children first, their own pressing problems take priority.

> *And when you've got children dependent on you it's very difficult to answer their needs because you're so wrapped up in your own. I don't want to be, I want to put them first, but I haven't been able to do that...*

(Parent suffering mental illness, quoted in Aldridge and Becker 2003, p.57)

When parents put their own needs above those of their children it can result in feelings of exclusion and worthlessness.

When my mum is using drugs it just makes me feel as if I am here myself – not got anyone else here.

(Jenny 15 years, quoted in Barnard 2007, p.88)

Parents' behaviour may also affect the relationship with their children because children feel let down, angry and embarrassed.

It annoys me and it makes me feel dead hurt, I feel as if I just want to batter her ... The way she just sits about and all that, when she's full of it and she just annoys me and she ... like a pure idiot man ... I pure hate it when she does it and then she tried to deny it and that's one of the worst things I hate about her...

(Jane 14 years, child of problem drug-using parent, quoted in Barnard 2007, p.89)

Witnessing domestic violence can have devastating effects on children's relationship with both their parents. In most cases adolescents express strong disapproval of the behaviour of the abuser. But feelings of anger may be directed at both abuser and abused. For example, children may react angrily towards their abusive father. *'Sometimes, y'know, I get really angry with my father ... I just want him to go and never come back'* (quoted in Joseph et al. 2006, p.36). But they may also feel anger towards their mother for accepting the behaviour. *'I don't know why she stays with him ... I don't understand why she doesn't leave him...'* (quoted in Joseph et al. 2006, p.36). In addition, most children continue to love their parents regardless of their behaviour, thus they are left with ambivalent and conflicting emotions.

Children's accounts of their lives exemplify the paucity of relationships and their unreliability (for maternal depression see Aldridge and Becker 2003; for problem drinking see Velleman and Orford 2001; for drug addiction see Barnard 2007; for learning disability see Cleaver and Nicholson 2007; for domestic violence see Covell and Howe 2009).

Conflict and threats were commonplace, and love or warmth too often given in a drunken haze and felt to be intrusive and unreliable.

(ChildLine 1997, p.32)

Teenagers' friendships can be restricted when parents' unreliable behaviour makes them cautious of exposing their family life to outside scrutiny. Parents who drink excessively, have mental health problems or have a problem with drugs can become a source of embarrassment or shame (Kroll and Taylor 2003; Bancroft et al. 2004). As a result teenagers feel unable to bring friends home, wanting to keep their situation secret and fearing the state their parent might be in. This means that friendships are curtailed or restricted, leading to increasing isolation.

Mum gets drunk and she always leaves me to look after my two brothers. I had friends round one time and she came downstairs naked. All my friends make fun of me at school now.

(Jan, aged 11 years, whose mother had a drink problem, quoted in ChildLine 1997, p.25)

My friends have been there when he's hit my Mum ... I mean, in front of me it's not so bad, but he shouldn't do it in front of my friends.

(Child, quoted in NCH Action for Children 1994, p.39)

Alternatively, the silence about family difficulties may be self-imposed, or children and parents can collude to keep the family secret. In many instances children fear that if their family problems become known they will be stigmatised and their situation will deteriorate (Bancroft et al. 2004). A common fear is that the family will be broken up or that people will reject them. *'I didn't want to tell anyone because I was afraid of what social services would do'* (child's view, reported in Brisby 1997, p.14). Isolation from peers, extended family or outsiders may also be imposed by a parent. *'He says that if we ever tell anyone he will kill us ... I'm scared ... it's getting worse'* (Tracy, aged 12, whose father drank and was violent, quoted in ChildLine 1997, p.23).

By contrast some teenagers were able to use friends and relatives as confidants and sources of support. Research suggests that positive features in one relationship can compensate for negative qualities in another, and mutual friendships are associated with feelings of self-worth (Stocker 1994). US research has also highlighted the importance of friends in counteracting the negative impact of domestic violence on young people's mental health. A study involving 111 adolescents aged 14 to 16 years who had experienced family violence found the perceived support of friends was a significant protective factor (Levendosky et al. 2002).

Teenagers may also cope with the stress of parental neglect or violence by distancing themselves from their parents and home. For example, they may withdraw emotionally by listening to music, reading, playing video games, participating in online virtual worlds or watching TV. Or withdrawal may take a physical form, staying in their room, spending more and more time away from home or running away (Velleman and Orford 2001). The majority of adolescents (approximately 70%) who run away from home believe that their parents or carers do not care about them (Rees and Lee 2005). It must also be acknowledged that although some young people run away to escape the difficulties of home life, others are forced to leave by parents or carers (Rees and Siakeu 2004). Many children in these circumstances have started the pattern of going missing from home in early adolescence; 30% of runaways reported staying away overnight before the age of 13 years and 10% before their 11th birthday. Although the majority stay with friends or relatives, a small proportion (16%) of young people aged 14–16 reported sleeping rough (Rees and

Lee 2005). Children who wander the streets are shown to be very much at risk of detachment from school and involvement in crime (Wade et al. 1998).

The isolation (whether self-imposed or due to parental threats) can leave young people in a particularly vulnerable position. Edwards and Smith (1997) in their study reported that young carers felt there was nobody there for them and that professionals were working exclusively with the adults. They wanted someone to listen to their experiences and understand their difficulties. Despite the practice guidance for a more holistic family approach to assessment, which includes addressing the needs of young carers, research suggests that little has changed. Apart from the support received from young carers' projects, statutory professionals from mental health teams continue to adopt a patient-oriented approach (Aldridge and Becker 2003).

Although some teenagers may separate themselves from their families, for others parental problems may mean that separation is thrust upon them. When this happens, some adolescents may visit their parents when in treatment, an experience which can be extremely distressing and for which they may need considerable support to understand what they have observed.

> *I went once [to visit mum] and she was in this, in this like, it looked like a wacko room. It was all mats and everywhere ... It had a door that could be locked from the outside you know what I'm saying? It looked depressing and I mean I know she was in a stage where she was going about, you know going all funny but the way they pin 'em down, pin 'em down onto the floor ... They need help, they don't need to be locked away.*

(Girl aged 14, quoted in Aldridge and Becker 2003, p. 50)

Social presentation

Expected presentation

Physical appearance becomes increasingly important. Much time is spent in front of the mirror scrutinising the changes which puberty has brought. Teenagers become very conscious about their appearance, want to choose their own clothes and their hair style and are sensitive to criticism, particularly from peers. Adolescents without handicapping disabilities are able to look after their own personal hygiene.

Children in this age group can communicate easily with both adults and peers and are able to regulate their language and non-verbal behaviour to be appropriate to the situation.

Possible impact on social presentation

There are two major issues for this age group: the stigma and bullying which may result from the consequences of physical neglect, and learnt inappropriate behaviour such as violence, bullying and sexual abuse.

The first problem described is that of physical neglect. For example, when parents have learning disabilities and care for a child with profound learning and physical disabilities, they may not have the resources or capacities to meet the child's needs. Substance misuse, mental illness and domestic violence may also affect parents' capacity to care for their own and their children's needs. Although this can have devastating effects on young children, teenagers are not immune.

> *At one time I went through a depression that went on for about a year where I didn't bother do the housework, and I didn't bother to wash myself … I didn't give a shit about who said what about how the children looked … People must have known, people must have seen the way I was looking and the way the children were looking … but it's almost like once you get yourself into that, it's like you just sit and watch it.*

(Mother, quoted in NCH Action for Children 1994, p.47)

Perhaps equally important is the stigma associated with neglect. This may be acutely felt by children of this age because they are self-conscious about their appearance and sensitive to how others see them. When parental drinking or drug use diverts monies which would ordinarily be used for household essentials and clothes, or mental illness and learning disabilities restrict parenting capacity, children may find it difficult to keep up an acceptable appearance and friendships may be jeopardised.

> *They spend all the money on drink. There's no soap in the house and all my clothes are too small. I lost my girlfriend because she said I smell. Others call me names and make fun of me. It hurts.*

(Paul aged 14, quoted in ChildLine 1997, p.37)

Children are acutely aware of the stigma of mental illness, learning disability, problem substance misuse and domestic violence and most believe that it should be kept hidden within the family. Children's feelings of shame and a wish to keep it secret were clearly illustrated in Somers' (2007) study of parental mental illness, *'Keep it in the house, if people outside knew you would get a bad name'* (Somers 2007, p.1326).

A further problem results from children not learning the accepted social skills of interaction with adults outside the family. Growing up in families where violence is an accepted way of dealing with problems can result in some teenagers using violent or aggressive language and behaviour towards peers and adults. When children are unable to deal successfully with teachers, this can result in negative interactions and reinforces learning deficits and feelings of alienation (Gray 1993).

He's got problems at school 'cause he won't do what he's told at school, and on the bus going to school there's a problem there as well with it because he's just hitting other children on the bus and things like that you know.

(Grandparent, quoted in Barnard 2007, p.115)

Self-care skills

Expected self-care skills

At this age children are becoming increasingly competent. For example, when shopping for clothes 11-year-olds may still want a parent to accompany them, but by 13 the majority wish to shop with friends. Although they may not always do it willingly, the majority of adolescents are capable of clearing up their own rooms and carrying out simple household tasks.

Children of this age group feel confident in staying away from home for short periods and cope adequately with the routines and cultures of other families. They are increasingly able to prepare simple meals, look after themselves in many basic ways, and react appropriately in an emergency.

Possible impact on self-care skills

The impact of parental mental illness, learning disability, problem alcohol or drug use or domestic violence on adolescents' self-care skills is that they are forced to assume too much responsibility for themselves and other family members. As a result of parental problems the traditional roles of caring and being cared for may have been reversed and young carers may fail to look after their own developmental needs.

> *I would always have to mind the boys and tidy you know the whole house like. In a way it prepared us for later on, we learnt to cook and we're all tidy you know ... Because most girls our age – you know I mean we're only 15 – but a lot of girls do go clubbing and sneak out clubbing but like we don't.*
>
> (Girl of a mother with serious mental health problems, quoted in Aldridge and Becker 2003, p.66)

The experience of being a young carer may mean that children are extremely skilled in carrying out everyday household chores and looking after themselves. However, the feeling of overall responsibility and continual fear of what might happen in their absence results in some teenagers believing they must remain continually vigilant. As a result they are absent from home as little as possible and everyday events such as having lunch at school, visiting friends or joining school trips are forgone.

To sum up

Key problems for children aged 11–15 years

- Coping with puberty without support.
- An increased risk of mental health problems, alcohol and drug use.
- Education and learning not supported by parents.
- Education adversely affected by worries about the safety and welfare of parents and younger siblings, which mean that adolescents find it difficult concentrate.
- School is missed to look after parents or siblings.
- Education disrupted because of changes of school.
- Greater likelihood of emotional disturbance, including self-harm.
- Increased risk of social isolation and being bullied.
- Increased risk of conduct disorders including bullying.
- Increased risk for adolescent boys of being sexually abusive.
- Poor or ambivalent relationships with parents.
- Lack of positive role models.
- Poor self-image and low self-esteem.
- Friendships restricted or lost.
- Feelings of isolation and having no one to turn to.
- Increased responsibilities of being a young carer.
- Denial of own needs and feelings.

Protective factors

- Sufficient income support and good physical standards in the home.
- Practical and domestic help.
- Regular medical and dental checks including school medicals.
- Factual information about puberty, sex and contraception.
- Regular attendance at school.
- Sympathetic, empathic and vigilant teachers.
- Participation in organised, out-of-school activities, including homework clubs.
- A mentor or trusted adult with whom the child is able to discuss sensitive issues.
- An adult who assumes the role of champion and is committed to the child and *'acts vigorously, persistently and painstakingly on their behalf '*. (Cleaver 1996, p.24).
- A mutual friend.

- The acquisition of a range of coping strategies and being sufficiently confident to know what to do when parents are incapacitated.

- An ability to separate, either psychologically or physically, from the stressful situation.

- Information on how to contact relevant professionals and a contact person in the event of a crisis regarding the parent.

- Non-judgemental support from relevant professionals. Some children derive satisfaction from the caring role and their responsibility for and influence within the family. However, many feel that their role is not sufficiently recognised.

- An alternative, safe and supportive residence for mothers and children subject to violence and the threat of violence.

Children aged 16 years and over

Health

Expected health

Taking account of limitations due to disability or an ongoing health condition, there is an expectation that adolescents aged 16 or more can manage their own health needs. Young people should certainly be able to seek advice from parents, carers or doctors.

Many young women are unhappy about the shape of their bodies '...*by late teens and early twenties, up to half of girls have dieted, usually without success*' (Leffert and Petersen 1995, p.69). Research suggests the average prevalence rates for anorexia nervosa and bulimia nervosa among young females 15 to 24 years are 0.3 and 1%, respectively. Anorexia nervosa is a common disorder among young white women, but is extremely rare among young black women (Hoek 2006).

Illicit drug use increases with late adolescence. Hoare and Moon (2010) analysis of the British Crime Survey 2009/10 found around 2 in 5 young people aged 16 to 24 years had used illicit drugs at some stage in their lifetime. About 1 in 5 (20%) had used one or more illicit drugs in the year prior to the survey and 1 in 9 (11.6%) in the month prior to the survey. However, drug use among this age group had fallen. For example, young people using any illicit drugs in the previous year fell from 29.7% in 1996 to 20% in 2009/10. Cannabis was the most popular drug. Drug use is associated with social class. The higher the social class the more likely it is that the young person will have experimented with illicit drugs (Leitner et al. 1993).

Late adolescence is also a period of sexual experimentation. It is a time when many young people embark on their first sexual relationship. Provisional data for

2008 show conception rates for girls aged 15–17 years in England were 40.5 per 1,000 girls, a decrease of 3.1% from the 2007 rate and the lowest rate for over 20 years. Half (49.7%) of conceptions to this age group led to a legal abortion. The rate of conceptions for girls aged 15-17 years has declined by 6.1% since 1998 but, as already noted in relation to girls aged 11–15 years, the conception rate in England remains one of the highest teenage conception rates in Western Europe (Department for Education 2011). Teenage pregnancy is associated with negative outcomes for mothers and children. As noted earlier in the section for children aged 11-15 years, guidance to tackle the issue was put in place in 2010 (Department for Children, Schools and Families and Department of Health 2010).

Possible impact on health

There are three main health issues for older adolescents whose parents have problems: inappropriate role models, greater risk of accidents, and difficulties related to sexual relationships.

Parents are powerful role models for their children. There is considerable research which suggests that young people whose parents misuse substances develop a similar pattern of alcohol and drug use as a strategy to cope with difficult situations and negative feelings (Kroll and Taylor 2003; Covell and Howe 2009). For example, in a study of young heroin users half identified that a member of the family had a substance-misuse problem (Wisely et al. 1997 referred to in Kroll and Taylor 2003, p.181). What is less clear is the relative role and significance of genetic and environmental factors. For example, genetics may play a role in determining levels of consumption and metabolism of alcohol. Nonetheless, many young people are fearful that they will become their parents and find it hard to believe that they have choices. There is also some evidence to suggest that a father's alcohol misuse is more associated, than the mother's, with their child's alcohol use (Dunn et al. 2002).

> *I've been involved with drinking, drugs, fighting. I'm desperate to change. I don't want to be like dad.*
>
> (Roy aged 16 years, quoted in ChildLine 1997, p.33)

It is generally accepted that alcohol and drug use is the result of a combination of many factors such as culture, childhood experiences and social circumstances. Research has identified three issues which are significant predictors of young people's vulnerability to tobacco, alcohol and cannabis use: the affiliation with a delinquent or drug-using subculture, the wish for novelty, and parental illicit drug use (Velleman and Orford 2001). The picture is further complicated because parental attitudes may be more relevant to the adolescent's drug use than actual parental behaviour. Indeed, the relationship between extreme parental attitudes and behaviours and children's reactions is complex. For example, children may adopt equally extreme but opposite positions (Velleman 1993).

It (the parental situation) hasn't made me not drink, I still like to go out and have a laugh with my mates. But it has made me more aware of what happens when you take it too far, I've seen what it can do. I won't do that, I know my limits, I'm sensible.

(Gemma aged 18 years, quoted in Turning Point 2006, p.11)

Velleman and Orford (2001) found that evidence to support the 'Parental Modelling Theory' was rather less than anticipated. Comparing a group of offspring of drinking parents with a control group they found the offspring group were more likely to be involved in heavy, risky or problematic drug use (alcohol, tobacco, drugs or all three) but that the difference was not as great as expected. The authors conclude that *'In general they are as mentally healthy and as satisfied with themselves and their lives as young adults as are other people who have not had parents with drinking problems'* (Velleman and Orford 2001, p.249).

Excessive parental drinking may have an indirect impact on young people's health if it results in young people mirroring their parents' behaviour. Research has shown that children who start drinking at an early age are at greater risk of poor health and of being involved in accidents and accidental injury.

He smokes between 16–25 cigarettes a day, and has unsuccessfully tried to stop. At 16 he sniffed glue regularly (more than weekly) for a year ... At 18 he once took amphetamines and once LSD, and has taken hash monthly until the present ... At 17 he drank two pints once a week, and from 18, 2–4 pints three times a week with more on occasions ... Quite a few times in the last year he would have drunk roughly 15 pints, and he has ended up in hospital in intensive care.

(Velleman and Orford 2001, p.164)

Drinking is a contributory factor in 70% of all injuries resulting from assaults presented in accident and emergency departments in the United Kingdom (Institute of Alcohol Studies 2009). In addition, *'Young, inexperienced drivers are over-represented in deaths from drink-driving; nearly a third of pedestrians killed aged 16 to 19 had been drinking'* (Walker 1995).

US research that involved 710 respondents taken from a national survey found that witnessing domestic violence increased significantly the likelihood of adolescent girls aged 14 to 17 years engaging in 'risky' sexual activity (Elliott et al. 2002). Adolescents whose parents are absorbed in their own problems and are emotionally unavailable, insensitive or unaware of their children's needs may be at increased risk of pregnancy, getting someone pregnant or catching a sexually transmitted disease.

I am not that well. I have epilepsy and asthma, and I have throat problems. I am not on medication but I want to be. I smoke and drink. I don't eat proper meals. My sister and friends give me something. I have taken drugs in the past, and I use contraceptive injections. But my sister thinks I am pregnant, I've got a bump in my tummy. I don't know if I am pregnant. I haven't seen a doctor. I haven't got a boyfriend any more. He was 24 and I saw him for three years. He treated me like a pig, he wanted a baby but I wasn't ready. I hope I am not pregnant, but we will see.

(Eighteen-year-old daughter of mother with a learning disability, quoted in Cleaver and Nicholson 2007, p.89)

Having parents who are not physically or emotionally available or have learning disabilities can mean young people have not had the opportunity to discuss contraception or, equally important, how to develop strategies to act effectively in close personal relationships. Similarly, young people need a degree of self-confidence to be able to influence what happens to them in a sexual relationship. Growing up in a situation of domestic violence or with parents with alcohol or drug problems, learning disabilities or mental illness may have a negative impact on young people's self-confidence, which makes it more difficult for them to ensure their views are respected in intimate relationships.

Education and cognitive ability

Expected ability

The Education and Skills Act 2008 places a duty on young people to participate in education or training until the age of 18 (or until attaining a level 3 qualification).

National statistics showed that in 2007 the majority (78.7%) of young people aged 16 to 18 years were in full-time education or attended some form of training; however, 9.4% were still outside education, training or work (Department for Children, Schools and Families and Department for Innovation, Universities and Skills 2008). Most young people in compulsory education attend school regularly. Young people are more likely to be absent if they are from a deprived background. Young people need guidance to ensure their education is properly planned and suits their ambitions and abilities.

Examinations can cause many teenagers, particularly those who are prone to anxiety, considerable stress. Although the majority cope well, a mentor in the form of a parent or teacher who offers support (both academic and emotional) can obviate negative outcomes (Hodge et al. 1997).

Possible impact on education

There are several areas where parental problems can impact upon young people's performance at school: a failure to achieve their potential; behaviour which leads to school exclusion; and a lack of attainment which may affect long-term life chances.

Parental problems may mean that parents do not have the capacity to support older teenagers with their school work and during the stressful period of examinations.

Moreover, when parental attention is focused on themselves, they may be unaware of what is going on in relation to young people's education and schooling.

> *I didn't really get anywhere at school. I missed loads 'cause they (her parents) didn't bother telling me to go and then when I did go, I'd be worrying what was happening at home. When it came to exams, I never did any revision – you couldn't in our house, there was always something going on. I remember one exam, I'd been up 'til four in the morning 'cause the police were round and then they were fighting. It's no wonder I'm thick now.*
>
> (Fiona 17 years, quoted in Turning Point 2006, p.11)

For other young people school and education can offer a way out of their present situation, an opportunity to build a different life from what they are experiencing at home.

> *My parents' drinking ... I guess it did me a favour in one way ... made me not want to be like them, do something positive with my life. I knew I didn't want to turn out like that, on the social and everything. I got my exams and got a job straight after school.*
>
> (Gemma 18 years, quoted in Turning Point 2006, p.11)

The stresses of coping with parental problems and undertaking the care of younger siblings can take its toll on young people's education. Research suggests many young carers find it difficult to strike the right balance between home and education, and although some go on to further education, it is more common for young carers to have poor qualifications or none at all (Dearden and Becker 2003). As a result, although young carers often have greater maturity and coping ability, the consequences for their education and exam results of caring for a parent with severe problems tends to restrict them to lower-paid jobs.

When behaviour within school results in exclusion, young people need an adult to champion their cause, strive for their re-entry into education or ensure their learning continues (Cleaver 1996). This is important not only because academic and skill-based qualifications are strong predictors of future careers (Banks et al. 1992), but also because many excluded pupils have few if any friends (Galloway et al. 1982). However, securing a mentor may be hampered because many young people whose parents have mental illness, learning disabilities, drug or alcohol problems or live with domestic violence have mixed feelings about discussing their families with teachers.

> *I didn't like talking about things at school, I always thought they'd talk to other people, that everyone would know.*
>
> (Laura 17 years, quoted in Turning Point 2006, p.19)

Finally, a lack of educational attainment has long-term effects on children's life chances. Early school leavers who are unemployed have been shown to have much poorer mental health than those who have a job (Lakey 2001). Unemployment is also associated with increased likelihood of suicide, disability and obesity (Berry 2006). Practically half of all 16-year-olds who do not continue their education are unemployed (Department for Education and Employment 1997).

Emotional and behavioural development

Expected development

There is a considerable body of research which indicates that depressive feelings and depressive disorders increase during late adolescence (see Fombonne 1995 for an overview of this research). An American study of young people aged 19 to 25 years found practically 12% had a mood disorder (Blanco et al. 2008).

Emotional and mental distress can lead young people to self-harm. A survey of 818 young people in the United Kingdom found 22% of those aged 11 to 19 years admitted to self-harm. Young women are more likely than young men to harm themselves; practically one in three (32%) young women of this age group admitted to self-harm (Affinity Health Care 2008).

Suicide is also more common during adolescence. An analysis of the World Health Organisation mortality database showed global suicide rates to be 7.4 per 100,000 among adolescents aged 15 to 19 years of age. Gender appears to influence the outcome of suicide attempts; the rate for young men was 10.5 per 100,000 compared with 4.1 per 100,000 for young women (Wasserman et al. 2005). In contrast, girls outnumber boys in suicidal behaviour (Fombonne 1995). Suicide rates vary dramatically depending on the country studied and the time frame. For example, data for Scotland show a 42% reduction in suicide rates among 15–29 year-old men, from 42.5 per 100,000 in 2000 to 24.5 per 100,000 in 2004. The decrease was associated with a reduction in hanging deaths (Stark et al. 2008).

Possible impact on emotional and behavioural development

There are three major areas that affect young people's emotional and behavioural development: the emotional problems that result from self-blame and guilt and a possible increased risk of suicidal behaviour; vulnerability to conduct disorders and crime; and modelling parental behaviour.

The tendency to blame oneself, an issue already discussed in relation to younger children, remains throughout late adolescence. Young people continue to feel responsible for their parents' behaviour and believe they are unloved and unlovable.

...when I done things in school, it used to be, phew, well, nobody cares, my ma doesn't care, so...

(Nineteen-year-old girl of drug-using parent, quoted in Barnard 2007, p.92)

Self-harm is associated with feeling isolated, academic pressures, suicide or self-harm by someone close, family problems, being bullied and low self-esteem (Mental Health Foundation 2006). Many of these factors are issues confronting the children of parents with mental illness, learning disabilities, alcohol and drug misuse and domestic violence. Similarly, suicide in young people is related to an array of coexisting problems rather than a single issue such as parental mental illness or parental alcohol problems. For example, increased risk of suicide in young people is found to be associated with parental suicide or early death, hospitalisation for mental illness, unemployment, low income, poor schooling and divorce (Agerbo et al. 2002). More recent research by Brent and colleagues (2007) shows similar results; a family history of both depression and substance abuse and lifetime history of parent–child discord were most closely associated with adolescent suicide.

Young people whose parents have a multiplicity of serious problems are more at risk of coming into contact with the law. This may result because young people feel the need to acquire funds for what are seen as essential purchases. When money for everyday household goods is spent on gratifying parental drinking or drug needs, young people may resort to illegitimate methods to obtain money. Alternatively, they may come in contact with the law because of their antisocial behaviour. It could be argued that because young people feel bad about themselves they are less likely to care about the consequences of their behaviour. As a result they are more at risk of conduct disorders and criminal behaviour. *'I go and do something – get caught ... it just started me being bad and all that'* (Laybourn et al. 1996, p.81).

Not all young people feel that they have enduring problems as a result of their own parents' disorders. Young people cope in different ways depending on a multitude of factors including personality or disposition, the presence of a supportive and harmonious family environment and an external support system such as schools, career and other important adults (Velleman and Orford 2001). The following quotation illustrates how different members of one family coped with their parents' substance misuse.

We all coped differently ... I coped by believing everything my mother said was right ... my dad was bad. My brother coped by rebelling but he might have rebelled anyway ... My sister just kept herself to herself and studied incessantly.

(Young adult, quoted in Laybourn et al. 1996, p.82)

Identity

Expected identity

Young people aged 16 to 18 experience a growing self-awareness and struggle to sort out their own potential and limitations. Their sense of identity is made up of a combination of 'given' elements, an understanding and interpretation of past events, and the impact of present incidents and expectations for the future. Many young people experiment with a range of different identities, some of which may come into conflict with parental expectations.

The young person's sense of identity is linked to a feeling of belonging to their family. Even when young people reject family values and culture, long-lasting rifts are unusual (Rutter et al. 1976).

Possible impact on identity

There are two main issues in relation to the impact of parental mental illness, learning disability, problem alcohol or drug use and domestic violence on young people's sense of identity: low self-esteem and the consequences of inconsistent parenting.

The realisation and acceptance that they are not first in the lives of their parents continues, leaving many young people feeling isolated, unwanted and alone – emotions which compound feelings of low self-esteem.

> *That's how I'd feel all the time: I'd feel alone. Drugs were more important than me. I didn't come first in my mother's life ... she was more worried about drugs.*

(Felicia aged 17 years, quoted in Howard Thompson 1998, p.34)

> *I would feel like killing myself because I would think it's my fault, 'cos he drilled it in my head.*

(Seventeen-year-old woman, quoted in Mullender 2006, p.59)

However, research suggests that many children of problem drinkers, drug users, parents with mental illness or learning disability, and those who were raised in violent households, outgrow their problems.

> *...there is no evidence here that offspring [of problems drinkers] would describe their marriages and their lives overall in more negative terms than comparisons. Nor was there any support for the prediction that offspring would have lower self-esteem than comparisons.*

(Velleman and Orford 2001, p.180)

Family and social relationships

Expected relationships

Relationships with parents remain strong, although they undergo considerable change as the young person increasingly strives for more autonomy and parents demand greater levels of responsible behaviour. Parent-regulated behaviour tends to diminish and co-regulation and autonomous functioning presides (Leffert and Petersen 1995). Nonetheless, young people wish for harmonious relationships with parents and these remain an important source of emotional support and help in the transition to adulthood (Bailey 2006). Adulthood and independence (economic or otherwise) is a variable concept. For example, in England the age of criminal responsibility is 10 years, the age of consent 16, but you need to be 17.5 years to join the armed forces and 18 years to vote, buy or drink alcohol.

Friends become increasingly important and influential in the lives of young people, but this is not necessarily at the expense of parents. Rather, each is important in relation to different aspects of life. For example, young people will be more influenced by their peers in relation to fashion and music but are more likely to discuss careers and morality with their parents (Bailey 2006). Relationships with friends differ in quality from those of middle childhood and early adolescence. Friendships tend to be more intimate and involve more mutual exchanges of thoughts and feelings, and shared activities. Single-sex peer groups are on the decline.

Most late adolescents are striving to become confident in their sexual orientation. It is the age when many young people fall in love and embark on their first sexual encounter. The results of a survey of 11,161 young people found that 30% of young men and 26% of young women reported having intercourse before their 16th birthday. By the age of 20 years the vast majority of young people reported having had their first sexual intercourse (Wellings et al. 2001). The first love affair constitutes a most important emotional experience for teenagers and its break-up engenders considerable stress.

Possible impact on relationships

There are three issues with regard to the impact of parental disorders and young people's relationships. First, the experience of domestic violence and emotional neglect may affect young people's own dating behaviour. Second, young people report feelings of isolation from both friends and adults outside the family. Third, the wish to escape can place young people in dangerous situations.

Research suggests that witnessing the abuse of their mothers is associated with young men taking an aggressive, angry and abusing role during dates. Dating violence among young males is linked to a childhood experience of domestic violence (Moffitt 1993; Covell and Howe 2009). Teenage girls are also more susceptible to violence within intimate relationships when they have experienced a history of family violence (Barter et al. 2009).

The impact of emotional neglect (the likely result of the parental disorders under discussion) is illustrated by US research which involved a random sample of 402 young people receiving child protection services. The findings show that child emotional maltreatment was associated with heightened levels of post-traumatic stress symptoms and dating violence. Patterns differed for males and females, with post-traumatic symptoms accounting for dating violence perpetration among males and victimisation among females (Wekerle et al. 2009).

Parental problems may result in young people developing low self-esteem, making it more difficult for them to make friends. Young people also distance themselves from their peers because they wish to hide what is happening at home, or restrict their friendship patterns because they do not wish to burden friends with their problems. Research has shown that when reaching adulthood the offspring of problem drinkers socialise less than the comparison group (Velleman and Orford 2001).

> *I didn't really like to talk to my friends about it ... They didn't understand and anyway it was embarrassing, who wants to admit their families are alkies? I used to make things up to make it sound alright...*

(Ellie 18 years, quoted in Turning Point 2006, p.12)

Young people may also lose contact with friends, and their potential for support, when parental problems result in the need to move house and neighbourhood, whether planned or unplanned.

> *The hardest thing for me has been leaving my friends and knowing I have to make new ones where I live now. I also miss my belongings that I was unable to bring such as teddy bears from when I was born, clothes, jewellery and CDs and player, and really important my computer with all my course work on it...*

(Sophie aged 16 having entered a refuge, quoted in Barron 2007, p.17)

As discussed in relation to younger adolescents, relationships with peers may also be restricted because young people need to care for parents or younger siblings. For example, when young people fear for their parents' safety they may curtail substantially their leisure time, returning home during lunch breaks, immediately after school, college or work, and decline to join after-school activities or evening outings. Similarly, the need to look after younger siblings will restrict the ability to socialise.

> *I had to look after my brother, make sure he got up and went to school, had his tea ... if I didn't he wouldn't have. I couldn't go out after school 'cause he finished before me and I knew he'd be waiting, wanting to get in at home and my mum ... she wasn't always there or if she was, she'd be in bed.*

(Fiona 17 years, quoted in Turning Point 2006, p.15)

UNIVERSITY OF WINCHESTER LIBRARY

They may escape by withdrawing into themselves, characterised by long periods of day-dreaming, or time spent in their own room or out of the house.

> *In general, the most frequent ways of coping that these young people told us were that they: leave the room where fighting takes place (or sometimes they leave the house/apartment), they go to their room to listen to music, they visit friends, they lock themselves in their room, they cry with anger, or they take their anger and frustration out by hitting or breaking something.*

(Velleman and Reuber 2007, p. 41)

A more risky method of escape is to leave home altogether. The most common reason for a young person to run away from home is a background of neglect associated with parental problem drinking or drug use (Wade et al. 1998). The reports of young people whose parents are problem drinkers reinforce this finding; 37% left home by the age of 17 years compared to 23% of the comparison group (Velleman and Orford 2001). Growing up with domestic violence is also associated with youth homelessness. Hester and Radford (1996) found a quarter (26%) of homeless 16- to 25-year-olds left home due to domestic violence. Moreover, the poor relationships between young people and parents with learning disabilities, which may result from childhood abuse and neglect, can result in young people leaving home early.

> *I can look after myself. I sleep around wherever I can when I am not at mum's, which is not often now. I sleep at friends and sometimes at my sisters. I think I drink too much because I am around all over the place. I don't get on with my mum. She keeps on telling lies about me. I would like to get into a relationship with my mum. But I don't think it will happen now. My mum has problems, she has a disability, and she can't read or write. She can be nice when she wants to. I get on really well with my sister; she is really good to me. My brother doesn't like me, but I am OK with four of my step brothers. I hate my step-father; he assaulted me and got away with it. He should not be free to do it to other children. I was only 6 when he started. Most of my friends are men. I prefer to be with men than women.*

(Cathy aged 18 years, unpublished material Cleaver and Nicholson 2008)

It was estimated that there were 75,000 young people experiencing homelessness in the United Kingdom in 2006/7. Young people who are homeless have poorer health, particularly mental health and are more likely to misuse drugs and alcohol. The experience of homelessness compounds these problems and impedes participation in employment, education or training (Quilgars et al. 2008).

Alternatively, young people may seek escape and solace from family problems in drugs and alcohol. Establishing a relationship with a caring person that is characterised by mutual trust and respect can help young people to find less damaging ways of coping with family stress. Unfortunately, many who have grown up in very dysfunctional families have learnt to distrust adults (Cleaver and Walker with Meadows 2004).

Not all young people suffer isolation and loneliness when their parents have a serious disorder. Some teenagers do find a friend or relative in whom they can confide. Research which includes the views of young people highlights how friends and relatives, if carefully selected, can provide social support and help young people cope with the difficulties they experience (Bancroft et al. 2004; Velleman and Reuber 2007).

> *I speak to my aunt, who listens and calms me down.*
>
> *My friend cheers me up. And I know someone who has been through a similar experience, and that's helpful. And my teacher is trained to help – he listens and gives advice, which is great.*

(Two young people, quoted in Velleman and Reuber 2007, p.41)

Although relationships between parents and children can suffer because of parents' difficulties, this is not always the case. Indeed, research on parental mental illness has found that parents and children may report strong and positive relationships.

> *We are still the best of friends. We do really have a strong relationship and also I feel that I've matured a lot quicker which to me I think is a good thing because I've got a different outlook to a lot of other girls that are my age...*

(Ruth 18, quoted in Aldridge and Becker 2003, p.84)

Social presentation

Expected presentation

Young people aged 16 to 18 years are able to take care of themselves. They can take control for their own clothes, hair and skin care and rarely take advice on what to wear. Young people's appearance continues to be an extremely important issue and many spend a considerable proportion of their disposable income on clothing and toiletries.

Young people are increasingly competent in adjusting their behaviour, conversation and dress to different situations.

Possible impact on social presentation

The problems for social presentation are a lack of guidance to moderate the extremes of dress and presentation, insufficient funds for adequate or appropriate clothing and toiletries, and the use of aggression inappropriately to solve problems.

When young people feel rejected or alienated from their families they may resort to extreme modes of dress, body mutilation or adornment in a gesture of independence.

Research in the US suggests body piercing is not uncommon among young men and women. A survey of undergraduates found 42% of men and 60% of women had body piercing. The majority of piercing, both for young men and women, was to the ears and for women the naval. More extreme piercing to the genitals or lips was rare. Infections and complications occurred in 17% of cases (Mayers et al. 2002). Parents with learning disabilities and those who are overwhelmed with their own problems may not be able to offer the necessary reassurance or guidance to moderate such extremes.

When money and household resources are used to satisfy parental needs for alcohol or illicit drugs, the remaining funds may be insufficient to ensure that young people can 'keep up appearances'. Because appearance is a priority and pressure from peers can be intense, those with little parental guidance may avoid peer ridicule by resorting to stealing what clothing, jewellery or other items they perceive to be essential.

To have grown up in a culture of family violence may result in young people resorting to aggression as a method of solving their own problems. Young people who cannot control their emotions and react aggressively to peers or adults not only jeopardise their friendships but place their school or work careers at risk through exclusion or encounters with the law.

Self-care skills

Expected self-care skills

By 16 years most young people are capable of looking after their own basic needs. For example, they can wash up, shop, cook a simple meal and look after their clothes. The majority of young people will know how to use public transport and can organise travel arrangements for themselves.

Young people should be able to function independently at a level appropriate to their age and cognitive and physical ability. But, however well they appear to cope, young people need an adult to whom they can turn to for help and advice when necessary.

Possible impact on self-care skills

As we have already noted for children aged 11–15 years, being a young carer results in the acquisition of practical skills well beyond their years. As adulthood approaches many young people feel increasingly responsible for their parents and younger siblings. The degree to which they assume the parenting role will fluctuate depending on the parent's mental and physical health, the level of alcohol or drug intake, and the extent of additional familial support.

> *When she [my mother] come back out of hospital and I was doing everything and I had the three kids as well and she went, what was it, she said something to me like 'Have we swapped roles?' I went, 'What do you mean?' and she went 'Well I'm not the mum anymore, you are'. I went, 'Well what do you mean?' She went 'Well look at all the things you're doing, I'm meant to be doing all them'.*

(Debbie 18 years, quoted in Aldridge and Becker 2003, p.88)

Although young people are often very able to care for their parents and younger siblings, the effects can be all-pervasive and influence every aspect of their lives. In most cases young people do not wish to surrender the role of carer and may see it not as a burden but as a source of pride (Roberts et al. 2008). Nonetheless, they want their contribution to be recognised, to be able to get practical help when needed, to have access to reliable and relevant information, and for professionals to involve and include them in their parents' treatment and care (Aldridge and Becker 2003).

In many cases, however, their contribution is unknown because, despite policy and guidance to encourage greater inter-agency working, divisions between adults' and children's services continue, and professional oversight of the needs of young carers is not uncommon (Cleaver et al. 2007). Research suggests that most professionals working in the statutory sector assume that the needs of children and young people are met by young carers' projects or that children are accustomed to their circumstances and roles and so don't need any additional support. *'I judged he [young carer] was coping well enough'* (intensive support worker, quoted in Aldridge and Becker 2003, p.121). Indeed, young carers' projects are particularly valued by young people, but sadly their experiences of other services are more mixed and many young people are left without practical or emotional support (Aldridge and Becker 2003). Sadly, research shows that because young carers' projects are primarily for children, young people aged 16 years and more are less likely to access their support (Dearden and Becker 2004). Services for young carers, particularly those looking after parents with alcohol or drug problems, will benefit from the £1 million grants programme 2006/7 and 2007/8 given by Comic Relief to the Princess Royal Trust for Carers (Princess Royal Trust for Carers 2009).

To sum up

Key problems for young people aged 16 years and over

- Inappropriate role models.
- Increased likelihood of early drinking, smoking and drug use.
- Greater risk of poor health, injuries and accidents as a result of early substance misuse.
- Pregnancy and teenage motherhood.
- Problems related to sexual relationships.

- A failure to achieve their potential because of a lack of parental support and difficulties in concentration.
- Absence from school due to caring for parents and younger siblings.
- Increased risk of school exclusion.
- Poor life chances due to exclusion and poor school attainment.
- Emotional problems as a result of self-blame and guilt.
- Increased risk of self-harm and suicide.
- Greater vulnerability to conduct disorders and crime.
- Low self-esteem as a consequence of neglect and/or inconsistent parenting.
- Increased isolation from both friends and adults outside the home.
- Young men at greater risk of taking an aggressive and abusive role within intimate sexual relationships.
- Inappropriate and extremes of dress and body ornamentation, and inappropriate behaviour alienating other young people and adults and jeopardising educational and work careers.
- Young carers' own needs and wishes sacrificed to meet the needs of their parents and young siblings.

Protective factors
- Sufficient income support and good physical standards in the home.
- Practical and domestic help.
- Regular medical and dental checks and prompt attention for any injuries or accidents.
- Factual information about sex and contraception.
- A trusted adult with whom the young person is able to discuss sensitive issues including how to act effectively in sexual and other close relationships.
- Regular attendance at school, further education or work-based training.
- Sympathetic, empathic and vigilant teachers.
- For those who are no longer in full-time education or training, a job.
- An adult who acts as a champion for the young person.
- A caring adult who establishes a relationship characterised by mutual trust and respect.
- A mutual friend.
- The acquisition of a range of coping strategies and sufficient confidence to know what to do when parents are ill or incapacitated.
- An ability to separate, either psychologically or physically, from the stressful situation.

- Information on how to contact relevant professionals and a named contact person in the event of a crisis regarding the parent.

- Un-stigmatised support from relevant professionals who recognise and value their role as a young carer.

- Assessments under the Children Act 1989 for young carers.

- Access to young carers' projects.

- Specialist support for 'older' young carers.

- An alternative, safe and supportive residence for young people subject to violence and the threat of violence and those who wish to leave home at an early age.

Identified unmet developmental needs in adolescence

As for the other age groups, a re-analysis of data of children referred to children's social care (Cleaver et al. 2007 and Cleaver and Nicholson 2007) was undertaken for adolescents, i.e. children aged 10 years and over.[12]

Table 6.1: **Proportion of adolescents with identified unmet needs**

Dimension	Parental substance misuse n=55	Parental learning disability n=16	Domestic violence n=51
Health	20%	62%	20%
Education	61%	63%	61%
Emotional and behavioural development	73%	73%	69%
Identity	31%	28%	44%
Family and social relationships	65%	79%	63%

The findings shown in Table 6.1 suggest a similar pattern of unmet developmental needs regardless of the parental disorder. A greater proportion of adolescents experience unmet needs in relation to their education, emotional and behavioural development and with regard to family and social relationships. Although, once again, the findings suggest parents with learning disabilities experience difficulty in meeting the educational needs of their adolescent children.

---

[12]   All information given in this section on the impact of parental disorders on children's developmental needs is the result of a re-analysis of data: Cleaver and Nicholson 2007 and Cleaver et al. 2007. The research did not cover children living with mentally ill parents and, consequently, such detailed information is not available.

Young people were classified as having severe needs when social workers identified unmet developmental needs in three or more of the five dimensions. The data suggest teenagers are likely to experience approximately the same degree of overall difficulty regardless of whether they are living with parents with alcohol or drug problems, domestic violence or with parents with learning disabilities. Results show that 42% of adolescents living with parental substance misuse, 48% of those living with domestic violence, and 54% of those living with a parent with a learning disability had severe developmental needs.

PART III: CONCLUSIONS AND IMPLICATIONS FOR POLICY AND PRACTICE

7 Conclusions

Mental health problems, learning disability, substance misuse and domestic violence are problems that may affect any one of us. This overview suggests that 16.6% of adults experience some form of mental disorder in any one week, approximately 2% of the adult population has a learning disability, 7% of men and 5% of women are higher risk drinkers, and 3.7% of the population are drug dependent. One in four women is subjected to domestic violence at some point in their lives.

Sadly, these issues do not generally exist in isolation and many with mental disorders also report alcohol or drug problems. Similarly, the majority of those with chronic alcohol or drug problems suffer poor mental health, as do some 40% of adults with a learning disability. Moreover, half of the perpetrators of domestic violence have a history of problem alcohol use. A single disorder can negatively affect parents' capacity to meet their children's needs, but the co-existence of these types of problems has a much greater impact on parenting capacity.

The impact may leave parents with a sense of apathy, blunted emotions and low self-esteem. The ability to control emotions may also be affected, leading to extreme mood swings, unpredictable violence and irritability, unresponsiveness and anger. These are all factors that affect the parent–child relationship and particularly the attachment process. Parents may also experience difficulty in organising their lives and fail to sustain family rituals and routines – events key to cementing family relationships. Feelings of depression and despair and the effects of alcohol or drugs may result in parents neglecting their own and their children's physical needs. When problems become extreme, hospitalisation, imprisonment or residential treatment will also interrupt the parenting process.

The impact on children may be exacerbated through the social consequences of parental problems. Children's welfare may be compromised because too much family income is used to satisfy parental needs and the home and possessions damaged as a result of violent outbursts. Obtaining and sustaining a job can be difficult, and as a result parents may turn to criminal activities such as drug dealing or prostitution to obtain the necessary income. Such activities can expose children to unsafe adults and a criminal lifestyle.

The negative consequences for children of parental mental illness, learning disability, substance misuse and domestic violence are not a foregone conclusion. A detailed exploration of the impact of parental problems on children's health and development at different stages of life highlights the importance of looking at children, parents and other key family members as individuals. The short- and long-term consequences for children of growing up in a family where at least one parent is experiencing extreme difficulties will depend on the combination of resilience and protective mechanisms. For example, when parental mental illness, learning disability or problem drinking coexist, or are accompanied by domestic violence, or associated with poverty and social isolation, children are particularly vulnerable.

However, other factors, such as the availability of another caring adult in the home who does not experience a disorder, other relatives who act as agents of social control and provide a safe refuge for the child, and for older children the support of friends, can cushion the negative consequences. It is therefore important not to pathologise all children who live in families where a parent suffers from mental illness, a learning disability, problem drinking or drug use or domestic violence. However, these parental problems often result in an estrangement from family and friends, leaving children either with a lone parent who has difficulties or two parents who both suffer problems. The isolation of the family may be compounded because parents' behaviour may have led to stigma and rejection by the local community.

The challenge for practitioners is to identify both the strengths and difficulties within the family by carrying out a holistic assessment which covers the child's development, the parents' capacity to meet the child's needs, and the impact of wider family and environmental factors (Department of Health et al. 2000). Of primary importance is to identify whether the child is suffering, or likely to suffer, significant harm (HM Government 2010a).

In addition, practitioners need to identify:

- Which children need help and the level of concern – are they 'children in need'?

- Which aspects of development are being adversely affected and how?

- What are the strengths and resources within each child?

- What disorders and other difficulties are the parents experiencing and how are these affecting their parenting capacity?

- What are the strengths within the family, in what aspects are they doing well, and how can these be built on?

- What support is available within the wider family and community?

- What services are needed (and from which agencies and organisations) to help both the child and the family?

8 Implications for policy and practice

Early identification and assessment

- Growing up with parental mental illness, learning disability, substance misuse or domestic violence will have an impact on individual children differently; children's needs vary. While some cope well, others will benefit from advice, assistance and counselling. For a minority who experience a multitude of behavioural and emotional difficulties, intensive therapeutic intervention will be necessary to overcome the traumatic effect of parental disorders. Identifying children who would benefit from support may be difficult because children are ashamed of their circumstances and wish to keep the family problems secret, or are frightened of the consequences of revealing information about their family. As a result, some children may not have their needs for basic care, love and affection from their parents or carers adequately met and are left in dangerous and abusive situations.

- It is important to provide children and young people with opportunities to discuss their concerns and worries with adults whom they trust. ChildLine (a well-established organisation) has helped many children talk about abuse and neglect and, more recently, bullying. However, this method of communication may not suit all children and young people, and schools and other community services working with children should consider providing an identified worker with the necessary skills to listen to what children say in a non-judgemental way, and act appropriately. Targeted youth support, including youth mentors and befriending schemes, can also provide much-needed help.

- Insufficient understanding and information about the impact of these parental issues on children may result in professionals either unconsciously not seeing the child's problems (because they are not sure what to do if they do acknowledge them) or, if they are aware of the child's problems, referring them directly to children's social care. In many cases what the child needs is for that professional, be it a teacher, health worker or youth worker, to take an interest in the child and provide a listening and caring ear. Resources for practitioners continue to be developed (see for example www.alcoholandfamilies.org.uk/toolkits.htm).

- Safeguarding and promoting the welfare of children and young people is everyone's responsibility (HM Government 2010a). Collaborative working and information sharing is supported by legislation, statutory and practice guidance on the misuse of drugs and alcohol, domestic violence and learning disability, and new multi-agency methods of working. Use of the Common Assessment Framework (CAF) (Children's Workforce Development Council 2010) and the guide to target youth support (Department for Education and Skills 2007) should promote more effective, earlier identification of children's additional needs, including when parents' problems are affecting the child's welfare. Those working with children need to be vigilant in observing and acting upon any concerns they may have (Allen 2011). Managers in agencies working with children need to ensure statutory guidance on what to do when concerned that a child is being abused or neglected (HM Government 2010a) is followed.

- Mental illness, learning disability, problem alcohol and drug use and domestic violence affect adults' parenting capacity and impact on their children in variable ways. Skilled, holistic assessments which focus on the outcomes for children, involve children and family members and place equal emphasis on the child, family and their environment are essential (Department of Health et al. 2000; Department for Education 2010c; Children's Workforce Development Council 2010). Assessments should identify not only the child's developmental needs but also parents' acute and chronic difficulties which have an impact on their parenting capacity.

- Most practitioners in children's social care services are skilled in assessing children's developmental needs but may experience more difficulty in judging how learning disability, mental illness, substance misuse or domestic violence have an impact on parenting capacity. To safeguard and promote the welfare of children, assess their needs (including their role as young carers) and fully understand the family's circumstances, children's services practitioners should seek the expertise of adult services. Collaboration should be given greater priority because practitioners in domestic violence units, alcohol and drug services, mental health and learning disability services will have a better understanding than those working in children's services of how these issues impact on adult family members and family functioning.

- Collaboration between children's and adults' services will allow the expertise of practitioners in these specialist services to inform assessments, judgements and plans. Joint working is likely to result in a more proactive and integrated approach to the delivery of relevant and timely services for both children and parents. To ensure joined-up service provision, specific attention should be given to creating robust professional links between children's and adults' services.

- The varying effects of parental mental illness, learning disability, problem drinking and drug use and domestic violence demands the careful assessment of each child's developmental needs. For example, some children may take on caring responsibilities. Young carers' projects can enable access to services, support young people in key decisions, build self-esteem and confidence and put young people in touch with others in similar circumstances. These projects are greatly valued by young carers and often represent the only access to dedicated support that children have as carers. However, the majority are located within the voluntary sector and will require stable funding to ensure their continuity. Most young carers' projects focus on children; local authorities should consider providing some form of specialist support for young carers over the age of 16 years.

- Too often little attention is paid to identifying the needs of young carers. There are at present two ways whereby young carers may have their needs assessed. Firstly, they may be defined as children in need under the Children Act 1989, which would allow their needs to be assessed and services such as befriending, counselling, respite care and recreational facilities to be provided. Second, the Carers and Disabled Children Act 2000 offers an opportunity for carers over the age of 16 to receive an assessment and services, including payments, in their own right. The practice guidance for carers introduced in 2008 (HM Government 2008) was developed to help professionals identify the needs of young carers through a commitment to increase awareness of caring and the issues it raises across children's settings. There is insufficient training and training materials for relevant professionals. Service intervention should be designed to support children and young people and to minimise the burden and negative effects of being a young carer.

- Many parents and adult family members fear that revealing their problems will lead to punitive reactions by service providers. Practitioners should work with great delicacy to ensure that they do not alienate parents and are sensitive to parents' reactions so that they can be both supportive and robust in the messages they give.

- Interventions which reduce the stress that parents experience are likely to benefit children indirectly. 'Community mothers' programmes, voluntary befriending schemes, and other social support interventions for mothers of young children, such as those provided at Sure Start children's centres and Family Nurse Partnerships, can provide essential help. These more targeted community-based programmes are often funded by short-term grants. Stable funding streams would allow such projects and others which focus on supporting children and parents with specific issues such as mental health problems or learning disability, and community-based drug and alcohol services, to provide the necessary long-term ongoing support for families.

Joint working

- Professionals tend to focus on the needs of their specific client group. When these needs are at odds with those of others in the family, professionals may be persuaded to advocate on their client's behalf. This can result in polarised views which block effective joint working. It is vital that every service gives due consideration to the needs of all family members.

- In some cases the complexity, co-morbidity and longevity of parental problems means no single agency will be able to provide all the services and support necessary to address the parents' problems, keep children safe and promote their welfare while living at home. A number of different agencies serving both children and adults will need to work together alongside community-based services. For this to happen, local authorities need to ensure that thresholds for services and the diverse legal and ethical considerations do not hamper collaboration.

- Greater priority should be given to collaboration and inter-agency working between organisations providing services for adults (such as domestic violence, substance misuse, learning disability and mental illness) and those working with children. An organisational barrier to working together is the different understanding of confidentiality and data protection held by various professionals and agencies. Relevant authorities, such as local authorities, strategic health authorities and police authorities, need to build on existing inter-agency protocols for information sharing and ensure that agencies working with adults are included (HM Government 2010a). The development of joint protocols and procedures which cross the divide between adults' and children's services will support inter-agency working (see for example Department for Children, Schools and Families et al 2009). Protocols are important in guiding practitioners when making professional judgements about what to share, in what circumstances and for what purposes.

- The extent to which parents experience a number of different disorders such as mental illness and learning disability, substance misuse and domestic violence, means that it is equally imperative that protocols for information sharing and joint working are developed between agencies providing different types of services for adults.

- Children should be given a higher priority in all strategic local authority plans whose primary focus is adults, such as those produced by the Domestic Violence Forum, the Drug and Alcohol Action Team and the Community Safety Plan.

- Senior managers and those commissioning services should ensure the provision of services for children of parents with poor mental health, learning disabilities, substance misuse and domestic violence. It is equally important that business plans produced by the local safeguarding children boards address adequately the needs of these children and young people.

Flexible time frames

- Some children and families may require long-term support services. When families have diverse and enduring, complex and multiple needs which cross agency boundaries, short-term interventions are rarely effective. For example, when parents have a learning disability and other disorders such as problem alcohol abuse and depression, to ensure that children are safe and their welfare is promoted resources must be committed for the duration of the individual's childhood. A review of British research suggests outcomes for children can be improved where foster or residential care is provided as family support rather than a permanent alternative to living at home (Forrester et al. 2009). Local authorities need to take account of the resources required to ensure that support services, including good-quality out-of-home care, can be provided.

- Not all families will require long-term support from statutory services. For example, when parental disorders build up over time and overwhelm family resources, a package of time-limited services targeted at addressing specific needs can be very effective.

- In families where there may be no other problems except for the presenting one (for example, the recurrence of mental illness or a relapse into problem drinking) the presence of another caring adult within the household and the support of family members and friends may ensure that children are safe and their welfare is promoted. In these cases the input of a single agency may be all that is required. Nonetheless, the active agency should be alert to the needs of each family member.

- Following a referral to children's social care, the initial assessment should explore the strengths and difficulties within the family in order to decide whether a more in-depth core assessment is required. The analysis of the findings from the assessment should enable social workers, together with other professionals, to judge whether the child is suffering, or likely to suffer, significant harm. Research findings that have informed this book suggest that a significant proportion of children living in families who are experiencing complex and enduring problems do not currently have their needs adequately met and a proportion are experiencing abuse and neglect. Managers should ensure that the 'child/young person's plan' is based on an analysis of the findings from the assessment and has clear objectives. These should identify what actions are necessary to address the needs of the child and family, who is responsible for carrying these out, and what services or resources are required to meet the objectives within the agreed time frame.

- The best-laid plans of mice and men often go awry. Planned services may not materialise, children and parents may not attend the services provided, and even when services are taken up they may not necessarily be successful in improving the outcomes for children and young people. Social work managers should ensure that children in need plans are regularly reviewed and that children's progress is closely monitored to try and prevent children being left in circumstances likely to impair their emotional and physical health and which place them at risk of suffering significant harm.

- When the child protection conference review suggests that parenting capacity has improved, children's needs are being met, and families are able to cope, the case might be closed to children's social care. However, because in many cases the characteristics of the parents' disorders are that there is a likelihood of relapse, contingency planning is essential (Davies and Ward, 2011). Ongoing support may be provided by other statutory and community-based services. When parents experience difficulty in sustaining progress, when conditions deteriorate or crises occur, family members need to know that they can come back and ask for help from children's social care or other relevant agencies without feeling that they have failed.

Information for children and families

- Families and especially children and young carers require sensitively developed information telling them about the disorders that are affecting their parents, the circumstances in which they find themselves, and the implications of the disorders (HM Government 2010d).

- A key factor in safeguarding children when parents suffer mental illness, learning disabilities, substance misuse or domestic violence is the take-up of services. Families need to know what services are available in their local community, including how the interface between adults' and children's services can be bridged. The local authority directory of services makes this information available to all practitioners and those working in community and voluntary agencies, and in many local authorities to the general public. Practitioners need to work in partnership with families to ensure that parents understand what is available and are happy and able to attend the relevant specialist services.

- Information about services should be widely available, written in relevant languages, and produced in accessible formats. Additional consideration should be given to ensuring that information is produced in a form accessible to those with communication impairments and those with learning disabilities (for both adults and children).

- Knowing what to expect when approaching agencies for help can be very reassuring to families. Children and parents need information on how to gain access to services and what to expect when entering service systems.

- Some families are likely to have specialised requirements for information. For example, children who become young carers need an identified person as an 'anchor' who they can contact easily in times of crisis or for information when worried.

Training and educational requirements

- The general public should be better educated on the issues for families experiencing parental mental illness, learning disability, alcohol and drug problems and domestic violence. A higher level of understanding should encourage communities and extended family networks to provide more support to the children and their parents.

- Professionals who work with children need training to recognise and identify parents' problems, understand how different issues can co-exist and appreciate the impact that these issues may have on various aspects of children's and young people's lives.

- Local authorities and health authorities should ensure that practitioners working with adults understand the importance of identifying clients who are parents or carers of children. Managers should ensure staff routinely attend training courses that link safeguarding and promoting children's welfare with parental mental illness, learning disability, substance misuse or domestic violence. A key factor in safeguarding and promoting the child's welfare is the ability to understand the situation from the child's point of view. Training should also ensure practitioners in adult services have the necessary skills in communicating with children.

- Inter-agency training in safeguarding and promoting the welfare of children should include practitioners from statutory and third-sector agencies who are in regular contact with children and young people and with adults who are parents or carers, as well as those with a particular responsibility for safeguarding and promoting the welfare of children (HM Government 2007; HM Government 2010a). It is essential that practitioners providing mental health and learning disability services, those working with adults who have alcohol or drug problems and those providing services for domestic violence, are included.

- It has been established that many families experience a number of difficulties. For example, a parent with a learning disability may also experience poor mental health and live in a violent relationship; a mother living with domestic violence may also be self-medicating and suffer from depression; a violent man may have a problem with alcohol. There is little training which brings together practitioners from different agencies that provide services to adults. Practitioners need to understand how different disorders may interact, how co-morbidity may affect parenting capacity and how this may impede children's developmental progress. Greater priority should be given to providing specialist training targeted at practitioners both from children's services and from the many relevant agencies providing services for adults.

- Inter-agency training involving adults' and children's statutory and third-sector services is necessary to support the development and use of a common language; a better understanding of the roles and responsibilities of professionals working in different organisations; thresholds for services; the legal framework in which they each work; and issues surrounding confidentiality and information sharing. Training will be necessary to ensure that issues of race, culture and disability are taken into account so that sensitive ways of working are developed and taken forward into practice.

To sum up

- Early identification and assessment are essential to ensure children and young people living with parental mental illness, learning disability, substance misuse and domestic violence, are not left in dangerous and abusive situations. Early identification depends on ensuring children and young people have opportunities to discuss their experiences with a trusted adult.

- In complex cases the involvement in assessments of practitioners from specialist adult services will result in a better understanding of how parental problems impact on family functioning and parenting capacity. Robust professional links, joint protocols and procedures between children's and adults' services will help to ensure collaboration during assessments and service provision.

- Assessments should focus on the needs of each child within the family, and identify those who have assumed a caring role. Older young people may not be eligible for young carers' projects and other forms of local support may need to be developed.

- Stable funding for voluntary and community based programmes is required to provide the necessary long-term support to ensure children living with families with complex needs are safe.

- It is essential that professionals who work with a specific client group consider the needs of all family members, particularly the children. A higher priority should be given to children in all strategic local authority plans whose primary focus is adults.

- Flexible time–frames when working with children in need and their families are essential. Local authorities should take account of the resources required to supply both long-term support as well as more focussed time-limited services. When services are provided, children's progress should always be closely monitored. Improvements in parents' disorders do not always result in improved parenting.

- Families, including the children, require information about the disorders affecting parents and the services available to them. The information should be widely available and produced in a range of different formats.

- Educating the general public on the impact on children and families of parental mental illness, learning disability, substance misuse and domestic violence should encourage communities and extended families to provide more support.

- Key to the safeguarding and promoting of a child's welfare is the ability to understand the situation from the child's viewpoint. Practitioners from statutory and third-sector agencies who are in regular contact with children and adults who are parents (including those providing services for adults) should be included in inter-agency training. Training should link safeguarding and promoting the children's welfare with parental issues, and ensure practitioners in adult services have the skills to communicate with children. Training should encompass the development of sensitive ways of working to ensure issues of race, culture and disability are addressed.

Bibliography

Abel, E.L. (1998) 'Fetal Alcohol Syndrome: The American paradox.' *Alcohol and Alcoholism* 33, 3, 195–201.

Abel, E.L. and Sokol, R. (1991) 'A revised conservative estimate of the incidence of Foetal Alcohol Syndrome and its economic impact.' *Alcoholism: Clinical and Experimental Research* 15, 514–524.

Abrahams, C. (1994) *The Hidden Victims: Children and Domestic Violence*. London: NCH Action for Children.

Ackerson, B.J. (2003) 'Coping with the dual demands of severe mental illness and parenting: The parents' perspective.' *Families in Society* 84, 1, 109–119.

ADFAM: Families, drugs and alcohol (2008) *What should I do?* (www.adfam.org.uk/find_help/what_should_i_do/is_it_my_fault_) assessed 03.03.2011.

Advisory Council on the Misuse of Drugs (2003) *Hidden Harm: Responding to the Needs of Children of Problem Drug Users*. London: Home Office.

Affinity Health Care (2008) *New Survey Reveals Almost One in Three Young Females Have Tried to Self-Harm* (www.affinityhealth.co.uk/pdf/SHS.pdf) accessed 03.03.2011.

Agarwal, D.P. (1996) 'Racial/ethnic and gender differences in alcohol use and misuse', in Peters, T.J. (ed) *Psychological Medicine*. New Jersey: Harwood Academic Publishers.

Agerbo, E., Nordentorf, M. and Mortensen, P. (2002) 'Familial, psychiatric, and socioeconomic risk factors for suicide in young people: nested case-control study.' *British Medical Journal* 325, 74–79.

Ainsworth, M.D.S., Blehar, M., Waters, E. and Wall, S. (1978) *Patterns of Attachment*. Hillsdale, NJ: Erlbaum.

Alcohol Concern (2010) *Swept under the carpet: Children affected by parental alcohol misuse.* (www.alcoholconcern.org.uk/) accessed 03.03.2011.

Aldgate, J. (1992) 'Work with children experiencing separation and loss', in Aldgate, J. and Simmonds, J. (eds) *Direct Work with Children*. London: Batsford.

Aldgate, J. and Jones, D. (2006) 'The place of attachment in children's development', in Aldgate, J., Jones, D., Rose, W. and Jeffery, C. (eds) *The Developing World of the Child*. London: Jessica Kingsley Publishers.

Aldridge, J. and Becker, S. (1993) *Children Who Care: Inside the World of Young Carers.* Department of Social Sciences: Loughborough University.

Aldridge, J. and Becker, S. (2003) *Children caring for parents with mental illness: Perspectives of young carers, parents and professionals.* Bristol: The Policy Press.

Alexander, H., Macdonald, E. and Paton, S. (2005) 'Raising the issue of domestic abuse in school.' *Children and Society* 19, 3, 187–198.

Alison, L. (2000) 'What are the risks to children of parental substance misuse?', in Harbin, F. and Murphy, M. (eds) *Substance Misuse and Child Care.* Dorset: Russell House Publishing.

Allen, G. (2011) *Early Intervention: The Next Steps.* London: Cabinet Office.

Alvik, A., Heyerdahl, S., Haldorsen, T. and Lindemann, R. (2006) 'Alcohol use before and during pregnancy: A population-based study.' *Acta Obstetricia et Gynecologica Scandinavica* 85, 11, 1292–8.

American Psychiatric Association (2000) *Diagnostic and Statistical Manual of Mental Disorders* (DSM-IV-TR). Michigan: American Psychiatric Association.

Anglin, D., Lonk, B. and Phelan, J. (2006) 'Racial Differences in Stigmatizing Attitudes Toward People With Mental Illness.' *Psychiatric Services* 57, 6. (http://psychservices.psychiatryonline.org/cgi/reprint/57/6/857) accessed 03.03.2011.

Armitage, M. and Walker, S. (2009) 'Approaching Someone for Help', in Cleaver, H., Cawson, P., Gorin, S., and Walker, S. (eds) *Safeguarding Children: A Shared Responsibility.* Chichester: Wiley-Blackwell.

Arnone, D., Patel, A. and Tan, G.M. (2006) 'The nosological significance of Folie à Deux: a review of the literature.' *Annals of General Psychiatry* 5:11.

Avis, H. (1999) *Drugs and Life, 3rd edition.* Boston: McGraw-Hill.

Bailey, S. (2006) 'Adolescence and Beyond: Twelve Years Onwards', in Aldgate, J., Jones, D., Rose, W., and Jeffery, C. (eds) *The Developing World of the Child.* London: Jessica Kingsley Publishers.

Baladerian, N. (1990). *Overview of Abuse and Persons with Disabilities.* Culver City, CA: Disability, Abuse and Personal Rights Project, SPECTRUM Institute.

Bancroft, A., Wilson, S., Cunningham-Burley, S., Backett-Milburn, K. and Masters, H. (2004) *Parental drug and alcohol misuse: Resilience and transition among young people.* York: Joseph Rowntree Foundation.

Banks, M., Bates, I., Breakwell, G., Bynner, J., Emler, W., Jamieson, L. and Roberts, K. (1992) *Careers and Identities.* Buckingham: Open University Press.

Barnard, M. (2007) *Drug Addiction and Families.* London: Jessica Kingsley Publishers.

Barnardo's (2005) *Keeping family in mind: a briefing on young carers whose parents have mental health problems.* Essex: Barnardo's.

Barnett, B. and Parker, G. (1998) 'The parentified child: Early competence or childhood deprivation.' *Child Psychology & Psychiatry,* Review 3, 4, 146–155.

Barnow, S., Spitzer, C., Grane, H.J., Kessler, C. and Freyberger, H. (2006) 'Individual characteristics, familial experience, and psychopathology in children of mothers with borderline personality disorder.' *Journal of American Academy of Child & Adolescent Psychiatry* 45, 8, 965–972.

Barron, J. (2007) *Kidspeak: Giving Children and Young People a Voice on Domestic Violence.* Bristol: Women's Aid Federation England.

Barter, C., McCarry, M., Berridge, D. and Evans, K. (2009) *Partner exploitation and violence in teenage intimate relationships.* Executive Summary. London: NSPCC.

Beardsley, W.R., Schultz, L.H. and Selman, R.L. (1987) 'Level of social cognitive development, adaptive functioning and DSM-111 diagnoses in adolescent offspring of parents with affective disorder: Implications of the development of capacity for mutuality.' *Developmental Psychology* 23, 807–815.

Beckwith, L., Howard, J., Espinosa, M. and Tyler, R. (1999) 'Psychopathology, mother-child interaction, and infant development: Substance-abusing mothers and their offspring.' *Development and Psychopathology* 11, 4, 715–725.

Bee, H. (2000) *The Developing Child.* London: Allyn and Bacon.

Bell, M. (2001) 'Child protection case conferences', in James, A. and Wilson, K. (eds) *The Child Protection Handbook.* London: Ballerie Tindall.

Belsky, J. (1980) 'Child maltreatment: an ecological integration.' *American Psychologist* 35, 4, 320–335.

Belsky, J., Hsief, K. and Crnic, K. (1998) 'Mothering, fathering and infant negativity at age 3 years: Differential susceptibility to rearing experience?' *Development and Psychopathology* 10, 301–319.

Bentovim, A., Cox, A., Bingley-Miller, L. and Pizzey, S. (2009) *Safeguarding Children Living with Trauma and Family Violence.* London: Jessica Kingsley Publishers.

Bentovim, A. and Williams, B. (1998) 'Children and adolescents: Victims who become perpetrators.' *Advances in Psychiatric Treatment* 4, 101–107.

Berger, L.M. (2005) 'Income, family characteristics, and physical violence towards children.' *Child Abuse & Neglect* 29, 2, 107–133.

Berk, M., Dodd, S., Berk, L. and Opie, J. (2005) 'Diagnosis and management of patients with bipolar disorder in primary care.' *The British Journal of General Practice* 55, 518, 662–664.

Berry, M. (2006) 'Unemployment damages physical and mental health.' *Personnel Today Magazine.* (www.personneltoday.com/articles/2006/09/07/37084/unemployment-damages-physical-and-mental-health.html) accessed 03.03.2011.

Bewley, S., Friend, J. and Mezey, G. (eds) (1997) *Violence Against Women.* London: Royal College of Obstetricians and Gynaecologists Press.

Bifulco, A. and Moran, P. (1998) *Wednesday's Child: Research into Women's Experiences of Neglect and Abuse in Childhood and Adult Depression.* London: Routledge.

Blanco, C., Okuda, M., Wright, C., Hasin, D.S., Grant, B.F., Liu, S. and Olfson, M. (2008) 'Mental health of college students and their non-college attending peers.' *Archives of General Psychiatry* 65, 12, 1429–1437.

BMA (2007) *Domestic Abuse – A Report from the BMA Board of Science.* BMA: London. (www.bma.org.uk/health_promotion_ethics/domestic_abuse) accessed 03.03.2011.

Booth, T. and Booth, W. (1996) *Parenting under Pressure: Mothers and Fathers with Learning Difficulties.* Buckingham: Open University Press.

Booth, T. and Booth, W. (1997) *Exceptional Childhoods, Unexceptional Children: Growing Up with Parents who have Learning Difficulties.* London: Family Policy Studies Centre.

Booth, T. and Booth W. (2002) 'Men in the lives of mothers with intellectual disabilities.' *Journal of Applied Research in Intellectual Disabilities* 15, 187–199.

Booth, T. and Booth, W. (2004) 'Parents with learning difficulties, child protection and the courts.' *Representing Children* 13, 3, 175–188.

Booth, T., Booth, W. and McConnell, D. (2005) 'The prevalence and outcomes of care proceedings involving parents with learning difficulties in the family courts.' *Journal of Applied Research in Intellectual Disabilities* 18, 7–17.

Bowker, L.H., Arbitell, M. and McFerron, J.K.R. (1988) 'On the relationship between wife beating and child abuse', in Yllo, K. and Bograd, M. (eds) *Feminist Perspectives on Wife Abuse.* Newbury Park, California: Sage.

Bowlby, J. (1973) *Attachment and Loss, Volume 11, Separation, anxiety and anger.* London: Hogarth Press.

Boydell, J., van Os, J., McKenzie, K., Allardyce, J., Goel, R., McCreadie, R.G. and Murray, R.M. (2001) 'Incidence of schizophrenia in ethnic minorities in London: Ecological study into interactions with environment.' *British Medical Journal* 323, 1336–1338.

Bradshaw, J. (1990) *Child Poverty and Deprivation in the UK.* London, National Children's Bureau.

Brandon, M., Bailey, S., Belderson, P., Gardner, R., Sidebottom, P., Dodsworth, J., Warren, C. and Black, J. (2009) *Understanding Serious Case Reviews and their Impact: A Biennial Analysis of Serious Case Reviews 2005–7.* London: Department for Children, Schools and Families.

Brandon, M., Bailey, S. and Belderson, P. (2010) *Building on the learning from serious case reviews: a two-year analysis of child protection database notifications 2007-2009: research brief.* London: Department for Education.

Brandon, M., Belderson, P., Warren, C., Howe, D., Gardner, R., Dodsworth, J., and Black, J. (2008) *Analysing child deaths and serious injury through abuse and neglect: what can we learn? A biennial analysis of serious case reviews 2003–2005.* London: Department for Children, Schools and Families.

Brandon, M. and Lewis, A. (1996) 'Significant harm and children's experiences of domestic violence.' *Child and Family Social Work* 1, 1, 33–42.

Brent, D.A., Perper, J.A., Moritz, G., Liotus, L., Schweers, J., Balach, L. and Roth, C. (2007) 'Familial risk factors for adolescent suicide: A case-control study.' *Acta Psychiatrica Scandinavica* 89, 1, 52–58.

Breznitz, Z. and Friedman, S.L. (1988) 'Toddlers' concentration: Does maternal depression make a difference.' *Journal of Child Psychology and Psychiatry and Allied Disciplines* 29, 3, 267–279.

Brisby, T., Baker, S. and Hedderwick, T. (1997) *Under the Influence: Coping with parents who drink too much.* London: Alcohol Concern.

British Crime Survey (1996) London: Home Office.

Bronfenbrenner, U. (1977) 'Towards an experimental ecology of human development.' *American Psychologist* 32, 513–531.

Bronfenbrenner, U. (1979) *The Ecology of Human Development.* Cambridge. M.A: Harvard University Press.

Brophy, J. (2006) *Research Review: Child Care Proceedings under the Children Act 1989.* London: Department for Constitutional Affairs.

Brophy, J., Jhutti-Johal, J. and Owen, C. (2003) 'Assessing and documenting child ill-treatment in minority ethnic households.' *Family Law* 33, 756–764.

Brown, G.W. and Harris, T. (1978) *Social Origins of Depression.* London: Tavistock.

Burns, E.C. (1996) 'The health and development of children whose mothers are on methadone maintenance.' *Child Abuse Review* 5, 113–122.

Butcher, P.R., Wind, T. and Bouma, A. (2008) 'Parenting stress in mothers and fathers of a child with a hemiparesis: Sources of stress, intervening factors and long-term expressions of stress.' *Child Care Health and Development* 34, 4, 530–541.

C4EO (2010) *Effective practice to protect children living in highly resistant families.* London: Centre for Excellence and Outcomes in Children and Young People's Services (C4EO).

Campbell, S.B. (1999) 'The timing and chronicity of postpartum depression: Implications for infant development', in Murray, L. and Cooper, P.J. (eds) *Postpartum Depression and Child Development.* London: Guilford Press.

Carers and Disabled Children Act 2000. London: The Stationery Office.

Carers (Recognition and Services) Act 1995. Office of Public Sector Information (www.legislation.gov.uk/ukpga/1995/12/contents) accessed 03.03.2011.

Casanueva, C., Martin, S.L. and Runyan, D.K. (2009) 'Repeated reports for child maltreatment among intimate partner violence victims: Findings from the National Survey of Child and Adolescent Well-Being.' *Child Abuse* & Neglect 33, 2, 84–93.

Caspi, A., Sugden, K., Moffitt, T.E., Taylor, A., Craig, I.W., Harrington, H., McClay, J., Hill, J., Martin, J., Braithwaite, A. and Poulton, R. (2003) 'Influence of life stress on depression: Moderation by a polymorphism in the 5-HTT gene.' *Science* 18, 301 (5631), 291–293.

Cassin, A.L. (1996) 'Acute maternal mental illness – infants at risk: A community focus.' *Psychiatric Care* 2, 6, 202–205.

Cavanagh, K., Dobash, E. R. and Dobash, R.P. (2007) 'The murder of children by fathers in the context of child abuse.' *Child Abuse & Neglect* 31, 7, 731–746.

Centre de liaison sur l'intervention et la prévention psychosociales (2007) *Children Exposed to Domestic Violence. 2nd Edition Revised and Augmented.* Montreal: CLIPP.

Centre for Disease Control and Prevention (2004) *Pregnancy Risk Assessment Monitoring System (PRAMS): PRAMS and Postpartum Depression* (www.cdc.gov/prams/PPD.htm) accessed 03.03.2011.

CHANGE (2005) *Report of National Gathering of Parents with Learning Disabilities.* Leeds.

ChildLine (1997) *Beyond the Limit: Children who Live with Parental Alcohol Misuse.* London: ChildLine.

Child Trends (2004) *Learning Disabilities.* (www.childtrendsdatabank.org/archivepgs/65.htm) accessed 03.03.2011.

Children Act 1989. London: HMSO.

Children Act 2004. London: The Stationery Office.

Children's Workforce Development Council (2010) *The Common Assessment Framework (CAF)*. Leeds: Children's Workforce Development Council. (www.cwdcouncil.org.uk/caf) accessed 03.03.2011.

Christensen, E. (1997) 'Aspects of a preventative approach to support children of alcoholics.' *Child Abuse Review* 6, 24–34.

Cicchetti, D., and Toth, S.L. (1995) 'A developmental psychopathology perspective on child abuse and neglect.' *Journal of the American Academy of Child Adolescent Psychiatry* 34, 5, 541–565.

Cleaver, H. (1996) *Focus on Teenagers: Research into Practice*. London: HMSO.

Cleaver, H. (2000) *Fostering Family Contact*. London: The Stationery Office.

Cleaver, H, and Freeman, P. (1995) *Parental Perspectives in Cases of Suspected Child Abuse*. London: HMSO.

Cleaver, H. and Nicholson, D. (2007) *Parental Learning Disability and Children's Needs: Family Experiences and Effective Practice*. London: Jessica Kingsley Publishers.

Cleaver, H., Nicholson, D., Tarr, S. and Cleaver, D. (2007) *Child Protection, Domestic Violence and Parental Substance Misuse: Family Experiences and Effective Practice*. London: Jessica Kingsley Publishers.

Cleaver, H. and Walker, S. with Meadows, P. (2004) *Assessing Children's Needs and Circumstances: The Impact of the Assessment Framework*. London: Jessica Kingsley Publishers.

Cm 5730 (2003) *The Victoria Climbié Inquiry Report of an Inquiry by Lord Laming*. London: The Stationery Office.

Cm 7589 (2009) *The Protection of Children in England: Action Plan. The Government's Response to Lord Laming*. London: The Stationery Office.

Cm 7985 (2010) *Healthy Lives – Healthy People: Our strategy for public health in England*. Norwich: The Stationery Office.

Cohler, B., Grunebaum, H., Weiss, J., Gamer, E. and Gallant, D. (1977) 'Disturbance of attention among schizophrenic, depressed, and well mothers and their young children.' *Journal of Child Psychology and Psychiatry* 18, 115–164.

Coid, J. and Yang, M. (2006) 'Prevalence and correlates of personality disorder in Great Britain.' *British Journal of Psychiatry* 188, 423–431.

Coldwell, J., Pike, A. and Dunn, J. (2006) 'Household chaos – links with parenting and child behaviour.' *Journal of Child Psychology and Psychiatry* 47, 11, 1116–1122.

Coleman, R. and Cassell, D. (1995) 'Parents who misuse drugs and alcohol', in Reder, P. and Lucey, C. (eds) *Assessment of Parenting: Psychiatric and Psychological Contributions*. London: Routledge.

Collishaw, S., Pickles, A., Messer, J., Rutter, M., Shearer, C. and Maughan, B. (2007) 'Resilience to adult psychopathology following childhood maltreatment: Evidence from a community sample.' *Child Abuse & Neglect* 31, 3, 211–230.

Community Care (2006) 'Set up to fail as parents?' *Community Care* 8 June 2006.

Community Care (2009) 'Inspectors point to lack of help for disabled parents.' *Community Care* 26 February 2009.

Cook, P.W. (1997) *Abused Men: The Hidden Side of Domestic Violence*. Westport: Praeger.

Cooke, P. (2005) *ACTing to Support Parents with Learning Disabilities*. Nottingham: Ann Croft Trust.

Courtney, M.E., Barth, R.P., Berrick, J.D., Brooks, D., Needell, B. and Park, L. (1996) 'Race and child welfare services: Past research and future directions.' *Child Welfare League of America* LXXV, 2. 99–137.

Covell, K. and Howe, R.B. (2009) *Children, Families and Violence: Challenges for Children's Rights*. London: Jessica Kingsley Publishers.

Cox, C.E., Kotch, J.B. and Everson, M. A. (2003) 'A longitudinal study of modifying influences in the relationship between domestic violence and child maltreatment.' *Journal of Family Violence* 18, 1, 5–17.

Cox, T.A., Puckering, C., Pound, A. and Mills, M, (1987) 'The impact of maternal depression in young children.' *Journal of Child Psychiatry* 28, 917–928.

Craft, A. (1993) *Parents with Learning Disabilities*. Kidderminster: British Institute for Mental Handicap.

Crime and Security Act 2010. London: The Stationery Office.

Currie, C.L. (2006) 'Animal cruelty by children exposed to domestic violence.' *Child Abuse & Neglect* 30, 4, 425–435.

Daniel, B., Taylor, J. and Scott, J. (2009) 'Noticing and Helping the Neglected Child: Summary of a Systematic Literature Review.' *International Journal of Child and Family Welfare* 12, 4, 120.

Daniel, B., Wassell, S. and Gilligan, R. (2000) *Child Development for Child Care and Protection Workers*. London: Jessica Kingsley Publishers.

Dave, S., Sherr, L., Senior, R. and Nazareth, I. (2008) 'Associations between paternal depression and behaviour problems in children of 4–6 years.' *European Child and Adolescent Psychiatry* 17, 306–315.

Davies, C. and Ward, H. (2011) *Safeguarding Children Across Services: Messages from Research on Identifying and Responding to Child Maltreatment*. London: Jessica Kingsley Publishers.

Day, N.L., Goldschmidt, L. and Thomas, C.A. (2006) 'Prenatal marijuana exposure contributes to the prediction of marijuana use at age 14.' *Addiction* 101, 1313–1322.

Deane, S. (1977) *Reading in the Dark*. London: Vintage.

Dearden, C. and Becker, S. (1996) *Young Carers at the Crossroads: An Evaluation of Nottingham Young Carers Project*. Nottingham: Young Carers Research Group/Crossroads.

Dearden, C. and Becker, S. (2003) *Young Carers and Education*. London: Carers UK.

Dearden, C. and Becker, S. (2004) *Young Carers in the UK: The 2004 Report*. London: Carers UK.

Denny, D. (2005) *Risk and Society*. London: Sage.

D'Orban, P.T. (1979) 'Women who kill their children.' *British Journal of Psychiatry* 134, 560–571.

Department for Children, Schools and Families (2008) *Targeted Youth Support: Integrated support for vulnerable young people*. A Guide. Nottingham: Department for Children, Schools and Families.

Department for Children, Schools and Families (2009) *Referrals, Assessments and Children and Young People who are the Subject of a Child Protection Plan, England – year ending 31 March 2008*. (www.education.gov.uk/rsgateway/DB/SFR/s000811/index.shtml) accessed 03.03 2011.

Department for Children, Schools and Families (2010) *ICS improvement: ICS guidance package 2010*. (www.education.gov.uk/childrenandyoungpeople/safeguarding/socialworkreform/b0071081/integrated-childrens-system-ics-improvement/ics-guidance-packagemarch-2010) accessed 03.03.2011.

Department for Children, Schools and Families and Department of Health (2010) *Teenage Pregnancy Strategy: Beyond 2010*. Nottingham: Department for Children Schools and Families.

Department for Children, Schools and Families, Department for Health and National Treatment Agency for Substance Misuse (2009) *Joint Guidance on Development of Local protocols between Drug and alcohol Treatment Services and Local Safeguarding and Family Services*. London: Department for Children Schools and Families.

Department for Children, Schools and Families and Department for Innovation, Universities & Skills (2008) *Participation in Education, Training and Employment by 16-18 Year Olds in England*. (www.education.gov.uk/rsgateway/DB/SFR/s000792/index.shtml) accessed 03.03.2011.

Department for Education (2010a) *Guidance for local authorities and schools on setting education performance targets for 2012*. Nottingham: Department for Education.

Department for Education (2010b) *Statistical Release: Referrals, Assessments and Children who were the Subject of a Child Protection Plan (Children in Need Census – Provisional) Year Ending 31 March 2010*. London: Department for Education.

Department for Education (2010c) *Haringey Local Safeguarding Children Board; Serious Case Review 'Child A'*. London: Department for Education. (www.education. gov.uk/childrenandyoungpeople/safeguarding/a0065483/serious-case-review) accessed 03.03.2011.

Department for Education (2011) Under-18 and under-16 conception statistics. (www.education.gov.uk/childrenandyoungpeople/healthandwellbeing/ teenagepregnancy/a0064898/under-18-and-under-16-conception-statistics) accessed 03.03.2011.

Department for Education and Employment (1997) *School Leavers Destinations Surveys: Careers Service Activity Survey*. Darlington: Department for Education and Employment.

Department for Education and Skills (2007) *Targeted Youth Support: A Guide*. London: The Stationery Office.

Department of Health (1991) *The Care of Children: Principles and Practice in Guidance and Legislation*. London: HMSO.

Department of Health (1995a) *Child Protection: Messages from Research*. London: HMSO.

Department of Health (1995b) *Looking After Children: Assessment and Action Records, Age Three and Four Years*. London: HMSO.

Department of Health (2002a) *Mental Health Policy Implementation Guide: Dual Diagnosis Good Practice Guide*. London: HMSO (www.dh.gov.uk/en/ Publicationsandstatistics/Publications/PublicationsPolicyAndGuidance/ DH_4009058) accessed 03.03.2011.

Department of Health (2005) *Alcohol Needs Assessment Research Project (ANARP): The 2004 National Alcohol Needs Assessment for England*. London: DH Publications. (www.dh.gov.uk/en/Publicationsandstatistics/Publications/ PublicationsPolicyAndGuidance/DH_4122341) accessed 03.03.2011.

Department of Health (2008) *Code of Practice: Mental Health Act 1983*. London: The Stationery Office.

Department of Health (2009b) *Alcohol Advice*. (http://webarchive.nationalarchives. gov.uk/+/www.dh.gov.uk/en/Publichealth/Healthimprovement/Alcoholmisuse/ DH_085385) accessed 03.03.2011.

Department for Health (2010a) *Improving services for women and child victims of violence: The Department of Health Action Plan*. London: Department of Health.

Department for Health (2010b) *A Vision for Adult Social Care: Capable Communities and Active Citizens.* London: Social Care Policy Division.

Department of Health, Department for Education and Employment and Home Office (2000) *Framework for the Assessment of Children in Need and their Families.* London: The Stationery Office.

Department of Health and Department for Education and Skills (2004) *National Service Framework for Children, Young People and Maternity Services.* London: Department of Health.

Department of Health and Department for Education and Skills (2007) *Good Practice Guidance on Working with Parents with a Learning Disability.* London: Department of Health.

Department of Health (England) and the devolved administrations (2007) *Drug Misuse and Dependence: UK Guidelines on Clinical Management.* London: Department of Health (England), the Scottish Government, Welsh Assembly Government and Northern Ireland Executive.

Department of Health and National Treatment Agency for Substance Misuse (2006) *Models of Care for Alcohol Misusers (MoCAM).* London: Department of Health.

Department of Health, Home Office, Department for Education and Skills and Department for Culture, Media and Sport (2007) *Safe. Sensible. Social. The next steps in the National Alcohol Strategy.* London: Department of Health and Home Office.

Department of Health, Scottish Office Department of Health, Welsh Office, Department of Health and Social Service, Northern Ireland (1999) *Drug Misuse and Dependence – Guidelines on Clinical Management.* London: The Stationery Office.

Desforges, C. with Abouchaar, A. (2003) *The Impact of Parental Involvement, Parental support and Family Education on Pupil Achievements and Adjustment: A Literature Review.* Nottingham: Dfes Publications.

DeVoe, E. and Smith, E.L. (2002) 'The impact of domestic violence on urban preschool children.' *Journal of Interpersonal Violence* 17, 10, 1075–1101.

Dingwell, R., Eekelaar, J. and Murray, T. (1983) *Protection of Children: State Intervention and Family Life.* Oxford: Blackwell.

Dinsdale,l H., Ridler, C., Rutter, H. and Mathrani, S. (2010) *National Child Measurement Programme: Changes in children's body mass index between 2006/7 and 2008/9.* Oxford: National Obesity Observatory.

Dixon, L., Browne, K.D., Hamilton-Giacritsis, C. (2005a) 'Risk factors of parents abused as children national analysis of the intergenerational continuity of child maltreatment (part 1).' *Journal of Psychology and Psychiatry* 46, 1, 47–57.

Dixon, L., Hamilton-Giacritsis, C. and Browne, K.D. (2005b) 'Risk factors and behavioural measures of abused as children: a meditational analysis of the intergenerational continuity of child maltreatment (part 11).' *Journal of Child Psychology and Psychiatry* 46, 1, 58–68.

Dobash, R.E. and Dobash, R.P. (1980) *Violence against Wives*. Sussex: Open Books.

Dobash, R.E. and Dobash, R.P. (1984) 'The nature and antecedents of violent events.' *British Journal of Criminology* 24, 3, 269–288.

Dobash, R.E. and Dobash, R.P. (1992) *Women, Violence and Social Change*. London: Routledge.

Domestic Violence, Crime and Victims Act 2004. Office of Public Sector Information (www.opsi.gov.uk/ACTS/acts2004/ukpga_20040028_en_1) accessed 03.03.2011.

Dominy, N. and Radford, L. (1996) *Domestic Violence in Surrey: Towards an Effective Inter-Agency Response*. London: Roehampton Institutes/Surrey Social Services.

Dore, M.M. and Dore, J.M. (1995) 'Identifying substance abuse in maltreating families: A child welfare challenge.' *Child Abuse & Neglect* 19, 5, 531–543.

Dowdney, L. and Skuse, D. (1993) 'Parenting provided by adults with mental retardation.' *Journal of Child Psychology and Psychiatry* 34, 1, 25–47.

Downey, G. and Coyne, J.C. (1990) 'Children of depressed parents: An integrative review.' *Psychological Bulletin* 108, 50–76.

Doyle, R. (1994) *Paddy Clarke Ha Ha Ha*. Berkshire: Minerva.

Duncan, S. and Reder. P, (2000) 'Children's experience of major psychiatric disorder in their parent: An overview', in Reder, P., McClure, M. and Jolley, A. (eds) *Family Matters: Interfaces Between Child and Adult Mental Health*. London: Routledge.

Dunn, J. (2004). *Children's Friendships: The Beginnings of Intimacy*. Oxford: Blackwell publishers.

Dunne, L., Sneddon, H., Iwaniec, D. and Stewart, M.C. (2007) 'Maternal mental health and faltering growth in infants.' *Child Abuse Review* 16, 5, 283–295.

Dunn, M.G., Tarter, R.E., Mezzich, A.C., Vanyukov, M., Kirisci, L. and Kirillova, G. (2002) 'Origins and consequences of child neglect in substance abuse families.' *Clinical Psychology Review* 22, 1063–90.

Dutt, R. and Phillips, M. (2000) 'Assessing black children in need and their families', in Department of Health, *Assessing Children in Need and their Families, Practice Guidance*. London: The Stationery Office.

Education and Skills Act 2008. London: The Stationery Office (www.opsi.gov.uk/acts/acts2008/ukpga_20080025_en_1) accessed 03.03.2011.

Edwards, A. and Smith, P. (1997) 'Young carers and their parents with long term psychiatric disorders.' *Keeping Children in Mind: Balancing Children's Needs with Parents' Mental Health.* Report of the 12th Annual Conference hosted by the Michael Sieff Foundation. (www.michaelsieff-foundation.org.uk/content/confkeepinfchild14.pdf) accessed 03.03.2011.

Eekelaar, J. and Clive, E. (1977) *Custody after Divorce.* Oxford: Oxford Centre for Socio-Legal Studies, Wolfson College.

Egeland, B. (2009) 'Taking stock: Childhood emotional maltreatment and developmental psychopathology.' *Child Abuse & Neglect* 33, 1, 22–27.

Egeland, B. and Scroufe, L.A. (1981) 'Developmental sequelae of maltreatment in infancy.' *New Directions in Child Development* 11, 77–92.

Elliott, G.C., Avery, R., Fishman, E. and Hoshiko, B. (2002) 'The encounter with family violence and risky sexual activity among young adolescent females.' *Violence and Victims* 17, 95, 569–592.

Emerson E. and Hatton, C. (2008) *People with Learning Disabilities in England.* Lancaster: Centre for Disability Research, Lancaster University.

Emerson, E., Malam, S., Davies, I. and Spencer, K. (2005) *Adults with Learning Disabilities in England 2003/4.* Leeds: Health and Social Care Information Centre.

Emery, R.E. (1982) 'Interparental conflict and the children of discord and divorce.' *Psychological Bulletin* 92, 310–330.

Emery, R., Weintraub, S. and Neale, J.M. (1982) 'Effects of marital discord on the school behaviour of children of schizophrenic, affectively disordered, and normal parents.' *Journal of Abnormal Psychology* 11, 2, 215-228.

Ene, A.C., Ajayi, B.B. and Nwankwo, E.A. (2007) 'Prevalence of HIV neonatal infection amongst babies born to HIV positive parents in Maiduguri north-eastern Nigeria.' *International Journal of Virology* 3, 11, 41–44.

Epstein, T., Saltzman-Benaiah, J., O'Hare, A., Goll, J.C. and Tuck, S. (2008) 'Associated features of Asperger Syndrome and their relationship to parenting stress.' *Child Care, Health and Development* 34, 4, 503–511.

Equality Act 2010. Government Equalities Office. London: The Stationery Office.

Erol, A., Ersoy, B., Gulpek, D. and Mete, L. (2008) 'Folie a famille: case report.' *Anatolian Journal of Psychiatry* 9, 261–264.

Fahlberg, V.I. (1991) *A Child's Journey through Placement.* BAAF: London.

Falkov, A. (1996) *Fatal Child Abuse and Parental Psychiatric Disorder.* London: Department of Health.

Falkov, A. (1997) 'Adult psychiatry – Missing link in the child protection network: A response to Reder and Duncan.' *Child Abuse Review* 6, 41–45.

Falkov, A. (1998) *Crossing Bridges: Training Resources for Working with Mentally Ill Parents and their Children.* London: Department of Health.

Falkov, A. (2002) 'Addressing family needs when a parent is mentally ill', in Ward, H. and Rose, W. (eds) *Approaches to Needs Assessment in Children's Services.* London: Jessica Kingsley Publishers.

Family Law Act 1996. London: HMSO.

Famularo, R., Kinscherff, R. and Fenton, T. (1992) 'Parental substance abuse and the nature of child maltreatment.' *Child Abuse and Neglect* 16, 475–483.

Fantuzzo, J. and Fusco, R. (2007) 'Children's direct sensory exposure to substantiated domestic violence crimes.' *Violence and Victims* 22, 2, 158–171.

Fantuzzo, J.W. and Lindquist, C.U. (1989) 'The effects of observing conjugal violence on children: A review and analysis of research methodology.' *Journal of Family Violence* 4, 1, 77–94.

Farmer, E. (2006) 'Using research to develop practice', in Humphreys, C. and Stanley, N. (eds) *Domestic Violence and Child Protection: Directions for Good Practice.* London: Jessica Kingsley Publishers.

Farmer, E. and Owen, M. (1995) *Child Protection Practice: Private Risks and Public Remedies.* London: HMSO.

Farmer, E. and Pollock, S. (1998) *Substitute Care for Sexually Abused and Abusing Children.* Chichester: John Wiley and Sons.

Fenson, L., Dale, P.S., Reznick, J.S., Bates, E., Thal, D.J. and Pethick, S.J. (1994) 'Variability in early communication development.' *Monographs of the Society for Research in Child Development* 59 (5, Serial No. 242).

Fergusson, D.M., Horwood, I.J. and Lynskey, M.T. (1995) 'Maternal depressive symptoms and depressive symptoms in adolescents.' *Journal of Child Psychology and Psychiatry* 36, 7, 1161–1178.

Fergusson, D.M., Horwood, L.J. and Ridder, E.M. (2005) 'Partner violence and mental health outcomes in a New Zealand Cohort.' *Journal of Marriage and the Family* 67, 1103–19.

Field, T., Healy, B., Goldstein, S. and Guthertz, M. (1990) 'Behaviour-state matching and synchrony in mother-infant interactions of nondepressed versus depressed 'dyads'.' *Developmental Psychology* 26, 7–14.

Finney A (2004) *Alcohol and Intimate Partner Violence: Key Findings from the Research.* London: Home Office.

Flately, J., Kershaw, C., Smith, K., Chaplin, R. and Moon, D. (2010) *Crime in England and Wales 2009/10.* (http://rds.homeoffice.gov.uk/rds/pdfs10/hosb1210.pdf) accessed 03.03.2011.

Fombonne, E. (1995) 'Depressive disorders: Time trends and possible explanatory mechanisms', in Rutter, M. and Smith, D.J. (eds) *Psycholosocial Disorders in Young People: Time Trends and Their Causes.* Chichester: Wiley.

Fonagy, P., Target, M., Gergely, G., Allen, J.G. and Bateman, A.W. (2003) 'The developmental roots of borderline personality disorder in early attachment relationships: A theory and some evidence.' *Psychoanalytic Inquiry* 23, 412–459.

Forrester, D. (2000) 'Parental substance misuse and child protection in a British sample. A survey of children on the child protection register in an inner London district office.' *Child Abuse Review* 9, 4, 235–246.

Forrester, D., Goodman, K., Cocker, C., Binnie, C. and Jensch, G. (2009) 'What is the impact of public care on children's welfare? A review of research findings from England and Wales and their policy implications.' *Journal of Social Policy* 38, 3, 439–456.

Foster, G. (2008) 'Injecting drug users with chronic hepatitis C: Should they be offered antiviral therapy.' *Addiction* 103, 9, 1412–13.

Foundation for People with Learning Disabilities (2009) *Statistics about people with learning disabilities.* Glasgow: The Foundation for People with Learning Disabilities. (www.learningdisabilities.org.uk/) accessed 03.03.2011.

Frank, D.A., Augustyn, M., Knight, W.G., Pell, T. and Zuckerman, B. (2001) 'Growth, development and behaviour in early childhood following prenatal cocaine exposure. A systematic review.' *Journal of the American Medical Association* 285, 12, 1613–1625.

Fuller, E. and Sanchez, M. (ed) (2010) *Smoking, drinking and drug use among young people in England in 2009.* London: National Centre for Social Research.

Galloway, D.M., Ball, T., Blomfield, D. and Seyd, R. (1982) *Schools and Disruptive Behaviour.* London, Longman.

Galvani, S. (2004) 'Responsible disinhibition: alcohol, men and violence to women.' *Addiction Research and Theory* 12, 4, 357–374.

Galvani, S. and Forrester, D. (2009) *What works in training social workers about drug and alcohol use? A survey of student learning and readiness to practice.* Universities of Warwick and Bedfordshire (www.communitycare.co.uk/smstudy) accessed 03.03.2011.

Gardner, R. and Cleaver, H. (2009) 'Working effectively with parents', in Cleaver, H., Cawson, P., Gorin, S., and Walker, S. (eds) *Safeguarding Children: A Shared Responsibility.* Chichester: Wiley-Blackwell.

UNIVERSITY OF WINCHESTER
LIBRARY

Gath, A. (1988) 'Mentally handicapped people as parents.' *Journal of Child Psychology and Psychiatry* 29, 6, 739–744.

Gerada, C. (1996) 'The drug-addicted mother: pregnancy and lactation', in Gopfert, M., Webster, J. and Seeman, M.V. (eds) *Parental Psychiatric Disorder: Distressed Parents and their Families*. Cambridge: Cambridge Universities Press.

Gerhardt, S. (2004) *Why Love Matters: How Affection Shapes a Baby's Brain*. Hove: Brunner-Routledge.

Gharial, N. (2007) 'Alcohol as a problem for south Asian community.' *Alcohol Alert* 1, 20–22. Institute of Alcohol Studies.

Ghate, D. and Hazel, N. (2002) *Parenting in Poor Environments: Stress, Support and Coping*. London: Jessica Kingsley Publishers.

Gibbons, J., Conroy, S. and Bell, C. (1995) *Operating the Child Protection System: A Study of Child Protection Practices in English Local Authorities*. London: HMSO.

Gibson, E. (1975) 'Homicide in England and Wales 1967–1971'. *Home Office research study No.31*. London: HMSO.

Gilchrist, E., Johnson, R., Takriti, R., Weston, S., Beech, A. and Kebbell, M. (2003) *Domestic Violence Offenders: Characteristics and Offending Related Needs. Home Office findings 217* (www.homeoffice.gov.uk/rds/pdfs2/r217.pdf) accessed 03.03.2011.

Girling, M., Huakau, J., Casswell, S. and Conway, K. (2002) *Families and Heavy Drinking: Impacts on Children's Wellbeing – Systematic Review*. Wellington: Blue Skies Fund.

Glaser, D. and Prior, V. (1997) 'Is the term child protection applicable to emotional abuse?' *Child Abuse Review* 6, 315–329.

Gleeson, C., Robinson, M. and Neal, R. (2002) 'A review of teenagers' perceived needs and access to primary healthcare – implications for school health services.' *Primary Health Care Research and Development* 3, 184–193.

Goldberg, D.P. and Williams, P. (1988) *A User's Guide to the General Health Questionnaire*. Windsor: NFER-Nelson.

Goldsmith, T.D. and Vera, M. (2000) *The Physical and Emotional Injuries of Domestic Violence*. (www.achievesolutions.net/achievesolutions/en/Content.do?contentId=1927) accessed 03.03.2011.

Goodyer, I.M., Cooper, P.J., Vize, C.M. and Ashby, L. (1993) 'Depression in 11–16-year-old girls: The role of past parental psychopathology and exposure to recent life events.' *Journal of Child Psychology and Psychiatry* 34, 1103–1115.

Gorin, S. (2004) *Understanding what children say; Children's experiences of domestic violence, parental substance misuse and parental health problems*. London: National Children's Bureau.

Gottlieb, S. (2002) 'Drug therapy reduces birth rate of HIV infected babies from 19% to 3%.' *British Medical Journal* 324, 381.

Graham, P., Rawlings, E. and Rimini, W. (1988) 'Survivors of terror: Battered women, hostages and the Stockholm syndrome', in Yllo, K. and Bograd, M. (eds) *Feminist Perspectives on Wife Abuse.* London: Sage.

Gray, J. (1993) 'Coping with unhappy children who exhibit emotional and behaviour problems in the classroom', in Varma, V. (ed) *Coping with Unhappy Children.* London: Cassell.

Green, H., McGinnity, A., Meltzer, H., Ford, T. and Goodman, R. (2005) *Mental Health of Children and Young People in Great Britain, 2004.* London: Office for National Statistics.

Greenwich Asian Women's Project (1996) *Annual Report.* London: Greenwich Asian Women's Project.

Hackett, S. and Uprichard E. (2007) *Animal Abuse and Child Maltreatment: A Review of the Literature and Findings from a UK Study.* London: NSPCC.

Hague, G. and Malos, E. (1994) 'Children, domestic violence and housing; the impact of homelessness', in Mullender, A. and Morley, R. (eds) *Children Living with Domestic Violence.* Bournemouth: Whiting and Birch.

Hammen, C. (1988) 'Self cognitions, stressful events and the prediction of depression in children of depressed mothers.' *Journal of Abnormal Child Psychology* 16, 347–60.

Hammen, C., Gordon, D., Burge, D., Adrian, C., Jaenicke, C. and Hiroto, G. (1978) 'Communication patterns of mothers with affective disorders and their relationship to children's status and social functioning', in Hahlweg, K. and Goldstein, M.J. (eds) *Understanding Major Mental Disorder: The Contribution of Family Interaction Research.* New York: Family Process Press.

Hamner, J. (1989) 'Women and policing in Britain', in Hamner, J., Radford, J. and Stanko, E.A. (eds) *Women, Policing and Male Violence: International Perspectives.* London: Routledge.

Haringey Local Safeguarding Children Board (2009) *Serious Case Review: Baby Peter.* (www.haringeylscb.org/executive_summary_peter_final.pdf) accessed 03.03.2011.

Hassiotis, A., Barron, P. and O'Hara, J. (2000) 'Mental health services for people with learning disabilities.' *British Medical Journal* 321, 583–584.

Health and Safety Executive (2010) *Health and Safety Statistics 2009/10.* (www.hse.gov.uk/) assessed 03.03.2011.

Health Protection Agency (2010) *Shooting Up: Infections among injecting drug users in the UK. An update: November 2010.* London: Health Protection Agency.

Henderson, J., Kesmodel, U. and Gray, R. (2007) 'Systematic review of the fetal effects of prenatal binge-drinking.' *Journal of Epidemiology and Community Health* 61, 1069–073

Her Majesty's Court Service, Home Office, Criminal Justice Service (2008) *Justice with Safety: Special Domestic Violence Courts Review 2007–8* (www.cps.gov.uk/publications/equality/sdvc_review_exec_sum.html) accessed 03.03.2011.

Hester, M., Pearson, C. and Harwin, N. with Abrahams, H. (2007). *Making an Impact: Children and Domestic Violence.* A reader. 2nd ed. London: Jessica Kingsley Publishers.

Hester, M. and Radford, L. (1995) 'Safety matters! Domestic violence and child contact, towards an inter-disciplinary response.' *Representing Children* 8, 4, 49–60.

Hester, M. and Radford, L. (1996) *Domestic Violence and Child Contact Arrangements in England and Denmark.* Bristol: Policy Press.

Hill, J., Swales, M. and Byatt, M. (2005) 'Personality disorders', in Gillberg, C., Harrington, R. and Steinhausen, H. (eds) *A Clinician's Handbook of Child and Adolescent Psychiatry.* Cambridge: Cambridge University Press.

Hill, M., Leybourn, A. and Brown, J. (1996) 'Children whose parents misuse alcohol: a study of services and needs.' *Child and Family Social Work* 1, 3, 159–167.

HM Government (2006) *What to do if you're worried a child is being abused.* London: Department for Education and Skills.

HM Government (2007) *Statutory guidance on making arrangements to safeguard and promote the welfare of children under section 11 of the Children Act 2004.* London: Department for Education and Skills.

HM Government (2008) *Carers at the heart of 21st-century families and communities. 'A caring system on your side. A life of your own'.* London: Department of Health.

HM Government (2010a) *Working Together to Safeguard Children: A guide to inter-agency working to safeguard and promote the welfare of children.* London: The Department for Children, Schools and Families.

HM Government (2010b) *Drug Strategy 2010 Reducing Demand, Restricting Supply, Building Recovery: Supporting people to live a drug free life.* London: Home Office. (www.homeoffice.gov.uk/drugs/drug-strategy-2010/) accessed 03.03.2011.

HM Government (2010c) *Call to End Violence against Women and Girls.* (www.homeoffice.gov.uk/publications/crime/call-end-violence-women-girls/vawg-paper.) accessed 03.03.2011.

HM Government (2010d) *Recognised, Valued and Supported: Next Steps for the Carers Strategy.* (www.dh.gov.uk/en/Publicationsandstatistics/Publications/PublicationsPolicyAndGuidance/DH_122077) accessed 03.03.2011.

HM Government (2011) *No Health Without Mental Health: A Cross-Government Mental Health Outcomes Strategy for People of All Ages.* London: Department of Health. (www.dh.gov.uk/mentalhealthstrategy) accessed 03.03.2011.

Hoare, J. and Moon, D. (eds) (2010) *Drug Misuse Declared: Findings from the 2009/10 British Crime Survey, England and Wales.* London: Home Office Statistical Bulletin.

Hobson, R.P., Patrick, M., Crandell, l., García-Pérez, R. and Lee, A. (2005) 'Personal relatedness and attachment in infants of mothers with borderline personality disorder.' *Development and Psychopathology* 17, 329–347.

Hodge, G.M., McCormick, J. and Elliott, R. (1997) 'Examination-induced distress in a public examination at the completion of secondary schooling.' *British Journal of Educational Psychology* 67, 2, 185–198.

Hoek, H.W. (2006) 'Incidence, prevalence and mortality of anorexia nervosa and other eating disorders.' *Current Opinion in Psychiatry* 19, 4, 389–394.

Hoff, L.A. (1990) *Battered Women as Survivors.* London: Routledge.

Hogan, D. (1998) 'Annotation: the psychological development and welfare of children of opiate and cocaine users – review and research needs.' *Journal of Child Psychology and Psychiatry* 39, 609–619.

Hogan, D.M. (2003) 'Parenting beliefs and practices of opiate-addicted parents: Concealment and taboo.' *European Addiction Research* 9, 113–119.

Hogan, D. and Higgins L. (2001) *When Parents Use Drugs: Key Findings from a Study of Children in the Care of Drug-using Parents.* Dublin: The Children's Research Centre.

Holden, G.W. and Ritchie, K.L. (1991) 'Linking extreme marital discord, child rearing, and child behaviour problems: Evidence from battered women.' *Child Development* 62, 311–327.

Hollander, E. (1997) 'Obsessive-compulsive disorder: the hidden epidemic.' *Journal of Clinical Psychiatry* 58 (suppl 12): 3–6.

Holt, S., Buckley, H. and Whelan, S. (2008) 'The impact of exposure to domestic violence on children and young people: A review of the literature.' *Child Abuse & Neglect* 32, 8, 797–810.

Home Office (2002) *Statistics on Women and the Criminal Justice System.* London: Home Office.

Home Office (2009a) *National Support Framework. Delivering Safer and Confident Communities: Information sharing for community safety: Guidance and Practice advice.* London: Home Office. (http://www.homeoffice.gov.uk/publications/crime/info-sharing-community-safety/guidance?view=Binary) accessed 03.03.2011.

Home Office (2009b) *Domestic Violence*. London: Home Office (http://rds. homeoffice.gov.uk/rds/violencewomen.html) accessed 03.03.2011.

Howard Thompson, S. (1998) 'Working with children of substance-abusing parents.' *Young Children* 53, 1, 34–37.

Howe, D. (1995) *Attachment Theory for Social Work Practice*. London: Macmillan.

Hughes, H. (1988) 'Psychological and behavioural correlates of family violence in child witnesses and victims.' *American Journal of Orthopsychiatry* 58, 77–90.

Hughes, H., Graham-Bermann, S. and Gruber, G. (2001) 'Resilience in Children Exposed to Domestic Violence', in Graham-Bermann, S. and Edleson, J. (eds) *Domestic Violence in the Lives of Children: The Future of Research, Intervention and Social Policy*. Washington DC: American Psychological Society.

Hulse, G.K., English, D.R., Milne, E., Holman, C.D.J. and Bower, C.I. (1997) 'Maternal cocaine use and low birth weight newborns: A meta analysis.' *Addiction* 92, 11, 1561–1570.

Humphreys, C. (2006) 'Relevant evidence for practice', in Humphreys, C. and Stanley, N. (eds) *Domestic Violence and Child Protection*. London: Jessica Kingsley Publishers.

Humphreys, C. and Houghton, C. (2008) 'The Research Evidence on Children and Young People Experiencing Domestic Violence', in Humphreys, C., Houghton, C. and Ellis, J. (eds) *Literature Review: Better Outcomes for Children and Young People Experiencing Domestic Abuse – Directions for Good Practice*. Edinburgh: The Scottish Government.

Humphreys, C. and Mullender, A. (1999) *Children and Domestic Violence*. Dartington: Research in Practice.

Humphreys, C., Mullender, A., Thiara, R.K. and Skamballis, A. (2006) 'Talking to my Mum: Developing communication between mothers and children in the aftermath of domestic violence.' *Journal of Social Work* 6, 1, 53–64.

Humphreys, C. and Stanley, N. (eds) (2006) *Domestic Violence and Child Protection*. London: Jessica Kingsley Publishers.

Hunt, J., Macleod, A. and Thomas, C. (1999) *The Last Resort: Child Protection, the Courts and the 1989 Children Act*. London: The Stationery Office.

Hyton, C. (1997) *Black Families' Survival Strategies: Ways of coping in UK society*. York: Joseph Rowntree Foundation.

Institute of Alcohol Studies (2009) *Alcohol and Accidents IAS Factsheet* (www.ias.org. uk/resources/factsheets/factsheets.html) accessed 03.03.2011.

International Schizophrenia Consortium, The (2008) 'Rare chromosomal deletions and duplications increase risk of schizophrenia'. *Nature* 455, 237–241.

Jaffe, P., Wolfe, D.A. and Wilson, S. (1990) *Children of Battered Women*. London: Sage.

Jaffee, S.R., Caspi, A., Moffitt., T.E., Polo-Tomás, M. and Taylor, A. (2007) 'Individual, family and neighbourhood factors distinguish resilient from non-resilient maltreated children: A cumulative stressors model.' *Child Abuse & Neglect* 31, 3, 231–253.

James, G. (1994) *Department of Health Discussion Report for ACPC Conference: Study of Working Together 'Part 8' Reports*. London: Department of Health.

James, H. (2004) 'Promoting effective working with parents with learning disabilities.' *Child Abuse Review* 13, 1, 31–41.

Jenkins, J.M. and Smith, M.A. (1990) 'Factors protecting children living in disharmonious homes: Maternal reports.' *Journal of the American Academy of Child and Adolescent Psychiatry* 29, 1, 60–69.

Jones, D.P.H. (2009) 'Assessment of parenting', in Horwath, J. (ed.) *The Child's World: The Comprehensive Guide to Assessing Children in Need*. 2nd edition. London: Jessica Kingsley Publishers.

Jones, D., Bentovim, A., Cameron, H., Vizard, E. and Wolkind, S. (1991) 'Signficant harm in context: The child psychiatrist's contribution', in Adcock, M., White, R. and Hollows, A. (eds) *Significant Harm*. Croydon: Significant Publications.

Joseph, S., Govender, K. and Bhagwanjee, A. (2006) '"I can't see him hit her again, I just want to run away ... hide and block my ears": A phenomenological analysis of a sample of children's coping responses to exposure to domestic violence.' *Journal of Emotional Abuse* 16, 4, 23–45.

Jotangia, D., Moody, A., Stamatakis, E. and Wardle, H. (2006) *Obesity among Children under 11*. (www.dh.gov.uk/en/Publicationsandstatistics/Publications/PublicationsStatistics/DH_4109245) accessed 03.03.2011.

Juliana, P. and Goodman, C. (1997) 'Children of substance abusing parents', in Lowinson, J.H. (ed) *Substance Abuse: A Comprehensive Textbook*. Baltimore: Williams and Wilkins.

Julien, R.M. (1995) *A Primer of Drug Action: A Concise, Non-Technical Guide to the Actions, Uses, and Side Effects of Psychoactive Drugs, 7th Edition*. New York: W.H. Freeman and Co.

Kandal, E.R., Schwartz, J.H. and Jessell, T.M. (2000) *Principles of Neural Science, 4th edition*. New York: McGraw-Hill.

Karr, M. (1995) *The Liars' Club*. Harmondsworth: Penguin.

Kelly, B. (1995) 'Children, families and nursery provision.' *Early Child Development and Care* 108, 1, 115–136.

Kelly, L. (1988) *Surviving Sexual Violence.* Cambridge: Policy Press.

Kelly, Y., Sacker, A., Gray, R., Kelly, J., Wolke, D., Head, J. and Quigley, M.A. (2010) 'Light drinking during pregnancy: still no increased risk for socioemotional difficulties or cognitive deficits at 5 years of age?' *Journal of Epidemiology and Community Health.* (http://jech.bmj.com/content/early/2010/09/13/jech.2009.103002.abstract) accessed on 03.03.2011.

Kendell, R.E. (2002) 'The distinction between personality disorder and mental illness.' *British Journal of Psychiatry* 180, 2, 110–115.

Kendler, K.S., Aggen, S.H., Tambs, K. and Reichborn-Kjennerud, T. (2006) 'Illicit psychoactive substance use, abuse and dependence in a population-based sample of Norwegian twins.' *Psychological Medicine* 36, 7, 955–962.

Kershaw, C., Nicholas, S. and Walker, A. (2008) *Crime in England and Wales 2007/8: Findings from the British Crime Survey and Police Recorded Crime.* London: Home Office (http://rds.homeoffice.gov.uk/rds/pdfs08/hosb0708.pdf) accessed 03.03.2011.

Kessler, R.C., Berglund, P., Demler, O., Jin, R., Koretz, D., Merikangas, K.R., Rush, A.J., Walters, E.E. and Wang, P.S. (2003) 'The epidemiology of major depressive disorder.' *The Journal of the American Medical Association* 289, 23, 3095–3105.

Khaole, N., Ramchanddani, V., Viljoen, D. and Ting-Kai, L. (2004) 'A pilot study of alcohol exposure and pharmacokinetics in women with or without children with fetal alcohol syndrome.' *Alcohol and Alcoholism* 39, 6, 503–508.

Kidd, K.K. (1978) 'A Genetic Perspective on Schizophrenia', in Wynne, L.C., Cromwell, R.L. and Matthysse, S. (eds) *The Nature of Schizophrenia.* Chichester: John Wiley & Sons.

Kinsella, M.T. and Monk, C. (2009) 'Impact of Maternal Stress, Depression and Anxiety on Fetal Neurobehavioral Development.' *Clinical Obstetrics and Gynecology* 52, 3, 425–440.

Kirkwood, C. (1993) *Leaving Abusive Partners: From the Scars of Survival to the Wisdom for Change.* London: Sage.

Klee, H., Jackson, M. and Lewis, S. (2002) *Drug Misuse and Motherhood.* London: Routledge.

Klein, D., Clark, D., Dansky, L. and Margolis, E.T. (1988) 'Dysthymia in the offspring of parents with primary unipolar affective disorder.' *Journal of Abnormal Psychology* 94, 1155–1127.

Koenen, K.C., Moffitt, T.E., Caspi, A., Taylor, A. and Purcell, S. (2003) 'Domestic violence is associated with environmental suppression of IQ in young children.' *Development and Psychopathology* 15, 2, 297–311.

Kolar, A., Brown, B., Haertzen, C. and Michaelson, B. (1994) 'Children of substance abusers: The life experiences of children of opiate addicts in methadone maintenance.' *American Journal of Drug and Alcohol Abuse* 20, 159–171.

Komulainen, S. and Haines, L. (2009) *Understanding Parents' Information Needs and Experiences where Professional Concerns Regarding Non-accidental Injury were not Substantiated.* London: Royal College of Paediatrics and Child Health.

Kosonen, M. (1996) 'Siblings as providers of support and care during middle childhood: Children's perceptions.' *Children and Society* 10, 4, 267–279.

Kroll, B. and Taylor, A. (2003) *Parental Substance Misuse and Child Welfare.* London: Jessica Kingsley Publishers.

Kumar, R., Marks, M., Platz, C. and Yoshida, K. (1995). 'Clinical audit of a psychiatric mother and baby unit: Characteristics of 100 consecutive admissions.' *Journal of Affective Disorders* 33, 11–22.

Lakey, J. (2001) *Youth Employment, Labour Market Programmes and Health: A review of the literature.* London: Policy Studies Unit.

The Lord Laming (2009) *The Protection of Children in England: Progress Report.* London: The Stationery Office.

Lang, C., Field, T., Pickens, J., Martinez, A., Bendell, D., Yando, R. and Routh, D. (1996) 'Preschoolers of dysphoric mothers.' *The Journal of Child Psychology and Psychiatry* 37, 2, 221–224.

Latzin P., Röösli M., Huss A., Kuehnil C.E. and Frey U. (2008) *Air Pollution During Pregnancy and Lung Functions in Newborns: A Birth Cohort Study.* (http://erj.ersjournals.com/cgi/content/abstract/09031936.00084008v1) accessed 03.03.2011.

Laybourn, A., Brown, J. and Hill, M. (1996) *Hurting on the Inside: Children's Experiences of Parental Alcohol Misuse.* Aldershot: Avebury.

Lee, C.M. and Gotlib, I.H. (1989) 'Maternal depression and child adjustment: a longitudinal analysis.' *Journal of Abnormal Psychology* 98, 78–85.

Leffert, N. and Petersen, A.C. (1995) 'Patterns of development in adolescence', in Rutter, M. and Smith, D.J. (eds) *Psycho-social Disorders in Young People: Time Trends and their Causes.* Chichester: Wiley.

Leitner, M., Shaplan, J. and Wiles, P. (1993) *Drug Use and Drugs Prevention: The View and Habits of the General Public.* London: HMSO.

Leslie, B. (1993) 'Casework and client characteristics of cocaine crack using parents in a child welfare setting.' *The Journal of The Ontario Association of Children's Aid Societies* 17, 17–24.

Levendosky, A.A., Huth-Bocks, A.C. and Semel, M.A. (2002) 'Adolescent peer relationships and mental health functioning in families with domestic violence.' *Journal of Clinical Child and Adolescent Psychology* 31, 2, 206–218.

Lewis, C.E. and Bucholz, K.K. (1991) 'Alcoholism, antisocial behaviour and family history.' *British Journal of Addiction* 86, 177–194.

Li, C., Pentz, A. and Chou, C-P. (2002) 'Parental substance use as a modifier of adolescent substance use risk.' *Addiction* 97, 1537–50.

Lipinski, B. (2001) *Heed The Call: Psychological Perspectives on Child Abuse.* Los Angeles: Sojourner Press.

Little, M., Axford, N. and Morpeth, L. (2004) 'Research review: Risk and protection in the context of services for children in need.' *Child and Family Social Work* 9, 105-117.

Littlewood, R. and Lipsedge, M. (1997) *Aliens and Alienists: Ethnic Minorities and Psychiatry.* London: Routledge.

Loewenthal, K.M., MacLoed, A.K. and Cook, S. (2003) 'Alcohol and Suicide-Related Ideas and Behaviour Among Jews and Protestants.' *Israel Journal of Psychiatry* 40, 174–181.

Lou, H.C., Hansen, D., Nordentoft, M., Pyrds, O., Jensenn, F. and Nim, J. (1994) 'Prenatal Stressors of human life affect fetal brain development.' *Developmental Medicine and Child Neurology* 36, 9, 826–832.

Macleod, J., Hickman, M., Bowen, E., Alati, R., Tilling, K. and Davey Smith, G. (2008) 'Parental drug use, early adversities, later childhood problems and children's use of tobacco and alcohol at age 10: Birth cohort study.' *Addiction* 103, 1731–43.

Maidment, S. (1976) 'A study of child custody.' *Family Law* 6, 195–22 and 236-241.

Maitra, B. (1995) 'Giving due consideration to the family's racial and cultural background', in Reder, P. and Lucey, C. (eds) *Assessment of Parenting: Psychiatric and Psychological Contributions.* London: Routledge.

Malos, E. and Hague, G. (1997) 'Women, housing, homelessness and domestic violence.' *Women's Studies International Forum* 20, 3.

Manning, V., Best, D.W., Falulkner, N. and Titherington, E. (2009) 'New estimates of the number of children living with substance misusing parents: results from UK national household surveys'. *BMC Public Health* 9, 377. (www.ncbi.nlm.nih.gov/pmc/articles/PMC2762991/) accessed 03.03.2011.

Marcenko, M.O., Kemp, S. and Larson, N.C. (2000) 'Childhood experiences of abuse, later adolescent substance abuse and parenting outcomes among low-income mothers.' *American Journal of Orthopsychiatry* 70, 3, 316–326

Margison, F. and Brockington, I. (1982) 'Psychiatric mother and baby units', in Brockington, I. and Kumar, R. (eds) *Motherhood and Mental Illness.* London: Academic Press.

Marks, M. and Kumar, R. (1996) 'Infanticide in Scotland.' *Medicine, Science and the Law* 36, 4, 299–305.

Marmot Review (2010) *Fair Society, Healthy Lives.* (www.marmotreview.org/) accessed 03.03.2011.

Martins, C. and Gaffan, E.A. (2000) 'Effects of early maternal depression on patterns of infant-mother attachment: a meta-analytic investigation.' *Journal of Child Psychology and Psychiatry* 41, 6, 737–746.

Maybery, D., Ling, L., Szakacs, E. and Reupert, A. (2005) 'Children of a parent with a mental illness: Perspectives on need.' *Australian e-Journal for the Advancement of Mental Health (AeJAMH)* 4, 2, 1–11.

Mayers, L.B., Judelson, D.A., Moriaty, B.W. and Rundell, K.W. (2002) 'Prevalence of body art (piercing and tattooing) in university undergraduates and incidence of medical complications.' *Mayo Clinic Proceeding* 17,1, 29–34.

McCarthy, M. (1999) *Sexuality and Women with Learning Disabilities.* London: Jessica Kingsley Publishers.

McConnell, D. and Llewellyn, G. (2000) 'Disability and discrimination in statutory child protection proceedings.' *Disability and Society* 15, 6, 883–895.

McConnell, D. and Llewellyn, G. (2002) 'Stereotypes, parents with intellectual disability and child protection.' *Journal of Social Welfare and Family Law* 24, 3, 297–317.

McConnell, D., Llewellyn, G., Mayes, R. and Russo, D. (2003) 'Developmental profiles of children born to mothers with intellectual disability.' *Journal of Intellectual and Developmental Disability* 28, 2, 1–14.

McDonald, R., Jouriles, E.N., Tart, C.D. and Minze, L.C. (2009) 'Children's adjustment problems in families characterized by men's severe violence toward women: Does other family violence matter?' *Child Abuse & Neglect* 33, 2, 94–101.

McFarlane, J., Parker, B., Soeken, K. and Bullock, L. (1992) 'Assessing for abuse during pregnancy.' *Journal of American Medical Association* 267, 23, 3176–3178.

McGaw, S. and Newman, T. (2005) *What Works for Parents with Learning Disabilities?* Essex: Barnardo's.

McGaw, S., Scully, T. and Pritchard, C. (2010) 'Predicting the unpredictable? Identifying high risk versus low risk parents with intellectual disabilities.' *Child Abuse & Neglect* 9, 34, 699-710.

McGaw, S., Shaw, T. and Beckley, K. (2007) 'Prevalence of psychopathology across a service population of parents with intellectual disabilities and the children.' *Policy, Practice in Intellectual Disabilities* 4, 11–22.

McGaw, S. and Sturmey, P. (1993) 'Identifying the needs of parents with learning disabilities: A review.' *Child Abuse Review* 2, 101–117.

McGee, C. (1996) *Children's and Mother's Experiences of Child Protection Following Domestic Violence.* A paper given at the Brighton Conference: Violence, Abuse and Women's Citizenship International Conference.

McGee, C. (2000) *Childhood Experiences of Domestic Violence,* London: Jessica Kingsley Publishers.

McMenamin, M., Jackson, A., Lambert, J., Hall, W., Butler, K., Coulter-Smith, S. and McAuliffe, F. (2008) 'Obstetric management of hepatitis C-positive mothers: analysis of vertical transmission in 559 infant-mother pairs.' *American Journal of Obstetrics and Gynecology* 199, 3, 315e1–315e5, September.

McNamara, J., Bullock, A. and Grimes, E. (1995) *Bruised before Birth: Parenting Children Exposed to Parental Substance Abuse.* London: British Agencies for Adoption and Fostering.

McWilliams, M. and McKiernan, J. (1993). *Bringing it out in the Open: Women and Domestic Violence in Northern Ireland.* Belfast: HMSO.

Meier, P., Donmall, M. and McElduff, P. (2004) 'Characteristics of drug users who do or do not have care of their children.' *Addiction* 99, 8, 955–61.

Melzer, D. (2003) 'Inequalities in mental health: A systematic review.' *The Research Findings Register, Summary No. 1063.* London: Department of Health.

Meltzer, H., Gatward, R. with Goodman, R. and Ford, T. (2000) *The Mental health of children and Adolescents in Great Britain.* London: National Statistics.

Mencap (2008) *Facts About Learning Disability* (www.mencap.org.uk/page. asp?id=1703) accessed 03.03.2011.

Mental Health Act 1983. London: HMSO.

Mental Health Act 2007. London: HMSO.

Mental Health Foundation (2006) *Self Harm.* London: Mental Health Foundation. (www.mhf.org.uk/information/mental-health-a-z/self-harm/) accessed 03.03.2011.

Mental Health Foundation (2007) *Smoking and Mental Health.* (www.mentalhealth. org.uk/information/mental-health-a-z/smoking). accessed 03.03.2011.

Mental Health Foundation (2010) *MyCare: the challenges facing young carers of parents with a severe mental illness.* (www.mentalhealth.org.uk/publications/?entryid =38571&entryid5=83759&cord=DESC&char=M) accessed 03.03.2011.

Merikangas, K., Dierker, L.C. and Szatmari (1998) 'Psychopathology among offspring of parents with substance abuse and/or anxiety disorders: a high-risk study.' *Journal of Child Psychology and Psychiatry* 39, 5, 711–720.

Merikangas, K. and Spiker, D.G. (1982) 'Assortative mating among in-patients with primary affective disorder.' *Psychological Medicine* 212, 753–764.

Messinger, D.S., Bauer, C.R., Das, A., Seifer, R., Lester, B.M., Lagasse, L.L., Wright, L.L., Shankaran, S., Bada, H.S., Smerigilio, V.L., Langer, J.C., Beeghley, M. and Pooles, W.K. (2004) 'The maternal lifestyle study; cognitive, motor and behavioural outcomes of cocaine-exposed and opiate-exposed infants through three years of age.' *Pediatrics* 113, 6, 1677–1685.

Mezey, G. and Bewley, S. (1997) 'Domestic violence and pregnancy.' *British Journal of Obstetrics and Gynaecology* 104, 528–531.

Michael, J. (2008) *Healthcare for All: Report of the Independent Inquiry into Access to Healthcare for People with Learning Disabilities.* (www.dh.gov.uk/en/Publicationsandstatistics/Publications/PublicationsPolicyAndGuidance/DH_099255) accessed 03.03.2011.

Miller-Perrin, C.L., Perrin, R.A., and Kocur, J.L. (2009) 'Parental physical and psychological aggression: Psychological symptoms in young adults.' *Child Abuse & Neglect* 33, 1, 1–11.

Milne, A.A. (1971) *Now We Are Six.* London: Methuen Children's Books.

MIND (2007) *Statistics 1: How common is mental distress?* (www.mind.org.uk/help/research_and_policy/statistics_1_how_common_is_mental_distress) accessed 03.03.2011.

Mirrlees-Black and Byron, C. (1999) *Domestic Violence: Findings from the British Crime Survey self-completion questionnaire.* Research Findings No. 86. London: Home Office.

Misuse of Drugs Act 1971. London: HMSO.

Moffitt, T.E. (1993) 'Adolescent-limited and life-course-persistent antisocial behavior: A developmental taxonomy.' *Psychological Review* 4, 674–701.

Moffitt, T.E. and Caspi A. (1998) 'Implications of violence between intimate partners for child psychologists and psychiatrists.' *Journal of Child Psychology and Psychiatry* 39, 2, 137–144.

Moffit, T.E., Caspi, A., Harrington, H., Milne, B.J., Melchior, M., Goldberg, D. and Poulton, R. (2007) 'Generalized anxiety disorder and depression: childhood risk factors in a birth cohort followed to age 32.' *Psychological Medicine* 37, 3, 441–452.

Monck, E., Bentovin, A., Goodall, G., Hyde, C., Lwin, R., Sharland, E. with Elton, A. (1995) *Child Sexual Abuse: A Descriptive and Treatment Study.* London: HMSO.

Monck, E. and New, M. (1996) *Report of a Study of Sexually Abused Children and Adolescents, and of Young Perpetrators of Sexual Abuse who were Treated in Voluntary Agency Community Facilities.* London: HMSO.

Mooney, J. (1994). *The Hidden Figure: Domestic Violence in North London.* London: Islington Council.

MORI (2004) *MORI Youth Survey 2004.* (www.yjb.gov.uk/publications/Resources/Downloads/YouthSurvey2004.pdf) accessed 03.03.2011.

MORI (2009) *Safeguarding and Promoting the Welfare of Children: Perceptions of Senior Stakeholders on how Public Organisations have responded to Section 11 of the Children Act 2004.* London: Department for Children, Schools and Families. (www.scie-socialcareonline.org.uk/profile.asp?guid=1a6c27bf-1e18-481d-bcc3-222723cf291a)accessed 03.03.2011.

Morley, R. and Mullender, A. (1994) 'Domestic violence and children: What do we know from research?' in Mullender, A. and Morely, R. (eds). *Children Living With Domestic Violence.* London: Whiting and Birch.

Morris, J. and Wates, M. (2006) *Supporting Disabled Parents and Parents with Additional Support Needs.* Bristol: The Policy Press (www.scie.org.uk/publications/knowledgereviews/kr11.asp) accessed 03.03.2011.

Morris, M., Thompson, C. and Unell, I. (2004) 'Down but not out – a survey of homelessness, substance use and service provision.' *Drugs and Alcohol Today* 4, 3.

Mullender, A. (2004) *Tackling Domestic Violence: Providing Support for Children who have Witnessed Domestic Violence.* London: Home Office.

Mullender, A. (2006) 'What children tell us "He said he was going to kill our mum"', in Humphreys, C. and Stanley, N. (eds) *Domestic Violence and Child Protection.* London: Jessica Kingsley Publishers.

Mullender, A., Hague. G., Imam, U., Kelly, L., Malos, E. and Regan, L. (2002) *Children's Perspectives on Domestic Violence.* London: Sage.

Munro, E. (2010) *The Munro Review of Child Protection Part One: A Systems Analysis.* (www.eduction.gov.uk/munroreview) accessed 03.03.2011.

Munro, E. (2011) *The Munro Review of Child Protection Interim Report: the child's Journey.* (www.education.gov.uk/munroreview) accessed 03.03.2011.

Murray, L. (1992) 'The impact of postnatal depression on infant development.' *Journal of Child Psychology and Psychiatry* 33, 543-561.

Murray, L., Cooper, P. and Hipwell, A. (2001) 'The mental health of parents caring for infants', in Gordon, R. and Harran, E. (eds) *Fragile Handle with Care: Protecting Babies from Harm: Reader*. Leicester: NSPCC.

National Audit Office (2005) *Improving School Attendance in England*. London: The Stationery Office.

National Audit Office (2008) *Department of Health – Reducing Alcohol Harm: Health Services in England for Alcohol Misuse*. London: National Audit Office.

National Health Services and Community Care Act 1990. London: HMSO.

National Institute for Health and Clinical Excellence (2008) *Updated NICE guideline published on care and support that women should receive during pregnancy.* (www.nice. org.uk/media/E5D/8B/2008022AntenatalCare.pdf) accessed 03.03.2011.

National Institute for Health and Clinical Excellence (2009) *Antisocial personality disorder. Treatment, management and prevention. NICE clinical guideline 77.* London: National Institute for Health and Clinical Excellence. (http://guidance.nice.org.uk/ CG77) accessed 03.03.2011.

National Institute for Health and Clinical Excellence (2010) *Alcohol-use disorders: preventing the development of hazardous and harmful drinking.* NICE Public health guidance 24. London: National Institute for Health and Clinical Excellence. (www. nice.org.uk/nicemedia/live/13001/48984/48984.pdf) assessed 03.03.2011.

National Treatment Agency for Substance Misuse (2010) *Statistics from the National Drug Treatment Monitoring System (NDTMS) 1 April 2009- 31 March 2010.* London: Department of Health. (www.nta.nhs.uk) accessed 03.03.2011.

NCH Action for Children (1994) *The Hidden Victims: Children and Domestic Violence.* London: NCH Action for Children.

Netmums (2005) *Screening for Postnatal Depression.* (www.netmums.com/h/n/ SUPPORT/HOME/ALL/545//) accessed 03.03.2011.

Newman, L.K., Stevenson, C.S., Bergman, L.R. and Boyce, P. (2007) 'Borderline personality disorder, mother-infant interaction and parenting perceptions: Preliminary findings.' *Australian and New Zealand Journal of Psychiatry* 14, 7, 598– 608.

Ng Man Kwong, G., Proctor, A., Billings, C., Duggan, R., Das, C., Whyte, M.K.B., Powell, C.V.E. and Primhak, R. (2001) 'Increasing prevalence of asthma diagnosis and symptoms in children confined to mild symptoms.' *Thorax* 56, 312–314.

NHS Information Centre (2006) *Health Survey for England 2004. Updating of trend tables to include childhood obesity data.* London: The NHS Information Centre. (http://www.ic.nhs.uk/pubs/hsechildobesityupdate) accessed 03.03.2010.

NHS Information Centre (2009) *Statistics on Alcohol: England, 2010.* London: The NHS Information Centre.

NHS Information Centre (2010) *Statistics on Alcohol: England, 2010.* London: The NHS Information Centre. (http://www.ic.nhs.uk/webfiles/publications/alcohol10/Statistics_on_Alcohol_England_2010.pdf) accessed on 03.03.2011.

Nicholas, K.B. and Rasmussen, E.H. (2006) 'Childhood abusive and supportive experiences, inter-parental violence, and parental alcohol use: Prediction of young adult depressive symptoms and aggression.' *Journal of Family Violence* 21, 1, 43–61.

Noll, J.G., Trickett, P.K., Harris, W.W. and Putnam, T.W. (2009) 'The cumulative burden borne by offspring whose mothers were sexually abused as children: Descriptive results from a multigenerational study.' *Journal of Interpersonal Violence* 24, 3, 424–449.

Norton, K. and Dolan, B. (1996) 'Personality disorder and parenting', in Gopfert, M., Webster, J. and Seeman, M.V. (eds) *Parental Psychiatric Disorder: Distressed Parents and their Families.* Cambridge: Cambridge University Press.

NSPCC (1997a) *Long Term Problems, Short Term Solutions: Parents in Contact with Mental Health Services.* Brent: Brent ACPC.

NSPCC (1997b) 'Drunk in charge: Substance abuse.' *Community Care 11–17 September,* p.35.

Oats, M. (2002) 'Adverse effects of maternal antenatal anxiety on children: causal effect or developmental continuum?' *The British Journal of Psychiatry* 180: 478–479

O'Connor, R.C., Rasmussen, S., Miles, J. and Hawton, K. (2009) 'Self-harm in adolescents: self-report survey in schools in Scotland.' *The British Journal of Psychiatry* 194, 68–72.

Office for National Statistics (2003) *General Household Survey.* London Office for National Statistics. (www.statistics.gov.uk/ssd/surveys/general_household_survey.asp) accessed 03.03.2011.

Office for National Statistics (2005) *Prevalence of Treated Depression per 1000 Patients, by Age, Sex and Calendar Year:* 1994–98 (www.statistics.gov.uk/STATBASE/xsdataset.asp?vlnk=2341) accessed 03.03.2011.

Office for National Statistics (2006a) *Surveys of Psychiatric Morbidity among Adults in Great Britain.* London: The Stationery Office.

Office for National Statistics (2006b) *Labour Force Survey.* London: The Stationery Office.

Office for National Statistics (2009) *Health: Alcohol Deaths*. (www.statistics.gov.uk/cci/nugget.asp?id=1091) accessed 03.03.2011.

Office of Population and Censuses and Surveys (1996) *The Prevalence of Psychiatric Morbidity among Adults Living in Private Households*. London: HMSO.

Office of the Tanaiste (1997) *Report of the Task Force on Violence Against Women*. Dublin: The Stationery Office.

Ofsted (2009) *Supporting young carers: Identifying, assessing and meeting the needs of young carers and their families*. London: Ofsted.

Ofsted, Commission for Social Care Inspection, HM Crown Prosecution Service Inspectorate, HM Inspectorate of Prisons, Healthcare Commission, HM Inspectorate of Constabulary, HM Inspectorate of Court Administration and HM Inspectorate of Probation (2008) *Safeguarding Children: The Third Joint Chief Inspectors' Report on Arrangements to Safeguard Children 2008*. London: Ofsted.

O'Hara, M.W. (1999) 'The nature of postpartum depressive disorders', in Murray, L. and Cooper, P.J. (eds) *Postpartum Depression and Child Development*. London: Guilford Press.

O'Hara, M.W. and Swain, A.M. (1996) 'Rates and risks of postpartum depression – a meta-analysis.' *International Review of Psychiatry* 8, 1, 37–54.

Olds, D.L., Kitzman, H., Hanks, C., Cole, R., Anson, E., Sidora-Arcoleo, K., Luckey, D.W., Henderson Jr, C.R., Holmberg, J., Tutt, R.A., Stevenson, A.J. and Bondy, J. (2007) 'Effects of nurse home visiting on maternal and child functioning: Age-9 follow-up of a randomized trial.' *Paediatrics* 120, e832–e845.

Oliver, C. and Candappa, M. (2003) *Tackling Bullying: Listening to the Views of Children and Young People*. London: Thomas Coram Unit, Institute of Education.

Onyskiw, J. E. (2003) 'Domestic violence and children's adjustment: A review of research.' *Journal of Emotional Abuse* 3, 1/2, 11–45.

Orford, J., Johnson, M.R.D. and Purser, R. (2004) 'Drinking in second generation black and Asian communities in the English Midlands.' *Addiction Research and Theory* 12, 1, 11–30.

Owusu-Bempah, K. (1995) 'Information about the absent parent as a factor in the well-being of children of single-parent families.' *International Social Work* 38, 253–275.

Owusu-Bempah, K. (2006) 'Socio-genealogical connectedness: Knowledge and identity', in Aldgate, J., Jones, D., Rose, W., and Jeffery, C. (eds) *The Developing World of the Child*. London: Jessica Kingsley Publishers.

Owusu-Bempah, K. and Howitt, J. (1997) 'Self-identity and black children in care', in Davies, M. (ed.) *The Blackwell Companion to Social Work*. London: Blackwell.

Oyserman, F., Mowbray, C.T., Allen-Meares, P. and Firminger, K. (2000) 'Parenting among mothers with a serious mental illness.' *American Journal of Orthopsychiatry* 70, 296–315.

Panaccione, V. and Wahler, R. (1986) 'Child behaviour, maternal depression, and social coercion as factors in the quality of child care.' *Journal of Abnormal Child Psychology* 14, 273–284.

Parrott, L., Jacobs, G. and Roberts, D. (2008) *Stress and Resilience Factors in Parents with Mental Health Problems and their Children.* London: Social Care Institute for Excellence.

Peckover, S. (2001) 'Domestic violence and the protection of babies: The role of health care professionals', in Gordon, R. and Harran, E. (eds) *Fragile Handle with Care: Protecting Babies from Harm: Reader.* Leicester: NSPCC.

Pence, E. and McMahon, M. (1998) 'Duleth: A co-ordinated community response to domestic violence', in Harwin, N., Hague, G. and Malos, E. (eds) *Domestic Violence and Multi-Agency Working: New Opportunities, Old Challenges.* London: Whiting and Birch.

Plant, M. (1985) *Drinking and Pregnancy.* London: Tavistock Publications.

Plant, M. (1997) *Women and Alcohol: Contemporary and Historical Perspectives.* London: Free Association Books.

Plewa, M.C. (2008) 'Panic disorders.' *Emedicine* (www.emedicine.com/emerg/topic766.htm) accessed 03.03.2011.

Porath, A. J. and Fried, P. A. (2005). 'Effects of prenatal cigarette and marijuana exposure on drug exposure on drug use among offspring.' *Neurotoxicology and Teratology:* 27, 2, 267–277.

Portin, P. and Alanen, Y.O. (1996) 'A critical review of genetic studies of schizophrenia.' *Acta Psychiatrica Scandinavica* 95, 1, 1–5.

Pound, A., Puckering, C., Mills, M. and Cox, A.D. (1988) 'The impact of maternal depression on young children.' *British Journal of Psychotherapy* 4, 240–252.

Povey, D. (ed.) (2008) *Homicides, Firearm Offences and Intimate Violence 2006/7 Third Edition.* London: Home Office.

Powell, J. and Hart, D. (2001) 'Working with parents who use drugs', in Gordon, R. and Harran, E. (eds) *Fragile Handle with Care: Protecting Babies from Harm: Reader.* Leicester: NSPCC.

Princess Royal Trust for Carers (2009) *Vulnerable and Hidden Young Carers Targeted with New £1 Million Fund* (www.carers.org/news/vulnerable-and-hidden-young-carers-targeted-with-new-1million-fund,669,NW.html) accessed 03.03.2011.

Priory Group (2006) *Suffer the Children: Adult Children of Alcoholics.* (www. priorygroup.com/~/media/Migration/Root%20Folder/Locations/Acute%20 Hospitals/SufferTheChildren.ashx) accessed 03.03.2011.

Propper, C., Jones, K., Bolster, A., Burgess, S., Johnston, R. and Sarker, R. (2004) *Local Neighbourhood and Mental Health: Evidence from the UK, CMPO Working Paper Series No 04/099.* Bristol: University of Bristol.

Protection from Harassment Act 1997. The National Archive Protection from Harassment Act 1997. (www.legislation.gov.uk/ukpga/1997/40/contents) accessed 03.03.2011.

Quilgars, D., Johnsen, S. and Pleace, N. (2008) *Youth Homeless in the UK.* York: Joseph Rowntree Foundation (www.jrf.org.uk/node/2782) accessed 03.03.2011.

Quinton, D. (2006) 'Self development', in Aldgate, J., Jones, D., Rose, W., and Jeffery, C. (eds) *The Developing World of the Child.* London: Jessica Kingsley Publishers.

Quinton, D. and Rutter, M. (1985) 'Family pathology and child psychiatric disorder: A four-year prospective study', in Nicol, A.R. (ed.) *Longitudinal Studies in Child Psychology and Psychiatry.* London: John Wiley and Sons Ltd.

Radford, L. and Hester, M. (2006) *Mothering Through Domestic Violence.* London: Jessica Kingsley Publishers.

Radke-Yarrow, M., Richters, J. and Wilson, W.E. (1988) 'Child development in a network of relationships', in Hinde, R.A. and Stevenson-Hinde, J. (eds) *Relations Within Families, Mutual Influences.* Oxford: Oxford University Press.

Reading, A. (1983) *Psychological Aspects of Pregnancy.* London: Longman.

Reder, P. and Duncan, S. (1999) *Lost Innocents; a Follow-up Study of Fatal Child Abuse.* London: Routledge.

Rees, G. and Lee, J. (2005) *Still Running 2: Findings from the Second National Survey of Runaways.* London: The Children's Society.

Rees, G. and Siakeu, J. (2004) *Thrown Away; the Experiences of Children Forced to Leave Home.* London: The Children's Society.

Regier, D.A., Farmer, M.E., Rae, D.S., Locke, B.Z., Keith, S.J., Judd, K.L. and Goodwin, F.K. (1990) 'Comorbidity of Mental Disorders with Alcohol and Other Drug Abuse'. *Journal of the American Medical Association* 204, 19, 2511-2518.

Reiss, D. (2008) 'Transmission and treatment of depression.' *American Journal of Psychiatry* 165, 9, 1083–1085.

Rende, R. and Plomin, R. (1993) 'Families at risk from psychopathology: Who becomes at risk and why?' *Development and Psychopathology* 5, 4, 529–540.

UNIVERSITY LIBRARY

Resnich, P.J. (1969) 'Child murder by parents: A psychiatric review of filicide.' *American Journal of Psychiatry* 126, 325–334.

Reupert, A. and Maybery, D. (2007) 'Families affected by parental mental illness; A multiperspective account of issues and interventions.' *American Journal of Orthopsychiatry* 77, 3, 362–369.

Rivinus, T.M. (1991) *Children of Chemically Dependent Parents.* New York: Drunner/Mazel Publishers.

Riley, J.W. (1920) *Child-Rhymes.* Indianapolis: The Bobbs-Merrill Company Publishers.

Roberts, D., Bernard, M., Misca, G. and Head, E. (2008) *Experiences of Children and Young People Caring for a Parent with a Mental Health Problem.* London: Social Care Institute for Excellence.

Roberts, E. and Latifa, Y. (2002) 'Maternal-infant transmission of hepatitis C virus infection.' *Hepatology* 6, 5, Suppl. 1, S106–113.

Robinson, S. and Lader D. (2007) *Smoking and Drinking among Adults,* 2007. Newport: Office for National Statistics (www.statistics.gov.uk/downloads/theme_compendia/GHS07/GHSSmokingandDrinkingAmongAdults2007.pdf) accessed 03.03.2011.

Rogosch, F.A., Mowbray, C.T. and Bogat, G.A. (1992) 'Determinants of parenting attitudes in mothers with severe psychopathology.' *Development and Psychopathology* 4, 469–487.

Rondo, P.H.C. (2007) 'Maternal stress/distress and low birth weight, preterm birth and intrauterine growth restriction – A review.' *Current Women's Health Reviews* 3, 1, 13–29 (17).

Rose, W. and Barnes, J. (2008) *Improving Safeguarding Practice: Study of Serious Case Reviews 2001–2003.* London: Department for Children, Schools and Families.

Rosenthal, R. N. and Westreich, L. (1999) 'Treatment of persons with dual diagnoses of substance use disorder and other psychological problems', in McCrady, B.S. and Epstein, E.E. (eds) *Addictions: A Comprehensive Guidebook.* New York: Oxford University Press.

Ross, E.M. (1996) 'Risk of abuse to children of spouse abusing parents.' *Child Abuse and Neglect* 20, 7, 589–598.

Royal College of Obstetricians and Gynaecologists (2006) *Alcohol Consumption and the Outcomes of Pregnancy.* London: Royal College of Obstetricians and Gynaecologist. (www.rcog.org.uk/files/rcog-corp/uploaded-files/RCOGStatement5AlcoholPregnancy2006.pdf) accessed 03.03.2011.

Royal College of Physicians (1991) *Alcohol and the Public Health*. London: Macmillan Education.

Royal College of Physicians (1995) *Alcohol and the Young*. London: Royal Lavenham Press.

Royal College of Psychiatrists (2004a) *Mental Health and Growing Up, Third Edition: Factsheet 10; The child with general learning disability: for parents and teachers.* (www.rcpsych.ac.uk/mentalhealthinfoforall/mentalhealthandgrowingup/10learningdisability.aspx) accessed 03.03.2011.

Royal College of Psychiatrists (2004b) *Mental Health and Growing Up, Factsheet 17: domestic violence – its effects on children: information for parents, carers and anyone who works with young people* (www.rcpsych.ac.uk/mentalhealthinfo/mentalhealthandgrowingup/domesticviolence.aspx) accessed 03.03.2011.

Royal College of Psychiatrists (2010) *Postnatal Depression.* (www.rcpsych.ac.uk/mentalhealthinfoforall/problems/postnatalmentalhealth/postnataldepression.aspx) accessed 03.02.2011.

Royal College of Psychiatrists (2008) *Mental Health Information For All.* (www.rcpsych.ac.uk/mentalhealthinformation.aspx) accessed 03.03.2011.

Rutter, M. (1966) *Children of Sick Parents: An Environmental and Psychiatric Study.* Institute of Psychiatry Maudsley Monographs No. 16, Oxford: Oxford University Press.

Rutter, M. (1985) 'Resilience in the face of adversity. Protective factors and resistance to psychiatric disorder.' *British Journal of Psychiatry* 147, 598–611.

Rutter, M. (1989) 'Psychiatric disorder in parents as a risk factor for children', in Schaffer, D., *Prevention of Mental Disorder, Alcohol and other Drug Use in Children and Adolescents.* Rockville, Md: Office for Substance Abuse, USDHHS.

Rutter, M. (1990) 'Commentary: some focus and process considerations regarding effects of parental depression on children.' *Developmental Psychology* 26, 60–67.

Rutter, M. (1995) 'Clinical implications of attachment concepts: Retrospect and prospect.' *Journal of Child Psychology and Psychiatry* 36, 4, 549–571.

Rutter, M. (2007) 'Resilience, competence, and coping.' *Child Abuse & Neglect* 31,2, 205-210.

Rutter, M., Graham, P., Chadwick, O, and Yule, W. (1976) 'Adolescent turmoil: Fact or fiction.' *Journal of Child Psychology and Psychiatry* 17, 35–56.

Rutter, M., Moffitt, T. and Caspi, A. (2006) 'Gene-environment interplay and psychopathology: multiple varieties but real effects.' *Journal of Child Psychology and Psychiatry* 47, 3–4, 226–261.

Rutter, M. and Quinton, D. (1984) 'Parental psychiatric disorder; effects on children.' *Psychological Medicine* 14, 853–880.

Rutter, M. and Rutter, M. (1992) *Developing Minds: Challenge and Continuity across the Life Span.* Harmondsworth: Penguin.

SAMHSA (2007) NSDUH Report: *Gender Differences in Alcohol Use and Alcohol Dependence or Abuse 2004-2005.* (www.oas.samhsa.gov/2k7/AlcGender/AlcGender. cfm) accessed 03.03.2011.

Saunders, H. (2004) *Twenty-Nine Child Homicides: Lessons Still to be Learnt on Domestic Violence and Child Protection.* Bristol: Women's Aid.

Schagen, I., Benton, T. and Rutt, S. (2004) *Study of Attendance in England: Report for the National Audit Office.* Slough: NFER.

Schofield, F. (2006) 'Middle childhood: five to eleven years', in Aldgate, J., Jones, D., Rose, W. and Jeffery, C. (eds) *The Developing World of the Child.* London: Jessica Kingsley Publishers.

Scottish Executive Department of Health (1998) *The Scottish Health Survey* (www. sehd.scot.nhs.uk/scottishhealthsurvey/sh808-01.html) accessed 03.03.2011.

Scottish Government, The (2009) *Attendance and Absence in Scottish Schools* 2007/8. (www.scotland.gov.uk/Publications/2008/12/18120723/1) accessed 03.03.2011.

Self, A. and Zealey, L. (2007) Social Trends No 37. *Office for National Statistics.* London: HMSO.

Seljamo, S., Aromaa, M., Koivusilta, L., Rautava, P., Sourander, A., Helenius, H. and Sillanpää, M. (2006) 'Alcohol use in families: a 15 year prospective follow-up study.' *Addiction* 101, 984–92.

Sharland, E., Seal, H., Croucher, M., Aldgate, J. and Jones, D. (1996) *Professional Intervention in Child Sexual Abuse.* London: HMSO.

Sharp, D., Hay, D.F., Pawlby, S., Schmucker, G., Allen, H. and Kumar, R. (1995) 'The impact of postnatal depression on boys' intellectual development.' *The Journal of Child Psychology and Psychiatry* 36, 8, 1315–1336.

Shen, A.C. (2009) 'Long-term effects of interparental violence and child physical maltreatment experiences on PTSD and behavior problems: A national survey of Taiwanese college students.' *Child Abuse & Neglect* 33, 3, 148–160.

Sheppard, M. (1993) 'Maternal depression and child care: The significance for social work and social work research.' *Adoption and Fostering* 17, 2, 10–15.

Sheppard, M. (1997) 'Double jeopardy: The link between child abuse and maternal depression in child and family social work.' *Child and Family Social Work* 2, 2, 91–108.

Singleton, N., Bumpstead, R., O'Brian, M., Lee A. and Meltzer, H. (2001) *Psychiatric Morbidity among Adults Living in Private Households 2000.* London: The Stationery Office.

Skuse, D., Bentovim, A., Hodges, J., Stevenson, J., Andreou, C., Lanyado, M., New, M., Williams, B. and McMillan, D. (1998) 'Risk factors for development of sexually abusive behaviour in sexually victimised adolescent boys: cross sectional study.' *British Medical Journal* 317, 175–179.

Smith, J., Berthelsen, D. and O'Connor, I. (1997) 'Child adjustment in high conflict families.' *Child Care, Health and Development* 23, 113–133.

Smith, M. (2004) 'Parental mental health: Disruptions to parenting and outcomes for children.' *Child and Family Social Work* 9, 1, 3–11.

Smith, P.K. and Cowie, H. (1993) *Understanding Children's Development.* Oxford: Blackwell.

Smith, P.K. and Thompson (1991) 'Dealing with bully/victim problems in the UK', in Smith, P.K. and Thompson, D. (eds) *Practical Approaches to Bullying.* London: David Fulton.

Social Care Institute for Excellence (SCIE) (2005) *Helping Parents with Learning Disabilities in their Role as Parents* (www.scie.org.uk) accessed 03.03.2011.

Somers, J.M., Goldner, E.M., Waraich, P. and Hsu, L. (2006) 'Prevalence and incidence studies of anxiety disorders: A systematic review of the literature.' *Canadian Journal of Psychiatry* 51, 100–103.

Somers, V. (2007) 'Schizophrenia: The impact of parental illness on children.' *British Journal of Social Work* 37, 8, 1319–1334.

Spotts, J.V., and Shontz, F. C. (1991) 'Drugs and personality: Comparison of drug users, nonusers, and other clinical groups on the 16PF.' *International Journal of Addiction* 26, 10, 1019–1054.

Stafford, A., Stead, J., Grimes, M. (2007) *The Support Needs of Children and Young People Having to Move Home Because of Domestic Abuse.* Edinburgh: Women's Aid.

Stallard, P., Norman, P., Huline-Dickens, S., Salter, E. and Cribb, J. (2004) 'The effects of parental mental illness upon children: A descriptive study of the views of parents and children.' *Clinical Child Psychology and Psychiatry* 9, 1, 39–52.

Standing Conference on Drug Misuse (SCODA) (1997) *Working with Children and Families Affected by Parental Substance Misuse.* London: Local Government Association Publications.

Stanley, N., Cleaver, H. and Hart, D. (2009) 'The impact of domestic violence, parental mental health problems, substance misuse and learning disability on parenting capacity' in Horwath, J. (ed.) *The Child's World: The Comprehensive Guide to Assessing Children in Need.* 2nd edition. London: Jessica Kingsley Publishers.

Stark, C., Stockton, D. and Henderson, R. (2008) *Reduction in Young Male Suicide in Scotland.* BioMed Central Public Health, The Open Access Publisher. (www.biomedcentral.com/1471-2458/8/80) accessed 03.03.2011.

Statistics Canada (1993) *The Violence Against Women Survey.* Ottawa: Centre for Justice Statistics.

Stein, M., Rees, G., Hicks, L. and Gorin, S. (2009) *Neglected Adolescents: Literature Review.* London: Department for Children, Schools and Families.

Sternberg, K.J., Lamb, M.E., Guterman, E. and Abbott, C.B. (2006) 'Effects of early and later family violence on children's behaviour problems and depression: A longitudinal, multi-informant perspective.' *Child Abuse & Neglect* 30, 3, 283–306.

Stevenson, O. (2007) *Neglected Children and their Families.* Oxford: Blackwell.

Stewart, M.A. Deblois, C.S. and Cummings, C. (1980) 'Psychiatric disorder in the parents of hyperactive boys and those with conduct disorder.' *Journal of Child Psychology and Psychiatry* 21, 283–292.

Stocker, C.M. (1994) 'Children's perceptions of relationships with siblings, friends, and mothers: Compensatory processes and links with adjustment.' *Journal of Child Psychology and Psychiatry* 15, 8, 1447–1459.

Strategy Unit (2004) *Alcohol Harm Reduction Strategy for England.* London: Strategy Unit.

Stroud, J. (1997) 'Mental disorder and the homicide of children.' *Social Work and Social Sciences Review: An International Journal of Applied Research* 6, 3, 149–162.

Sullivan, C.M., Juras, J., Bybee, D., Nguyen, H. and Allen, N. (2000) 'How children's adjustment is affected by their relationships to their mothers' abusers.' *Journal of Interpersonal Violence* 15, 6, 587–602.

Surgeon General's Report (2004) *The Health Consequences of Smoking: Impact on Unborn Babies, Infants, Children and Adolescents.* (www.cdc.gov/tobacco/data_statistics/sgr/2004/highlights/children/index.htm) accessed 03.03.2011.

Svedin, C.G., Wadsby, M. and Sydsjo, G (1996) 'Children of mothers who are at psycho-social risk: Mental health, behaviour problems and incidence of child abuse at age 8 years.' *European Child and Adolescent Psychiatry* 5, pp.162–171.

Swadi, H. (1994) 'Parenting capacity and substance misuse: An assessment scheme.' *ACPP Review and Newsletter* 16, 5, 237–244.

Swofford, C. D., Scheller-Gilkey, G., Miller, A. H., Woolwine, B. and Mance, R. (2000). 'Double jeopardy: schizophrenia and substance use.' *The American Journal of Drug and Alcohol Abuse* 26, 343–353.

Tarleton, B., Ward, L. and Howard, J. (2006) *Finding the Right Support? A Review of Issues and Positive Practice in Supporting Parents with Learning Difficulties and their Children.* (www.baringfoundation.org.uk/FRSupportSummary.pdf) accessed 03.03.2011.

Testa, M., Quigley, B.M., Das Eiden, R. (2003) 'The effects of prenatal drug exposure on infant mental development: A meta-analytical review.' *Alcohol and Alcoholism* 38, 4, 295–304.

Thoburn, J. (1996) 'Psychological parenting and child placement: "But we want to have our cake and eat it"', in Howe, D. (ed.) *Attachment and Loss in Child and Family Social Work.* Aldershot: Avebury.

Thoburn, J., Lewis, A. and Shemmings, D. (1995) *Paternalism or Partnership? Family Involvement in the Child Protection Process.* London: HMSO.

Tienari, P., Wynne, L.C., Lahti, I., Laksy, K., Moring, J., Mikko, N., Pentti, N. and Wahlberg, K. (2004) 'Genotype-environment interaction in schizophrenic-spectrum disorder: Long-term follow-up study of Finnish adoptees.' *British Journal of Psychiatry* 184, 216–222.

Tompsett, H., Ashworth, M., Atkins, C., Bell, L., Gallagher, A., Morgan, M. and Wainwright, P. (2009) *The Child, the Family and the GP: Tensions and Conflicts of Interest in Safeguarding Children.* London: Department for Children, Schools and Families.

Torgersen, S., Kringlen, E. and Cramer, V. (2001) 'The Prevalence of personality disorders in a community sample.' *Archives of General Psychiatry* 58, 6, 590–596.

Tunnard, J. (2004) *Parental Mental Health Problems: Key Messages from Research, Policy and Practice.* Dartington: Research in Practice.

Turning Point (2006) *Bottling it up: The Effects of Alcohol Misuse on Children, Parents and Families.* London: Turning Point.

Tweed, S.H. (1991) 'Adult children of alcoholics: Profiles of wellness amidst distress.' *Journal of Studies on Alcohol* 52, 2, 133–141.

Tymchuck, A. (1992) 'Predicting adequacy of parenting by people with mental retardation.' *Child Abuse & Neglect* 16, 165–178.

Tymchuck, A. and Andron, L. (1990) 'Mothers with mental retardation who do or do not abuse or neglect their children.' *Child Abuse & Neglect* 14, 313–323.

Unell, I. (1987) 'Drugs and Deprivation'. *Druglink* 2, 6.

VanDeMark, N.R., Russell, L.A., O'Keefe, M., Finkelstein, N., Noether, D.C.D. and Gampel, J. (2005) 'Children of mothers with histories of substance abuse, mental illness and trauma.' *Journal of Community Psychology* 33, 4, 445–459.

Velleman, R. (1993) *Alcohol and the Family.* London: Institute of Alcohol Studies.

Velleman, R. (1996) 'Alcohol and drug problems in parents: an overview of the impact on children and the implications for practice', in Göpfert, M., Webster, J. and Seeman, M.V. (eds) *Parental Psychiatric Disorder: Distressed Parents and their Families.* Cambridge: Cambridge University Press.

Velleman, R. (2001) 'Working with substance misusing parents as part of court proceedings.' *Representing Children* 14, 36–48.

Velleman, R. (2004) 'Alcohol and drug problems in parents: An overview of the impact on children and implications for practice', in Göpfert, M., Webster, J. and Seeman, M. (eds) *Seriously Disturbed and Mentally Ill Parents and their Children, 2nd Edition* 185–202. Cambridge: Cambridge University Press.

Velleman, R. (2009a) *How do Children and Young People Learn about Alcohol: A Major Review of the Literature.* Bath: University of Bath.

Velleman, R. (2009b) *Influences on how Children and Young People Learn about and Behave towards Alcohol.* York: Joseph Rowntree Foundation.

Velleman, R. and Orford, J. (2001) *Risk and Resilience: Adults who were the Children of Problem Drinkers.* Amsterdam: Harwood Academic Publishers.

Velleman, R. and Reuber, D. (2007) *Domestic Violence and Abuse Experienced by Children and Young People Living in Families with Alcohol Problems: Results of a Cross European Study.* ENCARE. (www.apua.info/File/fb9c3027-2698-48b3-994c-349a0e491c7c/ALC_VIOL_ParentalAlcoholProblems_EN.pdf)   accessed 03.03.2011.

Velleman, R. and Templeton, L. (2007) 'Understanding and modifying the impact of parental substance misuse on children.' *Advances in Psychiatric Treatment* 13, 79–89.

Vranceanu, A.M., Hobfoll, S.E. and Johnson, R.J. (2007) 'Child multi-type maltreatment and associated depression and PTSD symptoms: The role of social support and stress.' *Child Abuse & Neglect* 31, 1, 71–84.

Wade, J. and Biehal, N., Clayden, J. and Stein, M. (1998) *Going Missing: Young People Absent from Care.* Chichester: Wiley.

Walby, S. and Allen, J. (2004) *Domestic Violence, Sexual Assault and Stalking: Findings from the British Crime Survey.* London: Home Office Research Study 276, Home Office Research, Development and Statistics Directorate.

Walker, F. (1995) *Young People and Alcohol, Highlight No 138*. London: National Children's Bureau.

Wasserman, D., Cheng, Q. and Jiang, G. (2005) 'Global suicide rates among young people aged 15–19.' *World Psychiatry* 4, 2, 114–120.

Weaver, T., Stimson, G., Tyrer, P., Barnes, T. and Renton, A. (2002) *Co-morbidity of Substance Misuse and Mental Illness Collaborative Study* (COSMIC). London: Department of Health.

Webster, A., Coombe, A. and Stacey, L. (2002) Bitter Legacy. *The Emotional Effects of Domestic Violence on Children*. London: Barnardo's.

Weissman, M.M. and Paykel, E.S. (1974) *The Depressed Woman: A Study of Social Relationships*. Chicago: University of Chicago Press.

Weissman, M.M., John, K., Merikangas, K.R., Prusoff, B.A., Wickramaratne, P., Gammon, G.D., Angold, A. and Warner, V. (1986) 'Depressed parents and their children: General health, social and psychiatric problems.' *American Journal of Diseases of Children* 140, 801–805.

Weissman, M.M., Prusoff, B.A., Gammon, G.D., Merikangas, K.R., Leckmanl, J.F. and Kidd, K.K. (1984) 'Psychopathology of the children (ages 6–18) of depressed and normal parents.' *Journal of the American Academy of Child Psychiatry* 23, 78–84.

Wekerle, C., Leung, E., Wall, A., MacMillan, H., Boyle, M., Trocme, N. and Waechter, R. (2009) 'The contribution of childhood emotional abuse to teen dating violence among child protective services-involved youth.' *Child Abuse & Neglect* 339, 1, 45–58.

Wellings, K., Nanchahal, K., Macdowall, W., McManus, S., Mercer, C.H., Johnson, A.M., Copas, A.J., Korovessis, C., Fenton, K.A. and Field, J. (2001) 'Sexual behaviour in Britain: Early heterosexual experience.' *The Lancet* 358, 9296, 1843–1850.

Werner, E.E. (1986) 'Resilient offspring of alcoholics: A longitudinal study from birth to age 18.' *Journal of Studies on Alcohol* 47, 1, 34–40.

West, M.O. and Prinz, R.J. (1987) 'Parental alcoholism and childhood psychopathology.' *Psychological Bulletin* 102, 2, 204–218.

Wilson K. (2006) 'Foster care in the UK', in McAuley, C., Pecora, P.J. and Rose, W. (eds) *Enhancing the Well-Being of Children and Families through Effective Interventions*. London: Jessica Kingsley Publishers.

Wolfe, D.A., Jaffe, P., Wilson, S.K. and Zak, L. (1985) 'Children of battered women: the relation of child behaviour to family violence and maternal stress.' *Journal of Consulting and Clinical Psychology* 53, 5, 657–665.

Wolkind, S. (1981) 'Pre-natal emotional stress – effects on the foetus', in Wolkind, S. and Zajicek, E. (eds) *Pregnancy: A Psychological and Social Study*. London: Academic Press.

Women's Aid (1995) *Domestic Violence, the Social Context*. Dublin: Women's Aid.

Women's Aid (2008) *The Survivor's Handbook*. (www.womensaid.org.uk/domestic-violence-survivors-handbook.asp) accessed 03.03.2011.

Woodcock, J. and Sheppard, M. (2002) 'Double trouble: Maternal depression and alcohol dependence as combined factors in child and family social work.' *Children & Society* 16, 4, 232–245.

World Health Organisation (1992) *The ICD-10 Classification of Mental and Behavioral Disorders: Clinical Descriptions and Diagnostic Guidelines*. Geneva: World Health Organisation.

Wynne, L.C., Pekka, T., Anneli, S., Ilpo, L., Juha, M. and Wahlberg, K. (2006) 'II Genotype-environment interaction in the schizophrenia spectrum: Qualitative observations.' *Family Process* 45, 4, 445–447.

Yates, T.M., Dodds, M.F., Scroufe, L.A. and Egeland, B. (2003) 'Exposure to partner violence and child behaviour problems: A prospective study controlling for child physical abuse and neglect, child cognitive ability, socioeconomic status, and life stress.' *Development and Psychopathology* 15, 1, 199–218.

Index

learning disability and   34, 35, 55, 199
prevalence   11, 28–33, 137, 159, 199
problem drinking and   29, 37, 56, 199
problem drug use and   29, 38, 56, 57, 199
smoking and   102
terminology   24
see also anxiety disorders; depression; parental mental illness; personality
        disorders; schizophrenia
methadone   16, 56, 57, 75, 104
mothers *see* women
multi-agency work *see* collaboration of support agencies
multiple problems
    child abuse and neglect   2, 31, 65–6, 86
    effects on children   73, 103, 142, 145, 171, 186
    effects on relationships   79
    families' typology   3
    learning disability   55, 65–6
    parenting capacity   2, 17, 65–74, 86, 199, 200
    personality disorders   54
    policy and practice implications   205–6
    prevalence   29, 37, 199
    problem drug use and   38, 65
    research limitations   16
    support services' collaboration   204
    training and educational needs   208

neglect *see* child neglect

obesity   137, 159, 185
obsessive-compulsive disorder   29, 53
opiates   56, 57, 72, 103, 112, 164
    see also heroin; methadone

panic disorder   29, 52, 58
'parent', definition   23
parent–child attachment relationships *see* attachment relationships
parental learning disability   54–5
    attachment relationships   72, 74, 112, 113, 115, 123
    child abuse   34, 35–6, 47, 65–6, 87, 173
    child neglect   34, 35–6, 65–6, 70–1, 117
    child sexual abuse   34, 36, 169, 173
    children and   2, 3, 73, 90, 92, 99, 199–200, 201

U...ITY OF W...
...ARY